Dear Bob and Sue: Season 2

Matt and Karen Smith

D1566736

To see color versions of the photos in this book and additional photos from our trip, visit our website:

www.dearbobandsue.com

OTHER WORKS BY MATT AND KAREN

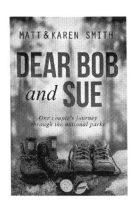 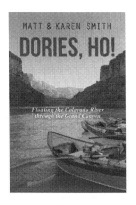

North Cascades National Park
August 3rd

Back at the campsite, we crawled into our tents again at ten o'clock. The nearly-full moon cast an eerie glow across the burned-out landscape as the light filtered through the thick smoke. Karen and Lolly must have found comfortable positions to sleep because I could no longer hear them fidgeting; John was snoring.

The wind began blowing, which I thought was unusual; there hadn't been so much as a gentle breeze all day. Within ten minutes the gusts were surprisingly strong. The rushing sound was making me drowsy and I dozed off, briefly. At 10:32 pm, I woke to a loud bang coming from the ridge where we'd just been hiking. I sat straight up in the tent. Another bang followed about a minute later. The noises sounded like gunshots. Karen sat up with a start, clutching her sleeping bag around her. She was terrified, sure that a deranged killer was on the loose. I was hoping she was wrong, but I couldn't think of another explanation. Why else would someone fire a gun at night in the wilderness?

I called out softly, "John. Lolly. Did you hear that?" John responded with an open-mouth snort, and I didn't hear a peep out of Lolly.

The bear spray was right where I put it, in the corner of the tent next to my pillow; it was our only protection. We laid back down and listened intently for more gunshots, or worse, the sound of someone coming down the trail toward our campsite. For the next two hours, I was wide awake looking up at the swaying, dead trees that surrounded us. At 12:30 am, we heard another bang, much louder and much closer than the ones before. This time the sound was more metallic; the report echoed off the surrounding hills.

Karen bolted upright and grabbed for her shoes. Where she thought she was going was a mystery to me. "Karen, wait! Those weren't gunshots. The wind is blowing down the dead trees!"

Lolly's silhouette appeared against the screen of her tent, and she shouted, "What wuth that!?"

"Lolly, it wuth the tweeth," Karen said.

"The what?"

"The tweeth! The tweeth!"

"Weally!? It thounded like a gunthot."

"You gals need to take out your mouth guards," I said. "You both sound like Sylvester the Cat."

"What are you talking about?" John asked.

"John, good, you're alive. I thought the first gunshots might have gotten you," I said.

"What gunshots?"

"The ones we heard two hours ago."

"I didn't hear gunshots two hours ago. Lolly, did you?"

"No. I wouldn't have been able to sleep if I had."

We all watched the trees above us move in the wind. At least a dozen big ones stood close to our campsite. John and Lolly's tent was directly underneath the biggest one. No matter which direction the trees were from our tent, every time the wind howled it looked like every one of them was about to fall on us.

"What are we going to do?" Karen asked.

"I don't think we have a choice other than to stay right here and ride it out," John said.

"Yeah, we're dead center in the middle of the burned-out area," I said. "Even if we moved our tents, there's nowhere else to put them that's safer. And we're not hiking out of here in the middle of the night."

"I'm not hiking in the dark, there are snakes out there," Lolly said.

"There are snakes everywhere, Lolly," I replied.

"Not helpful," Karen said.

By 3:30 am, I'd made peace with the idea that a tree would fall and kill us all. Too exhausted to stay awake any longer, I passed out.

INTRODUCTION

This book is a memoir about our travels during 2017. It's a follow up to the first book my wife, Karen, and I wrote together: *Dear Bob and Sue*, which we completed in 2013. The format is the same as our first book: a series of emails to our dear friends Bob and Sue.

In 2010, at the age of fifty and with our kids grown and out of the house, we quit our jobs and set off from our home in the Seattle area to visit the fifty-nine U.S. national parks. We encouraged Bob and Sue to travel with us, but they declined. While on trips to the parks—from 2010 to 2013— we occasionally emailed them describing our experiences. By that time, they'd moved from the Seattle area to Michigan.

The first *Dear Bob and Sue* wasn't a reproduction of actual emails. Neither is Season 2. We merely formatted our stories as emails. All of the events and activities we've written about happened, however we've edited the content to be more interesting for the reader. For instance, not every dialogue is a verbatim transcript; you wouldn't want to read a court stenographer's version of our travels—or anyone's.

Over the last couple of years, we've had the good fortune to travel with dear friends to many of the places we write about. In Season 2 you'll meet two couples: John and Lolly, and Craig and Aya. We're a bit surprised they still want to travel with us after knowing that whatever they say might end up in a book. It only takes one slip of the tongue while we're together and the next thing they know, I've scribbled a couple pages featuring their gaffe. Our friends are good sports. But we've also given them the chance to nix any passages before the book hits the presses.

Writing the first *Dear Bob and Sue* as a series of emails was an experiment; we had no idea how it would be received. It was never our intention to write another book in the same format. In fact, our second travel memoir, *Dories, Ho!*, which recounts our dory trip through the Grand Canyon, is written in a traditional style. But since we released *Dear Bob and Sue* several years ago, we've heard from many readers asking for a sequel.

Season 2 is different than its predecessor in one key way: *Dear Bob and Sue* is a chronicle of our journey to all of the U.S. national parks, and Season 2 is a collection of stories about our travels to destinations beyond places with a national park designation. We're now exploring public lands of all sorts: state parks, BLM areas, National Forests, and some of the four hundred-plus sites within the National Park Service (NPS) to name a few.

The other change you'll find is something that I didn't think I'd live long enough to experience. We're camping. That's right, Mrs. Smith is now sleeping outside and having her morning coffee while sitting on a stump in the middle of nowhere. I don't mean to sound like her aversion to camping was the sole reason we stayed in park lodges and Hampton Inns on our first tour of the national parks. I was perfectly happy with that arrangement as well.

In the fall of 2016, when we were on our dory trip, we had no choice but to camp on the sandy beaches along the river each night. After a couple of nights in a tent, and several more under the stars with nothing between us and the Milky Way, we were hooked. It was the nudge we needed. We still have a lot to learn about living without a fixed roof over our heads, but the important thing is we've started that journey.

As Karen said to me the other day, "We've become more comfortable being uncomfortable."

In the five-year gap between publishing *Dear Bob and Sue* and *Dories, Ho!*, I went back to work at a traditional corporate job. Karen and I continued to travel when we could, but it wasn't at the same pace as when we were on our national parks journey. After five years of being back at a corporate job, I decided to retire so we could travel and write full-time.

I say I'm retired, but I'm working as much now as I did when I had a demanding job, which begs the question, "Why are we traveling so much and working so hard writing about it?"

The short answer is we enjoy traveling, especially when it involves outdoor activity. The longer answer is that we find traveling and being outdoors to be good for our body, mind, and soul. The physical activity involved in hiking, scrambling over rocks, and setting up a campsite, keeps us feeling young. When we plan something that we know will challenge us, it gives us the motivation to stay in shape (or to get in shape) for that upcoming event. On top of that, we're continually learning. Between the research beforehand and the experience, travel expands our minds, and—we believe—helps maintain our acuity. And being in nature is good for the soul. I heard someone say that "wilderness redeems the soul." I believe it. There's something that draws us to nature, and we're better for being in it.

When we wrote our first book, we did it for the fun, novelty, and challenge of writing a book together. While writing our second book, we found that it doesn't get easier the more we do it. Had it not been for the feedback we received from readers, we probably wouldn't have continued. We've been overwhelmed by the number of people who've contacted us offering their encouragement, hiking suggestions, and hospitality to stay in their homes when we travel. They've even shared with us stories of their "OC without the D" behaviors. People have also told us that, after reading our books, they're planning to visit more parks, and not just national parks but state parks and other public lands as well. If our stories inspire people to have more outdoor experiences, then we'll keep writing.

These books are not intended to be guidebooks, but if you pick up useful information about the places we write about, great. Instead, we're simply trying to use humor to draw people into a story that ends with them being more likely to lace up their hiking boots, tennis shoes, snowshoes, or whatever, and head outdoors. Or, for those who want to experience these activities vicariously, we try to bring the essence of our travels to the written page.

In addition, we also hope to raise people's awareness about our incredible public lands so they will continue to be protected and preserved. All of us who've had the privilege of spending time in these places, some of which are the most beautiful on this planet, owe a debt to those who had the will and foresight a long time ago to set them aside for our enjoyment. We should do the same for future generations.

As you can see, reader feedback has made an impact on us, and we encourage you to continue sending us your thoughts. We'd love to hear from you. Our points of contact are listed below.

Thank you for joining us on this journey,
Matt Smith, 2018

Email: mattandkarensmith@gmail.com
Website: www.dearbobandsue.com
Instagram: mattandkarensmith
Facebook: Dear Bob and Sue

From: **Matt Smith**
Subject: **It's Been a Rough Year So Far**
Date: **January 1 (Sunday)**

Dear Bob and Sue,

Happy New Year, and Karen has lost her mind, not necessarily in that order. I went to make a ham sandwich today and couldn't find the leftover Christmas ham in the refrigerator. I asked Karen where it was, and she said, "At Target."

"No, not where did you get it, where's it now?"

"That's where it is now. And I didn't buy our Christmas ham at Target," she told me.

I had a feeling the story wasn't going to end well for the ham or me, but I had to ask, "Why is our Christmas ham at Target?"

"It was old. It was about to have a birthday, so I took it to Target and threw it away in the trash can in front of the store."

"Our Christmas ham! How could you? Every time I opened its shiny, gold foil, it was like opening a Christmas present. Whenever I made a sandwich and got an extra-large chunk of sugar crust, it was like winning the ham lottery. I loved that ham," I said.

"That's wrong. You shouldn't have such strong feelings for ham," she said with a furrowed brow.

"Wrong? Taking it to Target is wrong on so many levels I don't know where to begin," I said. "First, ham lasts forever. Second, it wasn't even close to having a birthday. Jesus had a birthday, not the ham. And C, you shouldn't be throwing away our trash at Target."

"Our trash pick-up is delayed until Saturday because of the holiday and I didn't want the ham sitting in the garage trash can for a week. It would smell up the place and the rat would be out there gnawing on it day and night," she said.

"What...rat?"

"That rat that we saw in our garage!"

"That was three years ago! We got rid of him, remember? There are no rats in our garage."

"Put a big, juicy ham out there for a week and there will be."

"I don't think Target would appreciate you bringing our family's Christmas ham to their store and disposing of it in their trash can."

"Their trash can was already filled with Starbucks cups, McDonald's bags, and dirty diapers. The ham classed it up if you ask me."

"Yeah, you should expect a thank you card in the mail from Target any day now."

Then a horrible thought popped into my head. "No, no, no! The pie! The leftover pumpkin pie! And the Cool Whip! You didn't, did you?"

"Take it easy, I didn't take the pie to Target, just the ham."

"Good, good. I'm down a ham, but I still have the pie and whipped cream."

What worried me most was that Karen thought taking our Christmas ham to Target was a perfectly acceptable thing to do. "Sweetie, please promise me you won't take any more of our trash to Target in the future."

"I promise. Until next Thanksgiving when it's time to throw away the turkey carcass."

"You haven't been taking our Thanksgiving turkeys to Target all these years, have you?" I asked. "And it's OK to lie to me."

"I think it's time for you to have a piece of pie," she replied. "With extra whipped cream. Why don't you turn on the football game and I'll get it for you?"

There you have it. We've had a bit of a rough start to the new year at the Smith home. I think Karen's been cooped up in our house too long without seeing the sun. These short Pacific Northwest days are taking a toll on the both of us. Hopefully, we can keep it together until we go on our first trip of the year to southern Nevada in a couple of weeks. Can't wait.

Your friend,
Matt

~.~.~.~.~.~.~.~

From: **Matt Smith**
Subject: **Vegas, Ho!**
Date: **January 15 (Sunday)**

Dear Bob and Sue,

Unless you count my trips to the beer fridge in our garage, the only exercise I've gotten in the last three weeks has been wrestling our over-sized Christmas tree out of the front room. It's rained non-stop for a month, and we can't remember the last time we saw the sun, so we flew to Vegas today to find it. We've been saying for years that we need to visit the parks down south in January. As much as we love the Pacific Northwest, the gray skies and the constant rain put us into a funk once the new year rolls around. The warning sign for me is when it's the middle of the day and I hesitate to change out of my pajamas. I figure, "What's the use? I'll be putting them back on in a couple of hours."

The Hampton Inn in Henderson, Nevada is our home base this week, but we're not going to the Las Vegas Strip while we're here. We plan to go to Lake Mead National Recreation Area, Red Rock (Red Rock Canyon National Conservation Area), Valley of Fire State Park (Karen keeps calling it Fire Valley, which in my opinion would be a better name for a park), and Mojave National Preserve.

I wanted to get a good night's sleep and be ready to head out early tomorrow morning for our first outing. The curtains in our hotel room weren't closing all the way and I knew the light from the parking lot would keep me awake. A trick I learned from years of business travel solved my problem: I took a couple of clothes hangers out of the closet—the ones that have those small pant grabbers on a bar—turned them vertical and attached the grabbers to both sides of the curtains, like sealing a large bag of Doritos with a chip clip. A hanger at the top and one at the bottom kept the curtains closed tight. Karen stood in awe watching me light-proof the room. I thought she was admiring my ingenuity, but instead, it was my OC that left her dumbfounded.

"Why are you putting pants hangers on the curtains?" she asked.

"I'm closing the gap here in the middle, so light doesn't shine in and keep me up all night," I replied.

"That's too weird. I *have* to take a picture of this and send it to Bob and Sue," she said.

"It's not weird; it's called being resourceful."

"No, it's called being OC with a capital D. You've already put duct tape over the microwave clock and the LED on the smoke detector, and unplugged the alarm clock," she said. "I'm surprised you haven't also duct taped the edges of the curtains to the walls."

I wish she hadn't mentioned putting duct tape on the sides of the curtains because that's not a bad idea. One tiny piece of tape every couple of feet on the outer edges would have made our room pitch black. I'm pretty sure, though, if I'd taped the curtains closed, she'd organize an intervention. If you get any photos from Karen, ignore them. She always makes fun of my odd behaviors, but I guarantee she'll sleep like a baby tonight.

Your friend,
Matt

~.~.~.~.~.~.~.~

From: **Matt Smith**
Subject: **Lake Mead National Recreation Area**
Date: **January 16 (Monday)**

Dear Bob and Sue,

Our first outing of the trip was to Lake Mead National Recreation Area, the very first national recreation area designated by Congress in 1936. Not many people show up to this park wearing hiking boots. Most of the recreating—boating, fishing, swimming—takes place on Lake Mead, the massive reservoir created by Hoover Dam. Karen had researched hikes in the area before we left home, and we were surprised to find out that there are lots of hiking trails; 87 percent of the park protects a big chunk of the eastern Mojave Desert.

The Alan Bible Visitor Center in Boulder City was our first stop. After we parked, I began rummaging through my backpack.

Karen asked, "What are you looking for?"

"My passport."

"Were you planning on swinging down to Mexico without telling me?"

"No, my national parks passport. Crap! It's not here. I must have left it at home."

"I thought we were done with that. We already have all fifty-nine stamps."

"I can't believe what I'm hearing. We're not *done*. We'll never be done; all the national park units have stamps."

"You could stamp a plain piece of paper and put in your passport later," she suggested.

"I could, but that would be lame. I'm going to buy another passport."

"And start over!"

"No, I'll stamp a page in the new passport and then put that page in my old passport when we get home."

"How's that different than what I suggested, besides costing ten dollars more?"

"I can't have random pieces of paper loosely stuffed between the pages of my passport. What I do is, I carefully cut the stamped page in the new passport at the edges where they connect to the spiral binding. Then I can slip it out, insert it into my *official* passport, and no one knows the difference."

"You realize no one is interested in knowing the difference, right?"

After I took care of my passport business, we went over to the information desk to talk with the ranger about the hikes we were thinking of doing. The volunteer ranger working the desk, who looked like he was in his sixties, was friendly but I'm not sure he'd spent much time outside. Karen asked him, "We're thinking about hiking the White Rock Canyon Trail today. It's a slot canyon, right?"

He replied, "Well, I don't know. I've never done one."

We looked at each other, at a loss for what else to ask him about the hike, when we were startled by a loud, hacking cough coming from behind him. An older gentleman was sitting behind the information desk with one arm leaning on a cane. He wasn't wearing a uniform and it wasn't clear to us why he was there.

"That's a real nice hike, especially this time of the year. It'll take you through a slot canyon all the way down to the river," he said between loud, wheezing coughs. (He was referring to the Colorado River that flows out of the Hoover Dam.)

"It's on the Arizona side of the park. You can also hike to the Liberty Bell Arch from that same trailhead," he added. Then he coughed so hard we thought he might pass out.

We turned back toward the ranger who was giving us a look that said, "Anything else I can do for you?"

"If we have time, we'd also like to hike up Fortification Hill," Karen said. "We've heard that the views from the top are incredible. How do we get to that trailhead?"

"Well, I'm not sure, I've never been there before. You know what you could do?" he asked. Neither Karen nor I said a word. "You could look it up on the Internet."

We heard another loud cough and a couple of long, exaggerated breaths. "You take Highway 93 and turn off at the first exit past the dam. Follow the gravel road to the north for a few miles." He wheezed, paused, and then said, "What kind of vehicle do you have?"

"It's a small SUV, a rental," I replied.

"You'll be fine if you go slow," he said.

This is how our time at the visitor center went. We'd ask the ranger a question and the guy behind him would answer. We never learned who he was, but I'm guessing he was a volunteer or an off-duty ranger who enjoyed hanging around to visit with people. "That'll be you someday," Karen said as we walked back to the car. "You'll park yourself behind a ranger's desk and answer all of the visitors' questions, even when they aren't talking to you."

"If that were me, I'd be at a doctor's office getting checked for pneumonia," I replied.

The trailhead for White Rock Canyon Trail was only a few miles south of the visitor center along Highway 93. We could see it from the road but drove right past it on our first try. It took us a couple of passes to figure out that the exit we wanted is only accessible when you're driving north on Highway 93. Once we turned around for the third time and avoided the other cars that nearly plowed into us while we slowed down to make the turnoff, we found a flat gravel area with plenty of room for parking.

Being the first day of our trip, we hadn't had a chance to do our regular stop for supplies for the week. All we had with us were the snacks in our backpacks left over from our last hike a month ago and a couple of full water bottles each. If it were later in the year, and warmer, I would have made sure we carried more water. This can be a hot hike, even in the spring. In fact, the park often closes the trail in summer months due to high heat danger. Today though, the weather was perfect—sunny and in the fifties when we started the hike.

A sign at the edge of the parking lot marked the beginning of the trail, informing us that we were at the start of the Arizona Hot Springs and Liberty Bell Arch trails. We were lucky that we knew ahead of time that White Rock Canyon Trail was also part of this system of trails or we might have thought we were in the wrong place. From the parking lot, the trail quickly descended a small hill, passed under Highway 93, and then continued southwest down a gently sloping wash.

We'd considered hiking the Liberty Bell Arch Trail; the views of the river at the end of the trail are supposed to be incredible. But that trail doesn't go all the way to the river, which is something we wanted to do. Ever since our dory trip through the Grand Canyon last September, we've wanted to see the Colorado River again. It was calling us back.

The farther we hiked down the wash, the narrower the canyon became. We love being in slot canyons where the walls are so close that you can touch both sides of the canyon at the same time. It surprised us how beautiful the trail was for a hike that we'd never heard of before. There was a time after we visited all of the national parks that we felt we might have already seen most of the exciting places on America's public lands. Now it seems quite the opposite: The more we travel, the more we realize that we've only scratched the surface of places to see.

The high walls of the canyon blocked our view of the river while we hiked, so we could never tell how close we were to the end of the trail. Just when we began wondering if the trail would indeed lead us to the river, the canyon opened and the river was a few hundred yards in front of us.

Colorado River at the end of White Rock Canyon trail.

At that point, the trail ended, and we picked our way through the gravel and small boulders leading to the water's edge. No other person was in sight. It felt good sitting in the sun on the bank of the river. The canyon walls rising up on both sides reminded us of the Grand Canyon on a slightly smaller scale. The water was calm, and the reflection of the far cliffs was a perfect mirror image. Slowly, the image began to fade; ripples appeared as a two kayakers rounded a bend and paddled by. We'll add that to our wish bucket: kayaking this stretch of the river.

After a short while, we heard a dog barking. We thought it might be with a group of hikers coming behind us on the trail, but no new hikers ever showed. When we finished our snack, we started walking downriver in the direction of the barking and stumbled upon a couple's campsite hidden behind several large boulders. It took them an uncomfortable amount of time to get ahold of their barking dog. I'm not good at determining dog breeds but if I had to guess I would say this one was a Short Hair Big and Angry with maybe a little Pit Bull mixed in.

We exchanged pleasantries while I kept my eye on their dog who I was sure would attack me as soon as he got the chance.

"I didn't know you could camp down here," Karen said. "This looks like fun. Did you hike in?"

"No, we canoed. We put in downriver and paddled up here with our camping stuff," the woman said, pointing to their canoe that was partially hidden behind a large rock.

"Is it difficult to get a permit to camp here?" I asked.

"We don't need a permit," the man said, holding the dog by the collar. The dog kept barking and tugging at the man's arm. My innocent question about a permit seemed to upset the man more than it should have. He was looking at me with a smirk that seemed to say, *Maybe I should let go of Butch here and see how fast these city folk can run.*

"OK, well, enjoy your camping trip," Karen said in a brisk tone. "We're going to go explore the river bank over this way," she said pointing farther downriver.

"Don't we want to go back in the direction we came from?" I asked.

"No, let's go this way," she said while giving me a cross-eyed look as if there was more she wanted to tell me once we were alone again. Confused, I followed her anyway. I was happy to be away from devil-dog, but a little concerned that we'd have to hike by their camp again to get back to our car.

Following a trail along the river, we put some distance between the dog and us. We went around an outcropping of rock that jutted out toward the water and then up over a large boulder, which was an ideal spot to sit and take in the view of the river. "Why did we hike this direction?" I asked. "Now we have to go back through their camp to get out of here."

"I was thinking," Karen started—I'm always fearful when she starts a sentence that way—"I was thinking we should take the Arizona Hot Springs Trail back to the car rather than backtrack on the White Rock Canyon Trail. We'll make it a loop."

"Why didn't you tell me this before?" I asked.

"Because there are a couple of things that I'm not sure of."

"Which are?"

"First, you have to climb a twenty-foot ladder that's leaning against a waterfall to get up to the trail from down here. I'm not sure I want to do that. I thought we could hike to the ladder and take a look at it first."

"OK, what's the other thing?"

"When I was researching the trail, I learned that you have to hike through some of the hot springs along the way. And..." she paused.

"And what?"

"And there's a small chance—a very small chance—that if you get any of the water from the hot springs up your nose, a brain eating amoeba could eat your brain."

"I'm out!"

"It's a miniscule chance. It travels to your brain through your nose, so you could swallow the water and still be fine," she assured me.

Now, I'm not a medical professional—or a professional of any kind—but I don't understand why doctors think it's safe to have brain-eating parasites in your stomach just because their preferred path to your brain is through the nose. They're brain eaters! They're probably pretty smart. They might figure out a way to make it from your stomach to your brain.

Karen continued, "I looked it up. It's a single-celled bug called Naegleria fowleri. It's only infected 143 people since 1962. And that's in the entire world—I think. Although, 139 of those folks died from the infection."

"I still don't like my odds. There can't be anything so incredible on that hike that would cause me to risk getting a brain-eating parasite up my nose."

"You know what's creepy?" she continued. "I've seen pictures of people sitting in those hot springs. They're up to their armpits in the water, smiling at the camera."

"That *is* creepy. How would a person know if they were infected?" I asked.

"The CDC website said early stage symptoms are a headache and nausea. Later stage symptoms are—get this— 'stiff neck, confusion, and lack of attention to people and surroundings.'"

"You just described me! I think I'm already infected!" I said.

"That's what I thought when I read the list of symptoms."

"Joking aside, let's review our options: In one direction we could get infected with a brain-eating amoeba, and in the other direction we could be mauled by a dog. Did I get that right?"

"We're not going to get *in* the hot springs," she pleaded. "Not above our knees anyway."

"What if I trip and fall into the water and it goes up my nose? Nope. I choose the dog."

"OK. OK. But I still want to go a little farther down the trail in the direction of the hot springs. I'd like to at least see the ladder."

"Fine, you can go as far as you'd like. I'll be here enjoying the peaceful view of the river," I said.

While Karen hiked farther down the trail, I sat gazing at the river. A pontoon boat coming from the direction of Hoover Dam passed by; only a single boatman was on it. This part of the river is a popular area for guided day trips. Seeing that pontoon boat reminded me of a time years ago when Karen and I did a tour of this section of the river on a boat like that one. We were attending a conference in Las Vegas and the entertainment for the day was a trip to the Colorado River and a boat ride for several miles below the dam. I remember enjoying that trip a lot, but I hadn't thought about it again until this morning when I saw that pontoon boat.

About twenty minutes later, Karen was back. "Let's go," she said. "I couldn't find the ladder."

When we got to the campsite with the unruly dog, our camper friends were busy talking with four new hikers who were looking for the Hot Springs Trail. The dog was surprisingly calm as the six of them stood chatting. That is, until he saw me. He lunged in my direction, but the owner kept him back with a firm grip on his collar.

"Really nice folks," I said to Karen as we picked up our pace past their campsite. "Too bad we can't stay and get to know them better. I'm sure we'd become lifelong friends."

"Why do dogs always want to attack you?" she asked.

"I've no idea. Maybe they sense that I'm the alpha male and they're looking to challenge my position in the pack."

"Yeah, that's really the only possible explanation," she replied. I could imagine her rolling her eyes as she said it.

We made it back to our car with plenty of daylight left. Driving north on Highway 93, we found the exit the mystery guy at the visitor center had told us about that led to the gravel road toward Fortification Hill. We drove a couple of miles down the road in our rental car, but saw nothing that resembled a trailhead. The farther we went, the worse the road conditions became. Storm clouds began to form in the east, which added to my concern. I could imagine us standing on the top of the hill with lightning flashing around us.

After the third time I almost slid off the road, we turned around and drove back to the visitor center. When we stopped there this morning, we'd seen signs for the Historic Railroad Trail, the only remaining section of the old railroad bed that ran from Boulder City to the Hoover Dam site. It was one of the hikes Karen had on her wish list for today. The compact gravel trail, a National Recreation Trail, is open to walkers, runners, bikers, and dogs. It turned out to be more of a pleasant walk than a hike, with some fantastic panoramic views of Lake Mead. Between mile one and mile two, we passed through five tunnels that engineers had blasted out of the surrounding cliffs, each one twenty-five feet wide to accommodate the huge equipment on the trains. Had we been there earlier in the day, we could have continued another mile or so to the Bureau of Reclamation property that surrounds Hoover Dam, but by the time we reached that section of the trail the gate was locked for the evening. Fortunately, nothing became of the dark clouds overhead, and within an hour, they'd moved on to the west.

I'd always thought of Lake Mead as a watersport only destination. Finding such a great hike through a slot canyon was a nice surprise. There are other hikes we'd like to come back and do in the future, but the Hot Springs parasite hike probably won't make it onto the list.

Your friend,
Matt

~.~.~.~.~.~.~.~

From: **Matt Smith**
Subject: **Red Rock Canyon**
Date: **January 17 (Tuesday)**

Dear Bob and Sue,

For the past several years we've had blinders on when it came to public lands. We're no longer limiting ourselves to visiting only national parks. There are incredible public lands also managed by the National Forest Service, Department of Natural Resources, Fish and Wildlife, and the Bureau of Land Management (BLM). And fantastic state parks exist as well.

Today we went to a BLM site, Red Rock Canyon National Conservation Area, about twenty miles west of the Las Vegas Strip. It's a beautiful parcel of land comprised of close to 200,000 acres tucked into a pocket of stunning red rocks in the Mojave Desert. We try to make it out there every time we're in Vegas.

From Henderson, we took Highway 215 to the suburb of Summerlin, and then turned west on Highway 159, which led us to the entrance to Red Rock Canyon. It was early in the day when we arrived, about nine thirty. The line of cars waiting to get in nearly reached the shoulder of Highway 159. The word must be out that this is an excellent spot for hiking; on our previous visits, we hadn't seen crowds like we saw today. With the large number of visitors to Las Vegas each year, it makes sense that some of those folks have found this outdoor playground. Red Rock can be a pleasant break from the casinos if you want to get away from the cigarette smoke and the hawkers handing out cards with pictures of naked women. When you're at the canyon, you wouldn't even know that the Strip is a short drive away; the area has the feel of a national park.

If you ever plan on going there, you should know ahead of time that the area only has one main road, and it's single-lane and one-way for thirteen miles. Aptly named a scenic drive, slow drivers will sandwich you between them and the impatient drivers behind you. Karen always suggests that I try adjusting my attitude and accept the fact that it will take as long as it takes to reach our destination, but that never works—mainly because I've never tried it. I can still see the tailgater in my rearview mirror who doesn't seem to understand that I can't drive faster than the line of cars in front of me.

Whoever built the road through the park didn't do drivers a favor by making it just wide enough for boneheads to think it's a two-lane road, but not wide enough to safely accommodate two cars side-by-side. Nor did they build any turn-outs so those who want to drive slower than I normally walk can pull over and let the cars behind them pass. Although, I noticed over the course of our trips to the parks that the slowest of the slow drivers never pull over and let the cars behind them pass. We were in a park once where the driver in front of us stopped in the middle of the road—right next to a turn out.

Karen thinks it's rude when I honk at slow drivers. I disagree. Not only is it not rude, it's my obligation. It's an unwritten rule of the road that the person directly behind the slow car must honk. The honk is on behalf of everyone stuck behind the slow car. A honk coming from the third car is only half as effective as a second car honk, and the fourth car—forget about it. This is why I honk. I consider it a public service, but Karen still thinks I'm being a jerk.

Twenty-six named hikes are on the map they give you at the pay station. Since we already knew which hike we wanted to do, we skipped our usual stop at the visitor center and proceeded to the scenic drive. Fortunately for me, we only had to drive half the loop to get to the trailhead; by then I was ready for a break from the traffic. We parked at the upper White Rock parking area and hiked the White Rock/La Madre Spring Loop.

This hike has a little bit of everything; the desert landscape changes on the back side of the loop to a forest of pinion and juniper. The trail circles White Rock Mountain and has a deceptive amount of elevation gain. On previous visits we've hiked this trail both clockwise and counterclockwise, and I swear it's mostly uphill whichever direction you go, but it does offer incredible views of the red rocks. Despite the numbers of cars we encountered earlier, we ran into few other hikers. After three hours, we'd hiked six and a half miles. It was a solid workout; we certainly felt that we earned our beers.

While still on our post-hike high, I eased our rental car back onto the scenic drive. I kept reminding myself to be patient with the other drivers, yet the traffic was more congested than a few hours earlier. "You don't have to follow so close to the car in front of us," Karen said to me.

"I'm not following too close; he keeps hitting his brakes every time he sees a bird."

"Then why don't you give him some room or pass him?"

"I would pass him, but the guy behind me keeps pulling up next to us as if he's going to pass us both."

"We're not in any hurry, so let's take our time."

"That's what I'm trying to do, but he keeps hitting his brakes. There he goes again! Now he's stopped. It's like he's never seen a robin before. God forbid that a jackrabbit runs across the road, we'll be stuck behind this guy for the rest of the day."

Karen was no longer speaking to me. She did deep yoga breathing until the cars in front of us got back to normal speed. Then another bird appeared, and the slow down began again. This is pretty much how the rest of the scenic drive went until we reached Highway 159 and headed back east toward Las Vegas.

After a nap and a shower, it was time to check out the state of the local microbreweries. Right here in the suburb of Henderson we found a couple of interesting ones that had excellent beer. At this point, too many breweries exist across the country for Karen and me to visit every one of them like we thought we might do, but we're going to hit as many as we can.

Your friend,
Matt

From: **Matt Smith**
Subject: **Valley of Fire**
Date: **January 18 (Wednesday)**

Dear Bob and Sue,

When we pulled up to the west entrance of Valley of Fire State Park this morning, several bighorn sheep had just crossed the main road and were climbing up the side of a hill. The ranger on duty at the entrance booth told us we still had plenty of time to get a good look at them. "They're moving slowly. There's a parking lot just up the road where you could stop to take pictures of them."

We parked the car, grabbed our phones, and stepped into the brilliant sunshine. "Whoa!" Karen said as the cold air hit her. We quickly found every item of clothing we'd squirreled away in our daypacks and put them on.

When we left Seattle three days ago, it was thirty-nine degrees at our house. We were looking forward to spending a week in warmer weather. "My phone says it's thirty-nine degrees here," I said to Karen.

"Yeah, but it's a dry thirty-nine," she said through chattering teeth.

The sun warmed us quickly, and we soon forgot about the cold as we were distracted by the bighorns. I climbed up the hill to get a better look at them. Another visitor was there doing the same, and for fifteen minutes, we leapfrogged each other moving closer to the sheep, trying to position ourselves for a clean shot. All we managed to do was scare them over the crest of the hill and out of sight. I looked back at Karen who was still standing at the bottom. She was waving me back to the car, saying something I couldn't hear that I assumed was along the lines of, "Let's go. You can't spend all day trying to get a picture of a sheep's butt! We have things to do!"

Karen had a long list indeed. I think she wanted to do every hike in the park, and we almost did. Our first stop was

Atlatl Rock, a petroglyph panel that sits about seventy-five feet off the ground; a metal staircase leads up to a platform next to the petroglyphs. *(A petroglyph is a rock drawing where the design has been scratched or pecked into the stone, as opposed to a pictograph, which is a rock drawing where mud or pigment has been used to make the design.)* When we reached the stairs, a woman was already halfway up looking back at her husband who was now standing next to us. "Are you coming or not?" she shouted.

"I can see 'em from here," he hollered.

"You can't see them from there. Get up here!" she yelled.

He turned to us and said, "I don't need to climb all the way up there to see a bunch of scratches on a rock." I sensed he wanted us to take his side in their dispute.

"I'm staying out it," I said.

As we started up the stairs, the woman was coming down to fetch her husband. We could hear them bickering as we took some quick photos of the petroglyphs. The drawings were typical of the petroglyphs we've seen throughout the Southwest, but what amazed me was they were seventy-five feet off the ground. How did the people who carved them get up there? They certainly didn't have a metal staircase with handrails.

When we were ready to leave, she appeared behind us on the top platform out of breath and husbandless. "Thirty years and I still can't get him to do anything," she said shaking her head.

"I know," Karen said sympathetically.

"You know?" I asked. "You know what?"

Karen moved her pinched figures across her lips as if zipping them shut and started down the stairs. I turned to the woman and said, "I'm up here, aren't I? What's this 'I know' stuff?"

Our next activity was a short loop hike to see petrified logs. Karen loves petrified wood. It fascinates her a little more than it should, but I'm not complaining. Chain link fences imprisoned each of the full-log specimens. It's understandable why the park put up the protective barriers; if they hadn't, it wouldn't take long before someone would be picking away at them with a rock hammer. But the chain link made it look like the petrified logs were in prison, and it was a bit of a buzzkill.

From there we turned off onto White Domes Scenic Byway. The road is a 5.7-mile national scenic byway, as you would expect by its name. I don't know the difference between a byway and a highway, but the road was undoubtedly scenic—*striking* is the word Karen used. The road went up and down like a roller coaster, and curved around huge boulders that looked as if they'd been intentionally dropped alongside the highway. She wanted me to stop the car every three feet, so she could get out and take pictures. It concerned me that she was so intent on taking photos that she might wander onto the road and the cars behind us would flatten her like a pancake, so I was strategic with my stops.

Our third stop was a hike called Mouse's Tank, named after an Indian renegade who used the area as a hideout in the 1890s after he was accused of killing two prospectors. It was an easy hike of about half a mile through a small canyon. The trail was mostly flat and sandy, and it led past several well-preserved petroglyph panels. Some were close to the path, and others required scrambling up slickrock to see. Looking for petroglyphs always feels like a treasure hunt. Sometimes they're so faded that you can be looking right at one for a couple of minutes before it comes into focus.

Karen could have spent all day back there. To her, petroglyphs are magical. "I'd love to know the meaning of these," she said as she stared at a panel with several carvings. "Look over here. There's a series of concentric circles and right below is a long wavy line. It could be a snake or an ancient code."

"Yeah, it's code alright. It's code for 'I'm so bored entertaining myself in the middle of nowhere with just a stick and half of an antler that I've resorted to drawing pictures on rocks.' A kid probably carved these five hundred years ago when his mother sent him out to play in the wilderness."

"There are some very strange-looking drawings of people, like that couple with the rectangular bodies holding hands. They're standing next to two human stick figures who are also holding hands. Maybe the rectangle people are aliens or maybe aliens carved these petroglyphs," Karen said.

"Well, that makes sense, because if aliens were intelligent enough to build a spaceship and visit earth, one of the things they would definitely do is draw stick figures on the sides of boulders before they blasted off for home," I said.

"I thought you liked petroglyphs."

"I like that you can stand in the same place where another person stood five hundred years ago pecking into the stone, and that you can still see their work in the rock. To me, that's pretty cool. Most of the images, though, are too bizarre to make any sense of. Except for the carvings of bighorn sheep. I like those."

A short distance farther down the park road was the trailhead for the highlight of the day: the Fire Wave hike. For the past several years we've been trying to score a permit to hike to a similar rock formation, The Wave in Coyote Buttes, on the border of Utah and Arizona. The photos we've seen of it are incredible: red and tan bands of sedimentary rock have been bent and sculpted over the years by wind and water leaving stunning, striated rock formations. We'd love to do that hike someday, but we've never been able to secure a permit. When Karen found pictures of the Fire Wave, the resemblance to The Wave amazed her.

From the parking lot, it was a three-quarter-mile hike to the Fire Wave rock formations. It's an easy hike, with an elevation drop of about two hundred feet on the way out. The trail is not well-marked, and there's not much to see until you get to the Fire Wave area. Once there, however, the views and scenery were well worth the trip. Streaks of red and beige sandstone make curved patterns in the undulating hills. The mounds were smooth slickrock, and with my grippy hiking boots I was able to climb to several high spots to get interesting photos of the patterned rocks below me. We were there at 11:30 am, and with the sun directly overhead, the colors of the rocks in our photos were a little washed out. I suspect that dawn or dusk would be better times to take photos if you want more vibrant colors and more contrast.

The Fire Wave, Valley of Fire State Park

We were glad we chose January to visit this site. Even with the cold temperatures at the start of the day, it was getting warm in full sun. (The average daily high temperatures in June, July and August are over one hundred degrees.) I wouldn't attempt this hike in the heat of the summer.

Fortunately, only one other twosome was on the trail when we reached the Fire Waves, so we got great pics without people in them. By the time we started back to the car, the area was getting crowded.

At the end of the byway is the White Domes Trail, a 1.25-mile loop that's perfect for anyone who wants to sample several types of desert hikes. It started with a short, sandy climb and then we descended into the canyon via a series of rock stairs built into the multi-colored sandstone. At the bottom of the stairs, the trail leveled off as we approached the ruins of a frontier cabin. The ruins looked a little too perfect for the setting because they're not authentic; they were part of a movie scene from the 1960s. Past the fake relics, the trail took us through a short slot canyon and then wound back to the parking lot.

Our next stop was The Cabins: a group of stone huts built in the 1930s by the Civilian Conservation Corps (CCC) as a shelter for people on the Arrowhead Trail between Los Angeles and Salt Lake City. Starting in the early 1910s, travel clubs would drive primitive roads across the desert, and the Arrowhead Trail was one of the popular roads. The rustic stone cabins provided one of the few shelters along the trail. Shortly after the CCC built the cabins, the state of Nevada made this area its first state park; it's also Nevada's largest state park at around 42,000 acres.

On our way out of the park, we made a final stop at the east entrance to see Elephant Rock. It's a natural arch that kind of looks like an elephant. It had been a long day already, and standing there, looking up at the elephant-like arch, I think I spoke for both of us when I said, "Alright, it looks like an elephant, let's go." Karen didn't hesitate to follow me back to the car.

After Elephant Rock, we'd done everything on Karen's list; it was time to head for the Hampton Inn. Driving out the east side of the park, I turned south on Highway 169, which put us into Lake Mead Recreation Area, heading toward Henderson. "What did you think of that park?" I asked Karen.

"It was wonderful. Great hikes, interesting sites. I might call it a 'hidden gem,'" she said.

"I would agree it's a hidden gem. Although it's been a park for over a hundred years. Maybe it's not so much *hidden* as we're morons for not knowing about it before now."

"I'd prefer to think of it as a hidden gem," she said.

Your friend,
Matt

~.~.~.~.~.~.~.~

From: **Matt Smith**
Subject: **Mojave National Preserve**
Date: **January 19 (Thursday)**

Dear Bob and Sue,

We've been to Mojave National Preserve three times now, and every time we tell people about it, we get a blank stare. It's pretty obvious they have no idea where or what it is, which is kind of hard to believe given that the park covers 1.6 million acres and is an hour or so from Vegas.

Soon after we crossed the California border on Highway 15, we took the Cima Road exit into the park, which runs through miles and miles of Joshua trees. This area has the world's largest concentration of them. A few years ago, we stopped at a parking lot along this road and hiked the Teutonic Peak Trail, which climbs 700 feet to an amazing view of the surrounding desert and mountains.

Today we continued farther into the park to the Hole in the Wall Information Center, which, coming from the north, entails driving on a rough dirt road for about ten miles. There are three campgrounds along this stretch of road, along with our favorite hike: the Barber Peak Loop Trail.

The skies were clear, and the temperature was in the fifties when we parked and started hiking from the information center. Walking through the nearby campground toward the trailhead, we saw a couple of RVs, but we didn't see any people. Karen says she'd like to camp there someday because it would be a great spot to view the night sky. She's probably right; it's far enough away from Las Vegas and other civilization that the stars must be brilliant on a cloud-free, moonless night.

The elevation change was slight on the moderately strenuous hike as we circumnavigated a massive rock formation in the middle of the desert. I assume the formation we hiked around was Barber Peak, although I've never found its name on a map. About halfway through the hike, cattle startled us as we suddenly came upon them. I think we surprised them as well; they took off trotting down the trail when they saw us. For about a mile they'd amble along the path, stop about every hundred feet, turn toward us to see if we were still following them, and then take off again. It never occurred to them that they could step aside and let us pass.

On the southwest side of the loop, we hiked over a rock ridge covered with desert vegetation in countless shades of pink and green. Huge barrel cacti lined the trail; each one looked perfect, as if a landscaper had arranged them along the trail and then came back to take care of them when no one was looking.

The last time we'd hiked this trail, we came around a bend and found ourselves face-to-face with half a dozen horses. We all froze and stared at one another. Had we hiked another thirty yards, we would have blocked their only way out of the canyon. We know that animals don't like having their only escape route blocked, so we backed up and waited a few minutes. A donkey was amongst the herd. He cocked his head and gave us a worried look; I could swear he squinted his eyes. Then he made a quick bolt toward the exit, stopped after a few yards, and watched us again. After another couple of minutes, he bolted for good, and the horses followed him out of the canyon. He looked like a big dog whose job it was to protect the herd. When we got to that same spot on the trail today, I was looking forward to seeing the horses and the donkey. No such luck; we were all by ourselves.

Matt climbing up the rings on Rings Loop Trail,
Mojave National Preserve

Rather than take the Barber Peak Loop Trail all the way back to the information center, we turned onto an adjacent path called the Rings Loop Trail. The attraction of the trail is that it runs through a short section of a slot canyon. At a spot where it's too steep to climb unaided, the park service attached large metal rings into the side of the canyon walls. It's awkward at first trying to climb up the narrow canyon using the rings because they're all on one side, and you have to stand on each one as you pull yourself up. But it doesn't take long to get the hang of it. At the top of the slot canyon there's a short hike to a paved road and a picnic area. From there, the road leads back to the information center.

In total, we hiked for about three hours. Afterward, we had plenty of daylight left and it was too early to head back to Henderson. Karen suggested we hike to the top of the Kelso Sand Dunes and watch the sun go down like we did in Death Valley years before. She said it would be romantic, and you know I'm all about the romance.

Sand dunes look inviting from a distance; they're so smooth and soft. You can imagine yourself getting to the top of a giant dune, laying back in the warm sand, and gazing at the landscape for miles. For me, though, walking in sand is a struggle. Hiking up hills of sand is worse; it's a slog.

"Are you enjoying this?" I called out to Karen about twenty minutes into our death march up the dunes. "Feeling romantic yet?"

She paused, panting heavily. "Well, um, let's just keep going a little farther. I want to get to the top so we can see the view to the other side of the dunes."

Ten minutes later when we reached the top, I was drenched with sweat and sand underneath my contact lens was irritating my right eye. I squinted through my good eye and asked, "How's the romance level now? Should we hold hands and kiss?"

"You're right. I've had enough," she replied while trying to empty the sand out of her shoe without taking it off her foot.

We stood there for a few minutes enjoying the view. It was a beautiful vista to the Southwest. The sun was low, and we were in the midst of the golden hour. Below us we could see a group of about twenty people gathered together. From our vantage point, it looked like a film crew and a five-person band. They must have been recording a music video. I'm sure the dunes made a great venue for the video, but I could imagine how difficult it must have been for them to lug all of their equipment through the sand.

As we started back down, it didn't take us long to realize we made the right decision to head back when we did; the sun was setting faster than we'd expected. Had we waited much longer, we would have been walking the last quarter of a mile in the dark. We got back to the car as the sun disappeared below the horizon.

We still have a lot to see and do in this park. Karen wants to come back and go into the Lava Tubes. I'm not sure what they are, but I think they're similar to caves. I can't wait.

Your friend,
Matt

~.~.~.~.~.~.~.~

From: **Matt Smith**
Subject: **Hoover Dam Tour**
Date: **January 20 (Friday)**

Dear Bob and Sue,

Our stretch of good weather came to an end today. We woke up this morning to gray skies and drizzle. Taking a tour of Hoover Dam hadn't been on our short list of things to do on this trip, but given the weather, it turned out to be the perfect indoor activity.

By 7:00 am I'd had my coffee, showered, dressed, and was staring at Karen. "What's the plan?" I asked.

Karen was still sitting up in bed. She took a sip of coffee and looked at me over her iPad. "There's no plan. It's still dark out. Don't you have something you can do to keep yourself busy?"

"We need a plan for the day," I insisted.

"Maybe we should have a day with no itinerary. We'll do whatever we want at the spur of the moment," she replied.

"Great, what do you want to do?"

Karen snorted and went back to reading her iPad. "Stop staring at me," she said without looking up.

"Alright, I'm going downstairs to make a waffle."

"Great idea. Take your time."

It shouldn't be a surprise when I tell you we were the first in line when they opened the doors of the Hoover Dam tour office at 9:00 am. The first tour started at 9:30 and while we were waiting for it to begin, we sat in the front row of the small theater to watch a short film about the dam. It was warm and cozy in the theater. When they dimmed the lights to start the film, my eyes shut; I fell asleep for a couple of minutes. Karen nudged me and whispered, "See, you should have slept longer this morning. It's too early for a nap."

"I think the waffles are making me sleepy," I replied.

"Waffles? Plural?"

Rookie mistake on my part. I quickly acted like I was asleep again.

Despite dozing, I found it interesting to learn about how the dam was constructed. Built during the Great Depression, men came to Boulder City from all over the country hoping to get a job. The number of workers on the project, at any given time, ranged from about 3,000 to 5,000. It was a dangerous project and the Bureau of Reclamation's official death count is listed as ninety-six. All of these deaths were accidental: drowning, falling, being struck by a rock, etc. The official count excludes deaths from heart attack, heat stroke, and men who were injured but died somewhere other than the job site. Also, more than forty men died of pneumonia, and some believe their respiratory problems were the result of working in poorly ventilated tunnels.

When it was built, the dam was the largest concrete construction project ever, and the engineers had to come up with novel ways to deal with such a massive pour. Their primary challenge was how to get the concrete to cool quickly so they could continue to pour slab on top of slab without trapping the heat the concrete generated as it cured. They solved this challenge by embedding one-inch steel pipes inside the newly poured slabs and running cold water through them to pull the heat out of the concrete. To cool the water, the engineers built the world's largest refrigerator. (I wonder where that refrigerator is today.) Probably the most surprising statistic we learned was the project finished over two years ahead of schedule; construction began in 1931 and the dam was completed in 1936.

After the film, an elevator took us 530 feet down through the dam to a room where massive generators were cranking out electricity. From there we walked through narrow passages and saw a couple of the internal stairwells that the construction workers used when building the dam. "Now, you'll notice that these stairs are very steep and the treads are narrow," our guide said. "That's because the workers back then were shorter than the typical man today."

"I call bullshit on that," I said softly to Karen. "They wanted to save money, that's why they built little tiny stairs."

She shot me a frown and shushed me.

I tried not to think too hard about where we were inside the dam relative to the enormous lake that it was holding back. When our guide told us how the dam engineers constantly monitor all of the cracks that have developed in the dam since its construction, a brief, creepy, claustrophobic wave of fear came over me. "See this one here?" he said pointing to a hairline fracture in the wall next to him. "This crack was discovered in 1961 and hasn't gotten any bigger since then. They catalog each one and monitor them to see if they've grown."

I said to Karen, "I don't think that crack was there five minutes ago."

She shushed me again.

"I'm serious. How much longer is this tour? I need some fresh air."

Shortly after our discussion about the cracks, our group took an elevator to the top and we were let out into the open air. It felt good to see daylight again.

The top of the dam is a two-lane road on which cars are allowed to drive, but they're prohibited from stopping to let out passengers. Besides this being a not-so-clever way to avoid the ten-dollar parking garage fee, it also is a not-so-smart way to get around the X-ray machines and metal detectors that all visitors must pass through as they enter the visitor center. Even so, while we were standing there, about every third car that came along tried to let someone out so they could take a quick look over the side of the dam. Security guards were posted along the road. It looked like their only job was to yell, "Sir! Get back in your car!"

The usual response was, "I just want to take one picture," which brought a quick response of "Sir! Get back in your car!"

As we were standing there watching this happen, a car stopped and an older gentleman got out and slowly walked toward the edge of the dam. The security guard barked his command, but the man just stared back at him with a blank look on his face.

"I don't think he understands you," I said to the guard.

"He understands me. Sir! You need to get back in your car!" he said shaking his head sternly.

The guard looked at me. "This is what I do—all day."

Since we'd paid the entrance fee as part of our tour, we were allowed to walk along the sidewalk at the top of the dam. On the Lake Mead side, the waterline was way below the level of the road. Years of low snowpack and drought have caused the lake to drop to a record low level. We tried to get a few photos, but the lighting was poor due to the overcast sky. And when it began raining, we decided we'd seen enough.

This trip was a great way to start the new year. It was a welcome relief to see the sun again, get some exercise, and have a reason to get out of my pajamas. We have a few more trips planned in the coming months. We'll keep you posted on how those go. If you ever want to join us, you're more than welcome.

Your friend,
Matt

~.~.~.~.~.~.~.~

From: **Matt Smith**
Subject: **Indian Canyons – Palm Springs**
Date: **February 17 (Friday)**

Dear Bob and Sue,

Greetings from Palm Springs! Most people come down here for the golf and tennis, but we've discovered a lot of great hikes in the area. It's become a ritual for us every time we're here to visit Indian Canyons on the Agua Caliente Indian Reservation, about seven miles directly south of downtown Palm Springs. You have to pay an entrance fee to get onto the reservation, but it's worth it to hike their network of well-maintained trails through the desert.

Today we hiked a three-hour loop starting at the visitor center. I'd tell you how many miles we hiked, if I knew. We always get the color-coded map at the entrance station when we pay our fee, but once we get about a mile along the trail we're never sure where we are. There's something about the Palm Springs area that causes me to lose my sense of direction; I get my north and south mixed up once we arrive and I'm confused the entire time we're here.

The hike always starts the same; from the visitor center we hike down a moderately steep trail for a quarter mile to an oasis covered with lush palm trees. From there the Palm Canyon Trail snakes through the narrow, treed area for about a mile at which point you have a choice of paths leading off into the desert. Karen and I always follow the East Fork Trail up a wash that has several mildly challenging dry falls, requiring some hand-over-hand scrambling. (A dry fall is a waterfall without water.) A couple of them are too high to climb, so we have to look for a side trail that bypasses them. I've noticed that every time we come, it takes a few more grunts and groans to get over them than the time before.

We hiked up the wash for about forty-five minutes until we came upon a trail marker that had arrows pointing to various trails. I was sure that both the direction of the arrows and the distances to each were incorrect. "I don't think they'd put incorrect trail markers out here in the middle of the desert," Karen said as I tried to explain to her that the trail we wanted was in a different direction than the marker indicated. Thankfully, I contained my belligerence—just this once—and followed her lead. Soon we were on top of a ridge that we recognized from our previous hikes in the area. The views up there are spectacular. The East Fork Trail is a loop that leads back to the visitor center. We continued on the Vandeventer Trail, which is an alternative arm of the loop that ends there as well.

It was an enjoyable hike. Three hours of sweating in the sun was what we needed after a long winter. The workout left us exhausted, and it felt good. We had just enough energy at the end to climb back up the quarter-mile section of trail to the parking lot.

At the turn of the last switchback, before we made it to the top, a man and woman were standing taking a picture of something in the vegetation just off the trail. Typically, when I'm worn out and hiking uphill, I ignore what's going on around me and focus on putting one foot in front of the other. But as I approached the couple, I sensed this might not be your typical scene of visitors trying to get close-up of a hummingbird. Maybe it was the woman standing in the parking lot right above them with one hand over her mouth and the other waving in the air nervously that made me think something unusual was happening.

The man was standing at the edge of the trail pointing his phone toward the object and taking shot after shot. Three feet away from where he stood—which was then three feet away from where I was standing—was a large, coiled, rattling rattlesnake. I quickly moved away and said to him, "No, no, no. Too close. Shouldn't be that close." Maybe I could have been more clear with my warning, but I was too tired to form complete sentences. The couple laughed at me and the man kept taking pictures.

I turned to Karen, who was still coming up the trail, and said, "Karen, rattlesnake, come this way," as I directed her to the uphill side of the trail.

At this point, the couple turned their backs to the rattlesnake and were taking selfies with it in the background. Karen kept looking back at them as we walked through the parking lot.

"Can you even believe them?" she asked.

"Yes. It's called natural selection. Now let's get out of here so the ambulance has somewhere to park."

Although we've gotten into a habit of hiking the same trail every time we visit, the reservation has other hikes worth doing. A couple of years ago we hiked to Seven Sisters Falls on the Murray Canyon Trail. It has a paved road to the trailhead, and it's only about two miles, one-way, to the falls.

We hiked it one sunny day in March. It was a weekday, and almost no one else was on the trail. About a mile and a half into the hike, we ran into a group of about twenty men who were working in an area along the trail where tall grass and weeds crowded the path. The men were cutting the vegetation and smoothing ruts. They each had a garden tool of some kind—rake, shovel, weed whacker—except one guy in the middle who was wearing a bright yellow vest. He stood and watched them work.

As we got closer, I noticed they were all wearing matching outfits. It was about then that I saw large, orange letters printed vertically on their pants. "Why are they all wearing the same thing?" Karen whispered.

"Here, walk in front of me," I said. "Just keep your head down and continue hiking. And do *not* stop to visit with them."

I made sure we didn't slow down as we passed them even though they were all friendly and polite. Each of them jumped out of the way when they saw us coming. Nearly every one smiled and said something kind to Karen as she walked by them.

"Hi, there!" the first one said as he almost fell backwards out of our way.

"Have a good hike, ma'am," the next one said.

"Enjoy your hike, ma'am."

"Excuse me, ma'am."

"Watch your step now."

"Beautiful day, isn't it?"

Once we were out of earshot, Karen stopped and turned toward me.

"What was printed on their pants? We were hiking so fast I couldn't read it."

"Prisoner," I replied.

After a long silence, Karen asked, "Are you sure? I only saw the 'P' and the 'ER' and the end. Maybe they were the Panthers."

"Yes, that's right. They were the Panthers. I've heard about them. They're a group of men who do volunteer work in communities and give each other tattoos. I feel so much better now. Prisoners? What was I thinking?"

"Do you think they're really prisoners?" Karen asked.

"Yes, they were prisoners! Why do you think they were so glad to see you? 'Enjoy your hike, ma'am!'"

After another long silence, Karen said, "Oh no, we have to walk past them again on our way out."

"No shit," I replied.

"Maybe they won't be there when we go back. It's late in the afternoon. Maybe their shift is about over."

"Sweetie, ma'am, they'll be there when we go back. I think you were the highlight of their day."

"What!? That's ridiculous," she said.

The rest of the hike through the canyon to the waterfall was pretty, with numerous creek crossings. We didn't spend much time looking at the falls at the end of the trail. The sun was setting fast, and it would be dark in about an hour.

Just as I'd told Karen, the trail crew was right where we'd left them. They were even more polite the second time. And coincidentally, right as we passed them, they all stopped working and fell in line behind us. "Sweetie, pick up the pace, they're coming," I said.

"Now that's creepy."

"Hey, if I were a prisoner, I'd follow you down the trail," I said. It wasn't the most well-thought-out compliment I've ever given my wife, but I was trying to lighten the mood.

"Did you happen to notice if the guard had a gun?" Karen asked.

"You mean like in one of those 1960s movies where the warden is holding a shotgun next to his chest while the chain gang breaks rocks?" I replied.

"Shhh, they'll hear you."

"You're the one who asked the question."

I tried not to worry about our new hiking buddies. Although, they seemed to have a lot of energy, and I could swear they were gaining on us—because they were. Soon, they were only a few feet behind us and making a lot of noise. I've never heard so much lively banter on a trail before.

"Karen, we need to stop," I said.

"I'm not stopping," she replied.

"Yep, let's move aside and let them pass."

She reluctantly stepped off the trail and I stood right next to her. "You guys sure hike faster than we do," I said in my most manly voice as they brushed past us.

I was relieved when they kept moving down the trail. A couple of them in the middle of the pack looked like they were slowing down to *visit*. A voice from the back shouted, "Keep it moving, gentlemen." The supervisor in the yellow vest was the last one in line. "These guys," he said, shaking his head. "It's like trying to keep a bunch of puppy dogs in a basket whenever we're out here."

"Puppy dogs? That's not the analogy that first comes to my mind when referring to convicts," I said under my breath.

Karen poked me in the ribs. "They were friendly. They seemed like a nice group of guys."

"Yeah, the Panthers are a real fine group. I hear they do children's birthday parties. They're prisoners, ma'am!"

"Matt, there's no way they'd let murderers and rapists out of their cells to work on a trail. Those guys probably forgot to pay a parking ticket or something like that."

"Yeah, I'm sure you're right. I hear they throw you in jail in Palm Springs if you 'forget' to pay a parking ticket."

When we reached the parking lot, the Panthers were loading into their white, county-issued van. A few of them waved and whistled at Karen one last time as their supervisor was trying to herd them into the van. "Let's go, gentlemen!" he said.

"Did you want to go over there and give them our home address before we leave, you know, so we can be pen pals?" I asked as we pulled out of the parking lot.

"They were nice," Karen said.

"Yep, nice guys."

Now that I've told you this story, I remember why we always hike the trails up by the visitor center when we visit the Agua Caliente Indian Reservation.

Your friend,
Matt

From: **Matt Smith**
Subject: **Becoming Campers**
Date: **March 7 (Tuesday)**

Dear Bob and Sue,

Back in January, before we'd taken our first trip of the year, Karen and I were sitting at the kitchen table drinking our morning coffee. Outside it was dark, cold, and rainy. Karen looked up from her laptop and said to me in a booming, confident tone, "You know what we're going to do this year?"

"Drink our coffee without startling each other?" I asked.

"Nope. This is the year we learn to camp."

"Do you know what camping is?" I asked.

"It'll be fun. We'll be out in nature. We can sit around the campfire and sleep under the stars."

"Alright, then we should put on our headlamps, go out to the deck, and finish our coffee while sitting in the rain. After coffee, you can brush your teeth in the backyard and spit into the bushes—because that's what camping is."

Despite my ribbing, her resolve was firm. She was ready to venture beyond the comfort of Hampton Inns and sleep outside. I wasn't sure why she was suddenly interested in camping. In the past when I'd suggested it, she'd scrunch her face and say, "You can't be serious." Maybe she changed her mind because of our experience in the Grand Canyon last year. When we floated the Colorado River through the canyon for a week, we camped every night. That trip was a blast, and it must have given her the confidence to try camping again. Whatever had made the difference, she was now ready.

Most of the equipment I'd bought more than fifteen years ago when our son and I camped was obsolete, broken or missing. At one time we had a tent, but I couldn't find it. I think maybe you borrowed it and never returned it. Regardless, I now had a valid excuse to buy new stuff, which is the most important reason to start a new activity in the first place. We knew at the very least we needed to buy two sleeping bags, pads and a tent.

Over the last couple of months, we've made several visits to REI to outfit our new adventure. I can't believe how much the camping section has expanded in the last fifteen years. The selection of beverage containers alone takes up several aisles, a far cry from when I first bought camping gear and there were only two choices: a red tin cup or a blue tin cup. On our last trip to REI, I found Karen standing in front of a display with her arms crossed.

"Look at all these wine glasses, Matt. There's a stainless steel stemless one, an acrylic one with a detachable stem, and an insulated wine tumbler with a lid. I don't know which one to get."

"Why don't you get the insulated tumbler and you can use it for coffee *and* wine."

"But what if I'm drinking both at the same time?"

"Then you have a bigger problem than which beverage container to choose."

Other necessities made their way into my shopping bag as well, like an extra-long titanium spoon for eating out of pouches of freeze-dried food. Karen dug the spoon out of my bag, looked at it, and said, "Do you really need a nine-dollar spoon?"

"It's a special spoon. It's longer than normal, which lets me reach the bottom of the food pouch without having to put my hand down in there," I replied.

"Should I get one?"

"You can get one if you want, but you have your spork."

"Yeah, but my spork isn't long like that one."

"We only need one long spoon. Once the food is fully cooked in the bag, I'll scoop your portion of the meal out and put it in a plastic cup. A spork is fine for eating out of a plastic cup." She held the translucent plastic cup up to the light so she could read the measurements marked on the side, then looked at me with suspicion, like I was cooking up an elaborate scheme to cheat her on meal portions. "You can be in charge of rationing out the food, I promise," I said.

Of all the items we had to buy, the tent footprint was the one Karen couldn't get her head around. When she saw it in my shopping bag, she had to ask, "What is a tent footprint? And why does it cost sixty dollars?!"

"It's a piece of fabric that you put down on the ground and then put your tent on top of it. That way your expensive tent doesn't get dirty," I replied.

"But it's a tent. You take it camping. It's going to get dirty."

"Not if you have a footprint."

"So, instead of your expensive tent getting dirty, your expensive footprint gets dirty?"

"No, I got a tarp to lay down that we can put our footprint on."

"You can't be serious. Eventually, something you own will have to touch the dirt."

I've resorted to hiding my purchases from Karen because our debates about each item were endless. My new strategy is to wait until the moment when we absolutely need a particular item and then whip it out. When I do this, she usually responds with, "That's genius! You are so smart to bring a lantern!" She doesn't need to know about all the stuff I have in the storage bins in the back of my truck.

Now that we have the basic equipment, it's time to try it out; we're going to become campers. Tomorrow we leave for a road trip to Utah. We're hoping that by going this early in the year, it won't yet be unbearably hot during the day. Karen wants to try a couple of hikes in Canyonlands National Park, one of them in the remote Needles District of the park. That's where we're hoping to camp for the first time. We'll keep you posted on how it goes.

Your friend,
Matt

From: **Matt Smith**
Subject: **Little Wild Horse Canyon and Goblin Valley**
Date: **March 10 (Friday)**

Dear Bob and Sue,

Happy Friday! We're writing to you from one of our
favorite states: Utah! It would probably be *the* favorite if they
sold beer stronger than 3.2 percent. Whenever we drive to
Utah, we always bring a cooler of craft beer from home. The
problem arises when we eat out. The last time I ordered a
beer in a Utah restaurant, I said to the waiter, "I think there's
something wrong with my IPA."

He replied, "Yeah, it was made in Utah."

Karen and I took a couple of days to drive from Seattle to
Green River. Along the way, we debated whether we'd find
snow on the hiking trails. I said to her, "You know, there's a
real possibility that we'll be hiking through snow on this trip."

"There's no way we'll be hiking in snow. We're going to
the desert. It'll feel like summertime," she replied.

Driving south on Highway 191, north of Green River, I
pointed out my window and asked her, "Hey, what's that
over there, in the open field?"

She pretended she didn't see what I was pointing at. A
couple of miles later I said again, "See, there's snow in the
desert just off the highway."

This time she couldn't ignore my comment. "I don't think
that's snow."

"Then what is it?"

"It's white dirt. We've seen white dirt in the desert before.
It's all over."

"It's snow, sweetie."

The white dirt debate continued the rest of the way to
Green River; that's what comes from two full days of driving
without stops. When I turned off the highway at the Green
River exit, I was sure I was in the wrong place. I couldn't find

the town to save my life. Then Karen said, "That was Green River."

"What was Green River?"

"We just drove through it."

"You mean the gas station and the restaurant by the river? That was the town?"

"I'm pretty sure that was it."

She was correct; besides a few small motels, the John Wesley Powell River History Museum, and a gas station, there's not much else to the town. This concerned me as we pulled into our motel parking lot, because I'm always keenly aware of where my next meal is coming from, and I didn't see a lot of dining options. Fortunately, along the main drag we found a food truck parked in front of an abandoned gas station that served excellent burritos. Emergency averted.

This morning we were up early and ready for a break from the long drive. The weather was beautiful, and the temps were mild, forecasted for the fifties and sixties. Our first stop of the day was Little Wild Horse Canyon (LWHC). From the town of Green River, we drove west on I-70 for about fifteen miles and then took State Route 24 south toward Hanksville. The canyon is right next to Goblin Valley State Park.

The entire area west of SR 24 is part of a land formation called the San Rafael Swell, which was uplifted about fifty million years ago. Ever since, erosion has been carving canyons and odd land formations throughout the swell. Two of those canyons are Little Wild Horse Canyon and Bell Canyon. An eight-mile loop trail takes you through both.

To get to the canyons, we hiked north from the parking lot up a wash for about half a mile until we came to a sign that pointed straight ahead to Bell Canyon. We looked to our right and saw an opening in the curved rock wall we assumed was LWHC. We'd decided to hike the loop counterclockwise, so we turned and descended into the canyon. Almost immediately, the walls narrowed, and we were in the slot. We encountered several boulders that required scrambling over, and a few dry falls where I had to give Karen a boost. In other sections we had to take off our packs to squeeze through tiny openings. It was very cool.

Matt squeezing through the walls of
Little Wild Horse Canyon

The slot opened up after we had hiked for about two miles, and we ended up on the backside of the loop following a primitive road to the west. We knew from the map that we were supposed to go that way, but there were lots of other side trails and we were never sure where the turn off for Bell Canyon was. After about an hour, when we were positive we were lost, we came to a big arrow of rocks in the wash pointing us to Bell Canyon. That was a relief.

"Now that we know where we are, maybe we should stop for a snack," Karen suggested.

"Sure, I just need to get a few pictures first. You find a good spot to sit and I'll join you in a minute."

"What are you taking a picture of?" she asked in an annoyed tone. She knew the answer but wanted to ask anyway.

"Oh nothing, just a few patches of white dirt. I want to photograph them before they're all gone. It's almost as if this white dirt evaporates once the sun shines on it, and then there's a wet spot where it used to be. I've never seen dirt like that."

Karen sat on a rock and ate her peanut butter and jelly sandwich without responding to my white dirt comments. The sun was warm, and we imagined that it was summertime. It would have been easy for me to take a nap, but I couldn't find a flat rock big enough to lie down on. Also, we had more to do before heading toward Moab, and we needed to keep moving. Karen was excited to see Goblin Valley State Park.

After snack time, we hiked through Bell Canyon and then back to the truck. Bell Canyon was similar to LWHC, although it seemed a little shorter and had a fewer spots that required scrambling. I'd never heard of this area before Karen found it while doing her research for this trip. The trail and slots were beautiful and during the four hours we were hiking we saw maybe a handful of people. Slot canyons are becoming one of our favorite types of hikes. Toward the end of this trip we'll be visiting one of the most stunning slot canyons in the U.S.: Buckskin Gulch.

Goblin Valley State Park was a few miles from the LWHC trailhead. While the Bureau of Land Management manages most of the San Rafael Swell, the state of Utah manages Goblin. It's rather small, less than six square miles, but it has a campground. The main attraction is its thousands of small mushroom-shaped hoodoos. One of the first westerners to discover the park named it Mushroom Valley, but the state renamed it Goblin Valley in 1964 when they bought the land and made it a park to protect it from vandalism.

Karen wandering through Goblin Valley

Unfortunately, vandalism still happens. Because the hoodoo rock formations are small, they're delicate. It wouldn't take much to push one over, which is what someone did a few years ago. The person doing the pushing was a Boy Scout leader, no less. Another leader took a video of him pushing over the hoodoo, and these guys were so proud of what they did that they posted the video on Facebook. On top of being expelled from the Boy Scout organization, the two men were fined and charged with felonies for their vandalism. Eventually, they pleaded to lesser charges. The incident is a warning to anyone thinking about messing with the parks; the penalties can be severe.

I've seen trail maps of Goblin Valley, but mostly you can walk anywhere in the main valley without following a trail. We could see the parking lot from wherever we hiked. I never worried about getting lost. It's one of those unique landscapes that begs you to look around every corner and explore all of the rock formations. I followed Karen around watching her take pictures of the goblins. She loves fantasy landscapes. "It looks very Dr. Seuss-like, doesn't it?" she kept saying.

The drive from Goblin Valley SP to Moab took about two hours. We'll be here a couple of nights. Tomorrow, Karen has another bucket list hike she wants to do in Canyonlands National Park and the day after that will be our inaugural camping trip in the Needles District of Canyonlands. We're living the dream, wish you could join us.

Your friend,
Matt

~.~.~.~.~.~.~

From: **Matt Smith**
Subject: **False Kiva and Aztec Butte**
Date: **March 11 (Saturday)**

Dear Bob and Sue,

Several months ago, Karen saw a stunning photograph of the Milky Way taken from inside a rock alcove. The stars hung over a beautiful desert landscape, and a circle of stones in the foreground looked as if they were part of an ancient cliff dwelling. She showed me the photo and said, "We need to go here."

At the time she didn't know where "here" was, but as a result of some persistent research, she figured it out. The name of the place is False Kiva, and we were surprised to learn that it's in the Island in the Sky District of Canyonlands National Park—a park we've been to several times. We'd never seen False Kiva on the park map or on their list of suggested hikes. I'm not sure why they keep mum about it; I'm guessing that they're trying to minimize wear and tear on the ruins.

The picture that Karen had seen was Wally Pacholka's photo of the Milky Way taken from inside the alcove. False Kiva was a relatively unknown place before his photo became a NASA Astronomy Picture of the Day back in 2008. Since then, photos of the site are continually posted on social media.

At the visitor center, I was expecting the information desk ranger to discourage us from doing the hike, but when Karen asked about how to get there he gave us detailed instructions about where to park, how to find the trailhead, and tips on following the trail. After doing the hike, I don't think we would have found the alcove without the help from the ranger and the GPS coordinates we'd found online. In a couple of places it's tricky to figure out where the trail is, and it would've been easy to miss finding the site altogether.

False Kiva is in the northwest section of Canyonlands. I parked our truck on the side of the road to the Upheaval Dome parking lot, and we walked back along the road looking for the start of the trail like the ranger told us to do. No sign marks the trailhead; we found it mainly by stumbling through the brush until we came across a clear path through the scrub.

Being spring break, we'd expected to run into crowds. However, since we'd gotten an early start this morning, we found this area of the park mostly empty. Fortunately for us, we could see another couple in the distance hiking toward False Kiva; we figured if we lost the trail, at least we could use them as a rough guide as to where we should be going.

The weather was perfect: not too warm, not too cool, no wind, and brilliantly sunny. My fear of having to hike through white dirt was a distant memory. On days like today, Karen says to me, "Soak it in, Matt, we don't get these days back!"

Despite a few tricky turns, the hike wasn't strenuous. We made a steep uphill scramble right at the end, but it wasn't very long. The total distance of the trek, one way, was about a mile. It only took thirty minutes to reach the alcove once we left the road and got on the trail.

The couple who'd reached the site before us were taking a few final photos when we got there. We stayed out of their way while they finished, and after they left we had the place to ourselves. I stood at the edge of the alcove looking southwest over the park toward the Green River. A few miles in the distance I could see Candlestick Tower pointing up toward the blue sky as if to say, "See Milky Way here."

A large circle made of stacked stones about twenty-five feet in diameter and two to three feet high was in the center of the alcove. Not much is known about the site other than archeologists believe it was probably only used for a short time. From the looks of the rocks that formed the circle, the site had been well-treated by park visitors.

A spiral notebook at the back of the alcove was held down by a flat rock—a makeshift registry for visitors to write their names and leave remarks. An entry from the day before read, "Feeling lucky to be alive." Another read, "I can't help but feel slightly insignificant while in the presence of this massive natural landscape." My favorite was, "This false kiva was made by aliens!" I knew it.

One thing we realized, as we squinted our eyes to see the pictures we'd taken on our phones, was that morning isn't a great time to take photos at False Kiva. The alcove and the stone circle are in the shade, and the landscape in the distance is in full sun. It was impossible for us to get a good exposure of both. I did some research this afternoon when we got to our hotel and learned that just after sunset is the best time to take photos of this site. Or, if you really know what you're doing, long exposures in the middle of a clear night let you capture the alcove and the stars for a stunning picture. The problem with doing this is you'd need to be at the site in the middle of the night. I wouldn't want to attempt the hike—in either direction—in the dark, regardless of how good my headlamp was.

Karen didn't want to leave. She stood still, looking at the landscape, with her hands on her hips and said, "This is amazing." Looking southwest from the kiva, we couldn't see a single man-made object or mark on the land other than the trail we just hiked. Near the edge of the horizon, the canyon in which the Green River flows cut a gash across the desert floor. The red and tan desert scene was speckled with hints of springtime green.

Matt standing in front of False Kiva,
Canyonlands National Park

Our peaceful moment in the alcove ended when a group of four young men got to the site. They had a lot of energy and were climbing on everything, including each other. I kept waiting for one of them to fall off the cliff, trying to guess which one would go over first. I had my money on the one who stood next to Karen, took off his shirt and gave out a primal scream into the canyon below. His echo fascinated him and his friends. Each time he yelled, his voice repeated a second later, and his buddy would say, "Bro, that's lit."

Karen had a concerned look on her face. She whispered to me, "They shouldn't be lighting anything up here."

"Why do you think they're lighting something?"

"Didn't you hear that kid say it was 'lit?'"

"I think 'lit' means something is cool. I think. Either that or they actually lit something, not sure."

After the fifth holler into the canyon, Karen turned to me and said, "And we're outta here."

As we started back down the trail, I said to our new trail mates, "Later, dudes."

Karen laughed so hard I thought she was going to fall over. When she gathered her composure she asked me, "Were you trying to be cool back there? Because I don't think anyone has used the phrase 'later, dudes' since the Teenage Mutant Ninja Turtles were popular—like twenty years ago."

"It's called *old school*, sweetie. It's lit. But you wouldn't know what that means," I replied.

The rest of the day she'd randomly say, "Later, dudes," and then burst out laughing.

Not far from where we parked for the False Kiva hike was a trailhead for a hike to the top of Aztec Butte. We hadn't planned on doing it, but we had extra time and the weather was so pleasant we decided to give it a try. Aztec Butte is a 300-foot bump of land that sits north of the road to Upheaval Dome. On the trail to the butte is another rock outcropping to the west that has a few small Anasazi granary ruins. The trip to the top of the butte and back, including a side trip to the granaries, was only about one and a half miles. The views from the highest point on the butte were spectacular, similar to the views from False Kiva, but without the overhang of the alcove.

On our way back to Moab, we took a side-trip through Arches National Park. As we drove past Balanced Rock, I turned to Karen and said, "We have to soak it up."

"Soak it *in*, not soak it *up*," she said.

At the end of the main road we reached the parking area for Devil's Garden. The lot was overflowing, but we found a spot close to the trailhead. "Are you up for another hike?" I asked Karen.

"Sure, we can always turn around when we've had enough."

Being mid-day on a beautiful Saturday, the trail was crowded. Karen and I started down the Devil's Garden Trail, and a short distance before we reached the turn off to the Primitive Loop, I heard a loud buzzing sound. "Someone is flying a drone in the park," I said.

"But that's illegal," she replied. "Who would be stupid enough to fly their drone with all of these people around?"

"That guy, the one standing on top of that fin over there piloting it around those big rocks."

"I read that the park service can fine people as much as five thousand dollars for flying a drone in a park without a permit," Karen said.

"Well, this guy must not know that because he's also yelling to his friends and drawing a ton of attention to himself."

I tried to get a video of him flying his drone, but just as I hit *record*, he quickly packed it into his drone-carrying-case-backpack and began climbing down from his perch. Maybe he saw me take my phone out and got spooked. We've only come across one other drone-flying incident in a national park. In Death Valley a couple of years ago, we saw a man fly his drone right over a park ranger's head. The ranger ordered him to stop flying it and the man hovered his drone in the air for another couple of minutes until the ranger repeated his demand.

Our energy level was still high despite our earlier hikes and we managed to do the entire seven-mile Primitive Loop. It felt good to push ourselves and experience that trail-weary feeling in our legs. For the first time this season, it seemed like winter was over and summer was just around the corner.

Tomorrow we're driving to the Needles District of Canyonlands, an area of the park we've never been to. Karen has her heart set on a hike through the Needles, and with a little luck we'll get a campsite. We have the tent in the back of the truck and we're ready to become campers.

Your friend,
Matt

~.~.~.~.~.~.~.~

From: **Karen Smith**
Subject: **Not Becoming Campers**
Date: **March 12 (Sunday)**

Dear Bob and Sue,

We missed getting a campsite today by minutes, and I blame the Cheez-Its. All of them: the Original, the Four Cheese, the White Cheddar, the Reduced Fat, the Hot and Spicy, the Pepper Jack, the Cheddar Jack, the Extra Toasty, the BIG ones, the Grooves, the Duoz (whatever the hell those are), the Cheez-It Sandwich Crackers and the Snack Mix.

This morning, when we stopped in the grocery store in Moab to pick up supplies, I rounded the corner with my shopping cart and almost ran over Matt, who was standing in the middle of the aisle in a trance, staring at a wall of Cheez-Its.

I told him, "It's time to be making your final decisions. We need to get on the road."

Without turning his head to look at me, he said, "I can't choose. Look at 'em all. When did this happen? I consider myself a Cheez-It expert, but I've never seen half of these before."

"Yeah. Thrilling. Why don't you choose one so we can get going?"

"Look," he said in awe as he gestured with his hand. "Now they have different sizes. Dang! Some have grooves, some are sandwich crackers."

"How about this one? It's a Cheez-It cracker sandwich with cheese in the middle. You'd like that, wouldn't you?"

"Cheese on cheese? That seems indulgent, doesn't it? Do we really need cheese on top of our cheese? I like cheese as much as the next guy, but…"

"Just. Choose. One," I said, interrupting his stream of consciousness.

Then I lost him again. He was staring at the wall of red boxes mumbling to himself. "Reduced Fat? Man, they should have run that one by me before it got all the way to the grocery shelves."

"We're done here," I said. "How about we keep it real and stick with the original version." I grabbed a small box and threw it in the cart. "Let's start moving toward the front of the store." Matt continued to stand there.

"I'll meet you at the truck in five minutes," I said, pushing the cart past him. I checked out, loaded the groceries in the truck, and waited until he finally sauntered out with a bag clutched to his chest.

"What's in the bag, sweetie?" I asked as he put it in the back seat.

"Don't you worry about what's in my bag."

"You bought more Cheez-Its, didn't you?"

"You'll thank me later when we're in the middle of nowhere and that little old box you bought is empty. Plus, I got the snack mix. We need a little variety on this trip. It might be nice to have a mini-pretzel or cheese puff now and then, to keep things interesting."

And as it turned out, that small delay is the reason I'm sending you an email from a motel in Monticello instead of gazing up at the stars at a campsite in the Needles.

Your friend,
Karen

~.~.~.~.~.~.~.~

From: **Matt Smith**
Subject: **Lost in the Needles**
Date: **March 12 (Sunday)**

Dear Bob and Sue,

We didn't become campers today. A series of missteps and delays led to us missing out on a campsite. The Squaw Flat Campground in the Needles District has two loops: A & B. In the winter (until March 15) Loop A is available on a first come, first served basis, and Loop B is sometimes closed. I called Recreation.gov last night to find out the status of Loop B and the person I spoke with told me Loop B was still closed for the winter. Hearing that, we thought it would be almost impossible to get one of the fourteen sites in Loop A.

We also woke up to a cloudy, rainy day in Moab, and thought there was a good possibility that the weather tonight would be less than ideal for camping. With all of those discouraging developments, we took our time getting to the park this morning, resolved that camping was out.

By the time we reached the visitor center two hours south of Moab, the clouds had disappeared, and the weather was perfect. Just for grins, I asked the ranger at the information desk, "When do you open Loop B for the season?"

With a confused look on her face, she replied, "Loop B isn't closed, it's open right now."

"Seriously? Is it possible for us to get a site for tonight?"

"Uh, maybe. I was there ten minutes ago and a couple of sites were still open. If you want to camp there tonight, you should go right now and grab one," she said.

We hightailed it over to the campground, drove through both loops, and watched the car in front of us place a registration receipt on the post in front of the last open site. "We missed it by ten seconds," I said to Karen.

"Look on the bright side. You have two boxes of Cheez-Its in the back as a consolation prize."

"Cheez-Its! They cost us a campsite!"

"Yep," was all Karen said.

"Let's regroup. It's still a beautiful day. We can do your hike and figure out later where we're going to sleep tonight."

The hike Karen wanted to do was the Chesler Park Loop Trail. It takes you back through the Needles to a slot canyon called the Joint Trail. We could see a trail on our map that connected the campground to the series of trails that lead to the Needles. At the end of Loop B was a small parking area with a few empty spots. We parked the truck and loaded our backpacks.

The Needles District has many intertwined trails, and it can be confusing at trail intersections determining the right way to go. The Chesler Park Loop would have been about eleven miles round trip if we'd started from the Elephant Hill trailhead where most people begin the hike, but since we began at the campground, it added another two miles each way. We set out on the trail at 11:00 am, figuring we had plenty of daylight to do the loop and make it back to the truck before sunset.

Cairns marked the first mile of the hike across bare slickrock. Usually we could see the next several cairns, but a few times we had to stop for a minute or two to search for the next one. At one spot, the cairns led up the face of a large rock that was too steep to climb unaided. A series of metal posts had been inserted into the rock and a chain was attached to the posts to help hikers steady themselves as they climb. We were fortunate the rain clouds disappeared and that we were wearing well-treaded hiking boots. I wouldn't want to scramble over the slickrock when it's wet or in worn-out boots.

As we hiked farther into the park, the trail became more traditional, with a clear footpath through the desert and fewer cairns to mark the path. Every mile or so we'd come to a place where our trail intersected another. An hour and a half into the hike, the trail went into a tight slot canyon where the walls were high and vertical. After descending a set of steps, we walked across the flat sandy floor of the canyon for about fifty yards. It was dark and cool in there.

When we got to the other side, Karen pulled out the map and said to me, "This is weird. That must have been the Joint Trail. It looks just like the pictures I saw of it online. But that means we're on the back side of the loop already. Either this map is wrong or we went a different way than I thought we did."

I never gave her comment a second thought, until later in the day. After another hour of hiking we came to the base of one of the Needles. The Needles are rock spires that sit about two miles east of the Colorado River, south of the confluence of the Colorado and Green Rivers. Extending southward for miles, they are colorful sandstone pillars that look like cairns made of stacked, smooth stones, except they're hundreds of feet high. It's difficult to appreciate how spectacular they are unless you're standing at the base of one, looking up at it.

In the heart of the Needles, we reached a sign that read "Chesler Park 0.2 mile" with an arrow pointing to the left. We decided this was a good place to stop for lunch. The hike to that point had been more strenuous than we'd anticipated, and it felt good to take a break and relax. I laid down on a smooth, flat rock and watched large black birds circle above us and around the Needles. My peaceful break was soon interrupted by Karen shouting, "Go away. Go away! Matt!"

Without looking I knew what was going on. A bold chipmunk was making passes beneath Karen's legs as she sat and ate her sandwich on the rocks. "That's it. Lunch is over," she said. "I'm going to go to the bathroom behind that big rock over there and then we need to get going."

When Karen goes off to pee, I usually use that opportunity to place a couple of nuts at the base of her backpack so that when she returns there are chipmunks sniffing around her stuff. She has a suspicion that I do this, that's why the last thing she says to me before she heads behind the rock or bush is, "Don't feed them!"

"What do think, that I'm like, twelve?" Is my pat response, which always brings another warning, "I mean it. Don't." I shake my head, act like I'm not interested, and then I place nuts at the base of her backpack once she's gone. To answer my own question, yes, there's a twelve-year-old kid inside all of us. And that's a good thing.

Karen came back stomping her feet and waving her hands at her backpack to shoo away the rodents.

"I'm ready to move on, how about you?" she asked.

"Yep, I've had enough of a break," I replied.

"OK, since this trail is a loop, we'll be going a different way back to the truck. At the sign where the trails cross, we're going to take a right."

"But the arrow on the sign for Chesler Park points left to the top of this trail, where it goes through the Needles," I said. "Let's at least go up there and look at the view. Maybe we'll be able to see the Colorado River from the top."

Karen contemplating the view of the Needles,
Canyonlands National Park

Another couple hundred yards of steep climbing took us to the high point of the trail. When I looked to the southwest I'd expected to see the river, but instead there were more rock spires off in the distance about a half a mile away—and no river.

"I bet you could hike for days out there and never cross a road or any other sign of civilization," I said to Karen.

"Eventually you'd reach Bear's Ears National Monument to the south. You might not run into any towns, but you'd probably find some cliff dwelling ruins. They say there are thousands of them in the monument."

"Alright, we need to start heading back. We've been out here for about two and a half hours and there are only a few hours of daylight left."

"We'll be fine; the loop back is no longer than the hike we did to get here," she said.

For the next hour we hiked a sparsely marked trail that took us north along the base of the Needles. They are spectacular up close. We kept stopping to take pictures, but it was hard to capture their massive scale on our phone cameras.

We took a break to drink water and Karen pulled out her map. "I think we need to go this way," she said, pointing through a break in the Needles toward the Colorado River. Up to this point I hadn't paid much attention to where we were. I had confidence that Karen knew the way—she had the map. But I knew that hiking toward the Colorado River was the opposite direction of where we'd parked the truck.

"Are you sure we're supposed to go *that* way?" I asked.

"Positive," she replied.

I was leery, but followed her through the towering rocks and onto a trail that went west across a flat stretch of desert. After about two hundred yards I stopped and said, "Sweetie, I know I'm not the one with the map, but I'm 100 percent sure we're hiking in the opposite direction of the truck."

Karen pulled out the map and said, "No, we're here and the truck is there." She was pointing in the direction of where she thought the truck was.

I took the map from her, turned it a quarter rotation, and said, "No, we're here, and the truck is over there."

"That can't be right. There's a huge canyon between us and where you think the truck is."

"Uh, huh," I said with a look of concern. "That's the problem."

Karen wasn't convinced. She showed me the map again and said. "You see here? This is the Joint Trail that we hiked earlier, and then we ate lunch right here."

Again, I took the map from her and turned it a quarter turn. "Unless, the trail you thought was the Joint Trail wasn't the Joint Trail, which would put us over here."

"Well, that would explain why I thought the map was wrong."

We spent the next five minutes studying the map and trying to match it with where we thought we were in the park. Finally, I said, "Here's the deal, we're running out of daylight and we don't have time to make another wrong turn. If we retrace our steps all the way back to the truck, we have just enough time to get there before the sun goes down."

Then it dawned on her. "Did you bring your headlamp?"

"No, did you?"

"No," she said after a long pause. "Crap! We always have our headlamps. There's no way we'll be able to follow those cairns across the slickrock in the dark."

"That's why I'm saying we don't have time to make one more wrong turn. We need to go back the way we came, now."

I know it sounds easy, but retracing your steps through an unfamiliar wilderness area on a trail that isn't well-marked is harder than it sounds. Especially when you're in a slight panic. Several times on the hike back to the truck, we were sure we'd made a wrong turn and were going off on yet another new trail that would lead us to God knows where.

About fifteen minutes into our trek back, I said to Karen, "Shouldn't we have come to that section of the trail where we ducked under a tree and slid through those two large boulders?"

"Yeah, remember I called it a 'squeeze' when we went through it before? I was just thinking we should have reached that section by now."

"If we don't come to the squeeze soon, then we're definitely going the wrong way."

A half an hour later, still no squeeze. Fortunately, we kept hiking and didn't panic—too much. Fifteen minutes later when we reached the squeeze, we looked at each other and just shook our heads; it was clear we were losing our sense of time and distance. Another ten minutes down the trail we came to a sign that we recognized from earlier. "OK," I said. "We've been here before, I remember this sign."

"Yep, we ate lunch right over there."

"And I remember looking at my watch when we reached this sign earlier; we'd been hiking for two and a half hours. If we just follow the trail back to the truck, we should be there in two and a half hours."

"How much daylight do you think we have left?"

"About two and a half hours."

For the rest of the way back, the farther we hiked the more confident we became that we were on the same trail we'd hiked earlier. Our concern went from, *Where the hell are we?* to *Are we going to make back before it gets dark?*

When we reached the slickrock with the chains, our shadows were long, very long. But we knew we'd make it back while it was still light. At the truck I looked at my watch; except for our short stop for lunch, we'd been hiking for seven hours and two minutes.

"I don't think we've ever been that lost before," Karen said to me as I pulled our camping chairs out of the back of the truck.

"I know. I'm still not sure where we were exactly."

"One thing's for certain. I'm not going anywhere again without my headlamp. Anywhere. I'm taking it with me to the grocery store."

"That's a good plan," I said. "I'm always worried about not having enough water. I never thought about being stuck out there without a flashlight or headlamp."

Just enough daylight was left for us to sit in the parking lot in our camping chairs and drink a beverage. We both put on flip flops and sank into our chairs. Between eating handfuls of salty snacks to restore our sodium levels, we talked about how lucky we were that we made it back before the sun went down.

"I'm pissed that we never found the Joint Trail, though. That's the reason I wanted to hike the Chesler Park Loop; the videos I've seen of it are really cool," Karen said.

"It's still out there if you want to try again someday. I think we now know where it is. We just need to keep going straight when we get to Chesler Park."

"Yeah, we'll have to come back and try again. Maybe next spring. The weather is perfect in mid-March, we now know that the Loop B campsites are open this time of year, and you can be in charge of the map. Deal?"

"Deal."

After a long pause when the only sound was the crunching of Cheez-Its, Karen said, "We should camp right here, as in right here on the pavement of this parking lot."

"I think we should sleep in our camp chairs. I'm exhausted."

A minute later, a ranger came walking down the road toward us. We could tell he was a law enforcement ranger because we could see his gun. He was young and fit; he had a serious look on his face—all business.

When he got within earshot of us I said to him, "All the campsites are taken. We thought we'd camp right here in the parking lot."

He laughed. He knew I was joking. I asked him, "What are our options for camping tonight since all the sites in the park are taken?"

"You could try the Needles Outpost, just outside the park. It's a private campsite, but I think it has changed ownership recently and I'm not sure it's open for business. Your other option is to just drive down one of the gravel roads into the BLM land outside the park east of here and set up camp anywhere. The only thing is, there aren't any services—no water or bathrooms—so you're on your own out there."

"I don't like the idea of us being 'on our own' out in the middle of nowhere," Karen said.

"Yeah, well, you could always drive into Monticello and try to get a room at one of the motels in town," he said.

"Monticello, motel room, that's what we should do," Karen said to me with determination.

"I agree, but first we're going to sit right here for an hour or so and not move," I said.

"You can sit here for as long as you want," the ranger said. "If you don't fall asleep, you're not camping as far as I'm concerned."

By the time we found a motel in Monticello and had dinner at a restaurant down the street, the temperature had dropped into the low 40s. It would have been a cold night in the tent, and I'm not sure Karen would have loved it. Maybe we dodged a bullet.

Your friend,
Matt

~.~.~.~.~.~.~.~

From: **Matt Smith**
Subject: **Monument Valley**
Date: **March 13 (Monday)**

Dear Bob and Sue,

Monument Valley has been in Karen's wish bucket for years, yet we haven't been able to fit in a visit before now. The monuments, which are colossal rock towers rising as much as 1,000 feet above the desert floor, are mostly contained within Monument Valley Navajo Tribal Park, which straddles the Utah/Arizona border on the Navajo Indian Reservation.

Today our road trip dipped into Arizona where we'll be spending the next couple of days. From Monticello, we drove two hours southwest and are spending the night at the Hampton Inn in Kayenta, Arizona. We'd wanted to stay at

The View Hotel in Monument Valley, but no rooms were available there tonight.

When we arrived at the park's visitor center, I handed my national park annual pass to the woman at the entrance booth, and she handed it right back. Despite using my charm and powers of persuasion, I still had to fork over the twenty-dollar admission fee to get in.

From the parking lot, we climbed a set of stairs to a spacious patio with panoramic views of the surrounding monuments. Inside the visitor center was a restaurant and a huge gift shop, for which Karen immediately made a beeline. Their collection of Indian rugs, art and jewelry was impressive. I watched her examine every glass case of jewelry. After a couple of laps around the displays, she looked up at me and shook her head. "I don't need another piece of jewelry."

She must not be feeling well, I thought.

"Let's get out of here and go for a hike," she suggested.

There was only one trail we could find on the park map where visitors are allowed to hike without a Navajo guide: The Wildcat Trail. The trailhead was a short walk from the visitor center.

Despite the tourist congestion around the visitor center, once we got onto the trail, we were mostly by ourselves in the middle of a magnificent desert landscape. The trail started out sandy and dropped a couple hundred feet in elevation for about a half a mile as we hiked straight toward West Mitten Butte. Then it became a relatively flat, compact trail that looped around the butte in a big, gradual circle. The West Mitten—so named because when viewed from the south it looks like a giant mitten—was awe-inspiring up close.

Many movies dating back to the 1930s were filmed in Monument Valley; the first one was *Stagecoach*, starring John Wayne. It won two Academy Awards, made John Wayne a star, and put Monument Valley on the map, so to speak, as the iconic location for many future westerns. I read that when

John Wayne first saw the area, he said, "So, this is where God put the West."

Back then, Monument Valley was the authentic Wild Wild West; there was only one small trading post and the roads were primitive. As more and more tourists visited the area, ancient relics began to disappear, and native sites were being looted. To protect their land, the Navajo Tribal Council chose to adopt the national park model, and in 1958, they set aside 30,000 acres as a tribal park, allocating money to upgrade roads and build a visitor center.

Even if you've never visited Monument Valley, the vistas are instantly recognizable as icons of the American West. When the Road Runner abruptly stops at the edge of a cartoon cliff, and then watches the Coyote hang in the air before dropping to the desert floor below, the views into the distance were inspired by Monument Valley. What could be more American than that? It's one of those places everyone must see.

Monument Valley
West Mitten Butte (left), East Mitten Butte (center)

Storm clouds threatened to rain on us toward the end of the four-mile loop, so we picked up the pace on the way back to the car. We decided to drive the scenic Valley Drive through the park: a seventeen-mile dirt road loop. Thirteen miles of the road is one way, which gave us pause; once we made the commitment, there would be no turning back. From the visitor center we had seen the slow parade of cars snaking through the valley.

The drive took us about two hours, mainly due to the cars that stopped every three minutes while someone jumped out to take a picture, but it was worth it to see the monuments up close. Mostly, the road was in good shape, but it was rough in a few places with a fair amount of jostling as we made our way around the rock towers and buttes. I'm not sure I'd drive an RV back there, but we saw a few small ones attempting it anyway.

Tomorrow we're going to Page, Arizona, which is a hundred miles west of here, and then if the weather cooperates, we'll hike Buckskin Gulch the next day. Right now, we're off to find dinner. Kayenta is a small town, but I'm hoping there's a place that serves fry bread.

Your friend,
Matt

~.~.~.~.~.~.~.~

From: **Matt Smith**
Subject: **Page, Arizona**
Date: **March 14 (Tuesday)**

Dear Bob and Sue,

Karen is a bad influence, and I'm weak. We drove straight to a Mexican restaurant for lunch as soon as we got to town, which meant our arrival in Page quickly turned into a noon-time Mexican fiesta. Three minutes after we sat down, two fishbowl-sized margaritas were on the table in front of us.

"Wow, they're not kidding when they say 'grande,'" I said.

"We're. On. Vacation," Karen replied. I had to slide to the end of the booth and look around her margarita glass just to see her face.

"Fine, but I'm going to need a siesta after the fiesta."

Fortunately, when we finished our lunch we were able to check into our hotel room down the street. I set my duffel bag on the floor and flopped on the bed as soon as we got in our room. "No, no! Don't lay down, you'll fall asleep. We need to stay awake and go see the sites. It's a beautiful day," Karen said as she flung open the curtains.

"Sweetie, I'm going to fall asleep regardless. It's better if I'm lying down."

I heard a few deep yoga breaths, and then I was out. It was only a short nap, though; an hour later we were back in the car driving south toward Horseshoe Bend.

Located on the west side of Highway 89 about four miles south of Page, Horseshoe Bend is part of Glen Canyon National Recreation Area. We first visited the site five years ago on a summer afternoon when it was about a hundred and ten degrees outside. Karen, not knowing what Horseshoe Bend was, opted to stay in the car while I hiked to the overlook and took a few pictures. Later, when she saw my photos, she kicked herself for missing it. She couldn't wait to go back and see it for herself.

After that big lunch and the margarita, I was moving slowly as we climbed the hill toward the overlook. It's only three-quarters of a mile from the parking lot, but it wasn't an easy walk; the trail is sandy, and it felt like climbing a sand dune. You don't get a full view of the bend until you reach the very edge of the cliff. When I saw it for the first time, it was similar to the thrill I felt when I first saw the Grand Canyon.

Horseshoe Bend

Horseshoe Bend got its name from the horseshoe-shaped curve that the Colorado River carved millions of years ago as it meandered through the Colorado Plateau, leaving behind a massive sandstone rock formation in the middle. The water is a beautiful teal green that's striking against the red cliffs soaring above it. I've seen a lot of pictures of the bend, and all of them, including mine, have an unreal quality to them, almost like you're looking at a painting rather than a photo.

Surprisingly, the overlook has no fences or rails to keep people from falling a thousand feet to the bottom. A large crowd was milling about when we got to the rim, many of them sitting and standing dangerously close to the edge. I saw a few people taking selfies with their backs turned to the drop off.

Even with the crowd, it was easy for me to find a spot to take an unobstructed picture of the bend. I stood close to the rim and held my phone high to get the best shot. Karen, who is afraid of heights, was standing about twenty feet farther back. After each photo, I'd take a step closer to the edge to get a better angle. I took a few more steps forward and I felt Karen grab my shirt from behind saying, "Too close, too close."

"Just one more foot closer and I'll have it."

"That's far enough," Karen replied hanging on to my shirt.

"Got it," I said as I looked at the photos on my phone.

"You can look at those over here." She pulled me by the hand away from the overlook. "This is insane. Someone's going to go over the edge," she said.

As we were driving back to Page, we passed the turnoff to Highway 98, which reminded me of the time we visited Antelope Canyon. Like Horseshoe Bend, it's one of the best places in the Southwest for capturing stunning photos, and you'd never know it was there unless you were looking for it.

A couple of years ago, Karen and I went on tours of both Upper and Lower Antelope Canyons; they're across the road (Highway 98) from each other about six miles east of Highway 89. Both are on Navajo land. What makes these slot canyons unusual is the way wind and water carved the rock into irregular, wavy shapes. Light filtering down from above reflects off the walls and creates beautiful, subtle shadows and colors.

Back then, we did Upper Antelope Canyon in the morning and Lower Antelope Canyon in the afternoon. The time slots fill up fast, so we arrived at the Upper Canyon offices early and got reservations for a mid-morning tour. Karen tells me that Antelope Canyon has become so popular that you no longer can count on getting a tour reservation for the same day you show up. Often, you have to make your reservation months in advance to ensure your spot.

When Karen initially suggested we do the tour, the idea didn't thrill me. Having a guide drive us to a site where we stand around with ten strangers and take pictures seemed a little more passive than the types of activities we usually enjoy. I was a little grumpy as we loaded into the back of our Navajo guide's pickup truck. But after having done the tour, I would do it again in a heartbeat. It was one of the coolest things we've ever done.

In the bed of the truck were benches where three to five people could sit on each side; a metal roof shaded us on our two-mile drive through the desert to the entrance of the canyon.

When we arrived and piled out, our guide made sure we all stayed together and waited our turn by the entrance. Many groups were touring the canyon, both in front of us and behind us, and the guides appeared to be well-trained at moving their groups through on schedule. We never felt rushed, but it was clear we were on a tourist conveyor belt that ran like clockwork through the site.

While we were waiting our turn to enter, we got to know our guide a little better. He said to us, "Before we started giving tours of the canyon, nothing was back here. My grandmother used to raise sheep on this land. No one ever thought about taking people through the rocks. And now, look at how many people want to come and see the canyon."

He also gave us tips on how to photograph the rocks. When he started, I thought to myself, *How hard could it be to take pictures of rocks?* Then he borrowed my camera, stepped a few feet inside the shadows of the canyon to take a couple of pictures, and then showed them to the group. "You see how in this first picture there's too much light and all of the colors are washed out? Now in this second picture, I positioned the lens so that a small amount of light is coming in from the corner of the frame. That light reflects off the sandstone and creates very subtle colors. Do you see the difference?" he asked.

He gave us other helpful hints and then, one-by-one, took each of our cameras and calibrated the settings for the conditions inside the canyon. This was back before anyone used the camera on their phone to take photos. We all had digital cameras ranging from simple point-and-shoot models to sophisticated SLRs. It didn't matter what make or model the camera was; it took him about five seconds each to change the settings. He looked like a kid with lightning fast hands solving a Rubik's Cube. His fingers moved so quickly I couldn't tell what he was doing, but afterwards my photos of the canyon walls looked incredible.

When it was our turn to enter, we were able to walk right into the canyon; there were no ladders or stairs to navigate. The floor consisted of compact sand. Our guide would take us through a few bends in the canyon and then stop so we could take photos. Every couple of minutes we'd move a little farther and then wait again; the groups in front and behind us did the same for most of the way through the canyon. This allowed each group plenty of opportunities to take photos without people in them. Afterward, when looking at my pictures, most of them looked as if Karen and I had been the only ones there.

When focusing my camera, it took some trial and error to determine how the photo would turn out. The scenes that I photographed looked different with the naked eye than they did in my photos. I asked our guide, "Why are the colors and light so different in my photos than what I see just looking at the canyon walls?"

He said, "The walls of the canyon are made of sandstone, and the tiny particles in the rock are reflecting the sunlight in all directions. Then when the reflected light hits another wall it's reflected again and again. That's what's making the walls of the canyon look like they're glowing. Your camera is picking up more of that light than your eyes." The explanation sounded reasonable, but I'm still not sure I understand it.

A couple of places in the canyon were even more spectacular than the rest. One of those areas was a room where, at a certain time of day, a narrow beam of sunlight would shine into the canyon and reflect off the floor. Dust in the air would catch the beam and create a dramatic shaft of light. It made for a beautiful photo, but there was an obvious dilemma; with so many people milling around, it would be impossible to get a clear shot of the scene. As we were standing there, I could see the serious photographers in the crowd fidget with anxiety.

After a couple of minutes, one of the guides said, "What we're going to do is have everyone move to that side of the room. There's plenty of space back there. And, once the group in front of us moves around that next bend in the canyon, you can all take photos without anyone in the picture. There will be enough time for everyone to get the shots they want; trust me, we do this dozens of times a day."

Everyone moved back, and after the far side of the canyon was clear of people, we all got our chance to capture the magical scene. The ideal time for photographing the beam of light changes depending on the time of the year, but it's usually late morning to early afternoon because the sun needs to be directly overhead to shine between the narrow, vertical walls. We were there a little earlier than the optimal time, but we still got some good shots.

Midway through the photo shoot, one of the guides stepped into the middle of the room and said, "Everyone stop for a moment. You see how the dust in the air makes the beam of light show up better? I'm going to take a handful of sand and toss it into the air, right here in the middle of the room. And then I'll move out of the way, so you can take some more pictures. This is fun, watch."

He tossed the sand fifteen feet in the air and darted behind a wall jutting out from the far side of the canyon. Amongst the "oohs" and "ahs" we all snapped photos as fast as we could before the dust settled.

At another location in the canyon, one of the guides placed a couple of handfuls of sand on top of a slanted rock that was in the sun and protruding from the canyon wall. As the sand slowly poured off the rock it gave the appearance of a small waterfall. That made for another one-of-a-kind picture.

Once we reached the far end of the canyon, our guide turned us around and we made our way back to the entrance like fish swimming upstream through a river of tourists. I kept looking at the photos on my camera to make sure I got some good shots. I was amazed to see that nearly every one was stunning. Most of them looked like abstract paintings. I even took a few with the crowd partially in the frame for a sense of scale.

Back at our car, Karen took the opportunity to gloat a bit. "I'm sorry I made you do that horrible tour."

"The what?" I replied. I was still looking at the photos on my camera.

"The tour. It really sucked, I know."

"I'll be the first to admit that you were right and I was wrong."

"Then admit it."

"You were right."

"And…"

"I wasn't right," I said.

"Close enough. What do you want to do next?" she asked as we climbed into our car.

"Go get a quick lunch and come back to do the Lower Canyon tour."

"That's what I was thinking."

From the ticket booth at the Lower Canyon, we walked to the entrance instead of riding in a truck. As our guide led us across the slickrock just beyond the parking area I wondered, *Where's he taking us? There's nothing out here for as far as you can see.* He stopped at a crack in the ground where we descended a series of metal staircases about a hundred feet to the canyon floor.

Despite having to climb down into it, the canyon was spacious and could accommodate a large number of people. They had a more relaxed attitude toward their crowd control in the Lower Canyon. Our guide kept us together for the first few turns and then told us we could explore the rest of the canyon at our own pace, so long as we let him know when we were ready to leave.

There wasn't a "beam of light" spot in the Lower Canyon, but there was a rock formation Karen wanted to find that she'd seen pictures of. It's called the Lady in the Wind. Karen asked our guide where it was, and he replied, "I'll point it out to you when we get there."

He didn't have to. As we came around a bend in the canyon, Karen said, "There it is! There it is!" It was a stunning scene: a profile of a woman's head, neck and shoulders, her long hair blowing across the rocks behind her. Usually, when I see a beautiful photo and then I see the subject in person, the scene looks less remarkable. That wasn't the case with the Lady in the Wind. The photos we took looked every bit as good as the ones we'd seen taken by professional photographers. That's one of the appeals of the Antelope Canyons: Ordinary people with ordinary cameras can get breathtaking photos.

To see color versions of the photos in this book and additional photos from our trip, visit our website:
www.dearbobandsue.com

The Lady in the Wind, Lower Antelope Canyon

On our way back to the parking lot, we noticed a large, brass plaque along the trail. It was there to commemorate a tragedy that had occurred in the canyon in 1997. On August 12 of that year, a flash flood killed eleven people who were touring the Lower Canyon. Most of them were tourists from France.

Early on the day of the tragedy, heavy rain had fallen upstream creating a torrent of water and debris that flowed through the narrow canyon. No one toured the Upper Canyon that day, but twelve people were in the Lower Canyon—right where we'd just been—when the flood came. Only one of the twelve survived, and he was severely injured. Recovery workers found most of the bodies several miles away in Lake Powell. Two of the victims have never been found.

The lone survivor of the flood had been the tour guide for many of the victims. He later described the event saying the ground began to shake, the walls moved back and forth, and he heard a rumble louder than anything he'd ever heard before. Then a thirty-foot-wide, eleven-foot-tall barrage of debris came at them in the canyon. That's what makes flash floods so dangerous: People caught in the path are more likely to die from the impact of the churning mass of logs, rocks and water than they are from drowning.

August is monsoon season in the Southwest, and that's when the tragedy occurred. Since then, the tour operators have changed their procedures for monitoring the weather and keeping people out of the canyon when there's a threat of flooding. The story of the tragedy was a somber end to that visit, but I would love to do the tours again someday—when there's no rain in the forecast.

Buckskin Gulch is our destination tomorrow, depending on the weather. It's also a slot canyon and not a place to be when there's a chance of rain. We'll let you know how it goes.

Your friend,
Matt

~.~.~.~.~.~.~.~

From: **Matt Smith**
Subject: **Buckskin Gulch**
Date: **March 15 (Wednesday)**

Dear Bob and Sue,

Buckskin Gulch is the deepest and longest slot canyon in the Southwest—the narrows (where the canyon walls are very close to each other) extend for about fifteen miles. The gulch, which is in Paria Canyon-Vermilion Cliffs Wilderness, begins in Utah but ends at the Arizona border where it joins the Paria River. We've only hiked a half dozen miles of it each time we've been there, so we don't know what the canyon is like for its entire length. The section we've seen is spectacular.

To get to the trailhead this morning, we drove west from Page on Highway 89 for about forty minutes and then turned left (south) onto House Rock Valley Road, a dirt road that leads to Wire Pass trailhead. The first time we did this hike, we had a heck of a time finding House Rock Valley Road; the turnoff is at a sharp bend in the highway and easy to miss.

The road to the trailhead can be rough in places: deep potholes, loose gravel, sharp rocks—that kind of stuff. We've done it before in a small rental car. I'm not sure that was a smart thing to do, but we got away with it. I felt a lot more confident today driving our truck.

For eight miles we sent up a cloud of dust all the way to the Wire Pass trailhead parking lot. A few miles before we reached Wire Pass, we saw a sign for the Buckskin Gulch trailhead pointing down a side road. We don't start our hike from there; by starting at Wire Pass, we intersect Buckskin at a point where the gulch becomes more scenic, thereby skipping the less interesting part of the trail.

For being so far off a paved highway, the Wire Pass parking lot is large. We had no trouble finding a spot when we arrived mid-morning. Hiking in that area requires a permit, and the fee was six dollars per person, which you deposit in a metal box at the edge of the parking lot. The first time we hiked Buckskin, I only had a twenty-dollar bill on me and had to put that in our fee envelope. Now I make a habit of keeping a few small bills in my truck just in case we need them for fees in public lands.

The sky was overcast when we started our hike. We'd checked the forecast and learned that despite the clouds, there was no chance of rain in the area today. It's not that we were worried about getting rained on while we hiked, our concern was whether there was a chance of rain upstream from the gulch. Rain coming down fifty miles away could send a torrent of water and debris through Buckskin. About eight flash floods occur each year, and the hike through the gulch changes after each one, depending on the number and size of log jams and boulders left behind. Given the forecast, and the fact the heaviest rains in these parts typically fall in August and September, we felt safe going into the canyon.

For the first mile and a half, the trail followed a dry wash that meandered toward Buckskin Gulch. Two other hikers, a man and woman who looked to be about our age, were hiking close to us through the wash. One moment they were right behind us, and then they disappeared into the brush alongside the wash, reappearing a few minutes later in front of us. They obviously knew the trail well and were taking shortcuts through the tall scrub.

When we were all back together again on a wide stretch of gravel, Karen turned to them and asked, "Are you hiking to Buckskin Gulch?"

"No, we're turning off shortly and hiking up to The Wave," the man replied.

"Oh, good for you," Karen said. "We've tried to get permits to hike The Wave a few times, but we haven't had any luck."

I said, "Maybe we should join you and if we run into a ranger, you could say that you thought the permits allowed you to bring a couple of friends." It was clear I was joking, and they laughed—thankfully.

"I don't think that would be a good idea. We're the volunteers who patrol the trail and check that everyone has a permit," the man said.

"Busted!" Karen said, pointing at me and laughing. I hadn't seen the volunteer ranger emblems on their shirts.

"Do you catch many people up there without a permit?" I asked.

"Oh, yeah, all the time," he replied.

"Do they ever say they didn't know they needed a permit?" I asked.

"Yes. They either say that or they tell us they got lost and ended up on the trail by accident."

"What do you do? Do you let them off with a warning?"

"Nope, we give 'em a ticket anyway. It's kind of hard to buy those excuses since there's a sign right at the turnoff to the trail that says you need a permit to go past that point," he said. "And no one is going to hike several miles down a trail into the middle of nowhere thinking they were lost and then coincidentally end up at The Wave.

"In fact," he said, "there was a time when it was a real problem. People would hike the trail without a permit, we'd ticket them—and, by the way, it's a fifteen-hundred dollar ticket—they'd go in front of the judge and tell him they were on the trail by accident, and the judge was letting them out of the tickets. So, we brought the judge out here hiking with us one day and showed him the trail and the signs."

"Did that help?" I asked.

"For sure. Now when they tell him they were lost, he says, 'No you weren't, I've been there. That'll be fifteen-hundred dollars. Next.'"

"Is it a dangerous hike?" Karen asked. "We've heard that people have gotten lost and died out there."

"Yes, that's true. Heatstroke was the cause of most of the deaths. One man was out there in the middle of the day during the hottest part of summer. Apparently, he wasn't feeling well, sat down, leaned against a rock, and died."

"I think I read about that," Karen said.

"It's also a problem when photographers want to take pictures of The Wave at dusk. One man stayed until sunset, and of course, it was dark when he started back to the parking lot. He didn't have a flashlight or headlamp, so he couldn't find his way back. Hikers found his body the next morning at the bottom of Buckskin Gulch."

"Oh, that's horrible," Karen said. "He must not have seen the crack in the earth and just fell in?"

"Yeah, you have to know where you're going out there, especially when it's dark."

"Well, you're very lucky to be able to go to The Wave anytime you want," Karen said.

"We love it. We've been volunteering for years and get to see some great places," the woman replied.

We hiked with them and chitchatted about Buckskin Gulch until we reached their turnoff to The Wave. I was hoping that if we gave them our most pitiful puppy dog faces as we bid them goodbye, they might invite us to tag along with them for the day. Instead, they waved and said, "Good luck getting a permit in the future! Keep trying, it's an amazing hike." And then they were gone.

Shortly after parting with them, the wash tapered and began snaking between large boulders. Soon we were staring at the entry to a narrow side canyon, Wire Pass. Almost immediately we were stopped by a tight choke point with a boulder blocking the way, beyond which was an eight-foot drop. The only way I could make it past the choke point was to lie down on the boulder, slide on my stomach facing the opposite direction we were hiking, and lower myself into the canyon. On the sandy floor below the boulder were a couple of large rocks that served as booster steps. Lowering myself slowly, I blindly felt for the stepping stones with my feet. When I got to the point where I couldn't lower myself farther without losing my grip, I still couldn't feel them. Letting go of the boulder, I dropped, hoping that the fall wouldn't be too far and that I wouldn't turn an ankle by landing awkwardly. My free fall was about an inch, maybe an inch and a half.

Karen had an easier time navigating down the boulder. I was at her backside and guided her feet onto the stepping stones. From there on, the tricky parts became easier. It didn't take long before we were on flat ground for good and winding through the tight canyon.

The first time we did this hike, Karen and I thought this first slot canyon *was* Buckskin Gulch because it looked similar to the photos we'd seen of it. Wire Pass though, was only a preview of what lay ahead.

A couple of hundred yards before we reached the intersection with Buckskin, the canyon walls opened wide. The clouds from earlier had burned off and we were standing in full sun. Karen searched the right (south) wall of the canyon for the faded petroglyphs we'd seen the last time we were there. My favorite is a small carving a few feet above ground level of what looks like a bighorn sheep. It's hard to find, especially in the full sun because it's very faint. We've read there are other panels of petroglyphs on this hike, but we've never found them. We're usually too distracted by the incredible views in the canyon to look for the rock carvings.

Karen in Buckskin Gulch

Our plan was to continue hiking through Buckskin Gulch to the south and turn around whenever we felt like we'd had enough. Many descriptions we'd read about this hike mention pools of water on the trail; hikers sometimes have to swim through sections of standing water. A couple of years earlier during the month of May, we'd hiked for about six miles before turning back. On that hike, we never ran into pools of water or even mud on the trail. Today, however, we ran into an impassible pool less than a quarter mile after entering Buckskin.

Standing there looking at the thirty-foot long puddle, I asked Karen, "Do you want to try to wade through this one and keeping hiking?"

"How deep do you think it is?"

"I've no idea. We should have brought trekking poles to feel for the bottom."

"I didn't think we'd run into standing water or I would have. The last time we were here this trail was bone-dry, remember?"

I took a large rock and tossed it into the water hoping that it might not disappear completely under the surface or somehow give us an indication of how deep the pool was. It disappeared without a trace.

"I'm not going in there," Karen said. "The water's green and the stuff floating in it looks like it's alive."

I didn't want to turn around so soon, but Karen had a valid point about the green water. It looked like a breeding ground for bacteria. If we had waded through the pool, we'd be wearing a layer of green slime for the rest of the day. I was pretty sure that we wouldn't find clearer water farther down the trail to wash off with. And even if we had, we'd have to wade through the slime again on the way back to the truck.

The hike was not a complete bust, though, we got some great photos of the canyon. One that I particularly like is a photo of Karen standing in a narrow section of the canyon— the walls are about ten feet apart—and thirty feet above her head is a log balanced between the canyon walls. What makes the photo special is it gives you the sense of scale of the flash floods that come through the canyon. That log could have only gotten stuck up there one way: It was left by a flash flood. It's sobering to think about a wall of debris that high rushing through the canyon. I realize floods of that magnitude don't happen very often, but when they do, everyone in its path who can't climb to safety is a goner. In Buckskin, there's only one place to climb out: the Middle Route exit. Classified as a Class 3 scramble, it's located about six miles into the narrows at a spot where the canyon walls are only about one hundred feet tall. We looked for it on our last hike through Buckskin, but we never saw any spot where we thought we could climb out.

About the time we turned around, the clouds returned, and the temperature dropped. It was chilly inside the Wire Pass slot canyon as we hiked back to our truck. It's usually cooler in slot canyons than out in the open because they're nearly always shaded. Getting back over the large boulder took some trial and error. Finally, I had Karen boost me from behind, and once I was on top of the boulder, I pulled her up by the arms. Soon after, we were out of the canyon and back in the wash for our final leg back to the truck.

On our hike through Buckskin Gulch a couple of years ago, the temperature in the wash was over a hundred degrees, yet barely above eighty when we were in the shade of the canyon.

On that hike, I struggled with the heat once we came out into the full sun. After a long day of hiking, suddenly going from eighty degrees to a hundred degrees made me lightheaded. As Karen and I hiked back to the trailhead that day, I became worried that we'd taken a wrong turn because it seemed like we'd hiked far enough to reach the parking lot. I was so concerned I decided to keep track of the time, thinking to myself, *If we don't reach the car in twenty minutes, then we're lost for sure.* When I thought we'd hiked another twenty minutes, I looked at my watch to check the time. We'd only been hiking for four minutes. That incident was a good lesson for me. I'd always wondered how hikers can get disoriented so fast in the desert heat; now I know. It only took hiking in the heat for a mile for me to lose my sense of time. Fortunately, we found the car soon after that.

What we learned today is to either check with one of the local BLM visitor centers before heading out to Buckskin Gulch, or bring waders and a giant bottle of Purell. Most likely, the rangers at the visitor centers will know the current conditions of the trail and whether or not there's standing water. I suspect late spring is the best time for dry conditions, and we'll be sure to stay away during monsoon season in late summer.

Overall, this trip to Utah was a lot of fun, even though we're disappointed we didn't get to camp. I thought about cannonballing it back home tomorrow from here in Kanab. It would only be eighteen hours of driving, but Karen put the nix on that plan. We'll probably spend tomorrow night somewhere in eastern Oregon.

Your friend,
Matt

~.~.~.~.~.~.~.~

From: **Matt Smith**
Subject: **Matt and Karen Visitor Center**
Date: **April 20 (Thursday)**

Dear Bob and Sue,

You know I've always been at a loss for what to do with our formal living room. Nothing is wrong with it, except that it's sunken, which causes people to either fall into it or trip on their way out. And it's boring. For all practical purposes, it's wasted space.

Although it did come in handy when I needed a place to inventory our camping stuff before the Utah trip. I've even thought about setting up the tent in that room and living in there for a week just to get used to camping and to try out all of our gear. When I floated the idea by Karen, she said, "It would look like we're running a summer camp in our house."

"And what's wrong with a fifty-six-year-old man playing summer camp in his living room?" I asked.

"Everything. You're not living in a tent inside our house. Outside is fine."

Fortunately, the room has potential. The small fireplace centered on the back wall is in good shape. A chimney inspector told us the flue looks like the previous owners never used the fireplace. The ceilings are vaulted and high, giving the space an open feel. A large bay window, adjacent to the fireplace, lets in a ton of light. Other than a few cosmetic details, there's nothing wrong with the room— except we don't need a living room.

Then one day when Karen and I were staring at the room in silence, the idea struck.

"Visitor center," I said. "We should turn this room into a national park visitor center."

"How cool would that be?" Karen replied.

"We could redo the fireplace with stone and a log mantle."

"Yes!"

"We'll have hardwood floors put in."

"I love hardwood floors."

"Over here we could put a cabinet. You know, the kind that has large, shallow drawers for storing maps. We'll get an American flag for the front yard, and this corner over here is perfect for the interpretive pelt collection."

"The what?" she asked.

"My pelt collection. I'll make tags for each one so that visitors can learn about the different animals. It'll be just like the pelt collection we saw at the Old Faithful Visitor Center in Yellowstone."

"You don't have a pelt collection."

"I *do* have a pelt collection, it's small, but I'll get more. Having a visitor center will give me a good reason to add to it. By the way, I'll need my white rabbit pelt back." Karen uses it as snow when she decorates for Christmas.

"What do you mean by 'visitors'? We won't have actual visitors," she said.

"Of course we will."

"Who? Who's going to visit?"

"Grade school kids. It would be the perfect field trip."

"You hate children."

"I don't hate children. But you bring up a good point; you'll have to give the ranger-led tours for the field trips so I can work the backcountry permit desk on those days."

"We don't have room for a desk in here. And we don't have a backcountry."

"True, we need to save space for the reptile display."

"No reptiles. They'll scare the grandkids."

"That's the point. Why else would you have a reptile display?"

"No reptiles," Karen repeated.

"Then how about a beehive? The kind where the hive is inside the house in a Plexiglas box and the bees have a clear tube that runs outside so they can come in and out," I explained.

She looked at me with an expression somewhere between pity and disgust, and said, "No! Nothing live."

"What about a passport stamp station?" I asked.

"Now you're back on the right track. Let's get a passport stamp."

"I'll put it on a chain just like the real national park visitor centers do. That way the grade school kids aren't tempted to walk off with it. And I don't want them changing the date on the stamp! You'll have to keep your eyes on the stamp when you do the tours."

"We're not having busloads of grade school children in our house."

"That might be best now that I think about it. But our friends can visit. When they come over for dinner, we'll start with a ranger-led tour featuring the interpretive pelts, then drinks and so on. If the sky is clear we can do stargazing with the ranger—that's you—after dinner."

"Will we wear national park uniforms?"

After a long pause, I shook my head. I gave up my dream of owning an authentic ranger uniform when I learned that impersonating a national park ranger is a federal offense. "We can wear badges and matching clothes, but we can't wear government-issued park ranger uniforms."

Some renovation work needs to be done in the room first, and then we can add the finishing touches. We'll probably start in the fall by having the floors raised and hardwood installed. Then a stonemason can rebuild the fireplace after the new floor is in. If all goes well, by next spring Karen and I will be drinking our morning coffee in the visitor center. You should come and visit. You can stamp your passport and take your picture by the park sign that will be going in our front yard.

Your friend,
Matt

~.~.~.~.~.~.~.~

From: **Karen Smith**
Subject: **Back to the Basement**
Date: **May 11 (Thursday)**

Dear Bob and Sue,

My dream has come true. Next week we're going back to Carlsbad Caverns National Park. I didn't think I'd ever get Matt to do another cave tour. After he told you our first visit to Carlsbad Caverns was like being in a dimly-lit basement, I figured the chance of us ever going back there was zero. My lucky break came when we started planning our New Mexico trip with our friends John and Lolly; they want to visit as many national parks and monuments as possible during our week there. Over beers one night back in March, I casually mentioned Carlsbad Caverns.

Lolly was enthusiastic. "Yes! I've always wanted to go there!"

"Me too," agreed John. "That's a must-see."

Matt grunted and didn't say anything.

"It's unanimous then!" I said. "We'll do the self-guided Big Room tour, of course, but the rangers also guide a variety of other cave tours throughout the week. I'll do some research and see what's available. Some of the tours are limited to small groups, so we'll have to buy tickets online as soon as possible."

I felt like I should lock this into our itinerary before Matt nixed it. As soon as I got home, I connected to the Recreation.gov website and looked at the cave tours offered during the last week in May. There were several choices:

King's Palace. We did that one on our previous visit. It's a ninety-minute, moderately easy tour, with lots of kids and families. I thought it was great, but since this may be the last time I get Matt to go on a cave tour, I want to see something new.

Left Hand Tunnel. Rated moderately difficult. The description says you'll experience the cave the way the early explorers did—by the light of a flame. The park provides lanterns. "Not recommended for anyone who has difficulty seeing in dim-lit conditions." That sounded too close to Matt's "dimly lit basement" remark. I don't think he'd like it.

Spider Cave. Rated very strenuous. Doesn't matter, Matt won't do it just because of the name.

Slaughter Canyon Cave. Rated moderately strenuous. Again, not a great name. (The National Park Service might want to get some marketing help with their cave naming. If they change it to Triple IPA Cave, Matt will sign up in a heartbeat.) To access this cave, you follow the ranger in your car and then hike up a steep rocky hill for half a mile. One of the highlights is a sparkly, crystal-decorated column called the Christmas Tree. Any tour with the word "sparkly" in the description sounds perfect to me, but this one was only offered early in the week, and we'll be in the Santa Fe area then.

Hall of the White Giant. Rated very strenuous, described as "dirty, belly-crawling, squeezing through tight passageways and climbing slippery, vertical rock." It's the park's most challenging and strenuous cave tour. I didn't consider this tour seriously; Matt and I have a "no belly-crawling" policy when we travel.

Lower Cave. Rated difficult, the adventure begins with a fifteen-foot descent using a knotted rope. Then you continue down another fifty feet on three steep ladders. The park provides helmets with headlamps and gloves. A definite possibility.

"What do you think about this one?" I asked Matt as I showed him the description on my laptop.

"I thought we agreed on no belly-crawling."

"No, it's the next one down on the list, Lower Cave."

"Will there be other people besides the four of us on the tour?"

"Yes, there will be other people. We have to interact with others when we travel. What do you think?"

"About interacting with other people or the cave tour?"

"The tour," I replied.

"Looks like it wouldn't suck."

"You're OK with me booking it then?" I asked. When it comes to caves, Matt saying it "wouldn't suck" is a pretty high compliment.

"Book it! I can't wait," he replied.

I texted a copy of the description to John and Lolly. Within five minutes they replied with their approval and I bought four tickets for May 25. I'm so excited!

Your friend,
Karen

From: **Matt Smith**
Subject: **To ABQ**
Date: **May 19 (Friday)**

Dear Bob and Sue,

Greetings from New Mexico, the land of enchantment! So far, we've only seen the ABQ (Albuquerque) airport and the Hampton Inn, and while they are both charming, I don't feel enchanted yet. We're spending the night here before heading out tomorrow for a whirlwind tour of parks in New Mexico. If all goes well, we'll see Bandelier NM and Kasha-Katuwe Tent Rocks NM up by Santa Fe, and then White Sands NM, Carlsbad Caverns NP, and Guadalupe Mountains NP. We flew here this evening from Seattle with John and Lolly; they're joining us for the week.

By the time we got our rental car and found the nearby Hampton Inn, it was 10:00 pm. I was standing behind John as we were checking in, when I heard him ask the front desk clerk, "Do you have any recommendations for places to have dinner around here?"

"John!" Lolly said. "It's ten o'clock. We're going to bed."

"Did you ask Matt and Karen what they wanted to do? Maybe they're hungry also," he replied.

Karen looked at me and shook her head without saying a word. I nodded in agreement; all I wanted to do was go to bed. But once we got to our room, Karen said to me, "Maybe we should go out to dinner. It's the first night of our trip and I don't want them to think we're party poopers."

Karen sent a text to Lolly saying we'd changed our minds, and twenty minutes later the four of us were sitting at a high-top table at Buffalo Wild Wings.

"What flavor of wings should we order?" John asked.

"I just want to go on record as saying this is a bad idea," I said.

"Let's get one of each," Karen said.

"You don't even like chicken wings," I said.

"Relax. We're. On. Vacation," she replied.

When the server brought us the wings, we had to clear the menus and salt and pepper shakers off the table to make room for all of the baskets—and four twenty-one-ounce beers.

Once we began eating, our fate was sealed; soon we were ordering our meals.

"I'll have the Southwest chicken salad," I said to our server.

"Do you want grilled or crispy chicken?" she asked.

"You know, 'crispy' is just another word for 'fried,'" Karen said.

"Crispy it is," I replied to the server.

"I might as well enjoy the ride," I said to Karen. "And when fried chicken is in a salad, the lettuce cancels out any negative effects."

John nodded in agreement. He couldn't speak because he was finishing off the last of the spicy wings.

We walked out of there close to midnight, wishing we'd never walked in. It's still not clear to any of us why our rental car's navigation system took us on a route through the airport arrivals and departure gates—twice—before directing us back to the Hampton Inn, but it did.

Our room was cold when we finally got back. Karen pointed toward the air conditioner on my side of the room and said, "Could you please, you know?" Then she waved at me with the back of her hand.

"What? Use your words, sweetie," I replied.

"Uh, um, lower the blow," she said.

"Lower the blow? Did you just say, 'lower the blow?'"

"I'm tired, and cold," she said, laughing.

"Did you mean, 'turn down the fan?'"

"Yes! I'm freezing!"

"I will in a second, I just need to make a note."

"Do *not* tell Bob and Sue I said, 'lower the blow.' My brain froze, and I couldn't remember the word 'fan.'"

"Yep, got it," I said. Then I lowered the blow on the air conditioner. This will be our little secret.

Your friend,
Matt

~.~.~.~.~.~.~.~

From: **Matt Smith**
Subject: **Bandelier National Monument**
Date: **May 20 (Saturday)**

Dear Bob and Sue,

Here's a travel tip you might already know, but if not, here goes: Don't drink beer and eat spicy chicken wings right before bed, especially on the first day of a long road trip.

I said to John this morning when I saw him at breakfast, "Just so you know, in the future if you ever ask us if we'd like to go get something to eat right before going to bed, the answer is 'no!'"

"You're right, my bad. We should have skipped the greasy food last night," he replied.

"And the beers the size of my head," Karen said.

"We're not in our twenties anymore," I said. "We need to pace ourselves or we're not going to make it through this week."

"I feel fine," Lolly said.

"Good, then you can drive today while the rest of us sleep," I said.

"First, we have to stop and buy groceries for the week," Lolly said.

"Lolly's not driving, I'm fine," John said.

Another consequence of our poor judgment last night was that once we got to the grocery store, Lolly and Karen were intent on buying healthier food than they probably would have otherwise.

"We need to get stuff with fiber in it," Lolly said. "Would you eat dried fruit this week?" she asked me.

I looked at John with an expression of mild panic and said so only he could hear me, "We need to nip this in the bud before it gets out of hand. Karen has a bag of kale chips in her hand."

"Yeah, dried fruit would be great," I replied to Lolly with a polite smile.

She grabbed several bags off the shelf. "We can make our own trail mix."

I whispered to John, "I'm not eating any of that stuff. I'll go get a box of Cheez-Its. You try to keep their healthy food selections to a minimum while I'm gone."

With the back of our SUV loaded to the gills with food, John found the entrance to Highway 25 and we were off to Santa Fe. Actually, we went to Bandelier National Monument first and then to Santa Fe where we're spending a couple of nights.

Bandelier is a 33,677-acre NPS unit. Its main attractions are the Puebloan ruins that were built into the cliffs along Frijoles Canyon hundreds of years ago. Today, many of these archeological sites are open for visitors to explore, although you have to climb ladders to enter some of them.

In addition to the ruins, the park has over seventy miles of backcountry trails. Only a small percentage of visitors go into the backcountry, but those who do get to experience one of the true hidden gems of the National Park Service. Countless petroglyphs and other archeological ruins are spread throughout the park. The NPS doesn't have maps of these treasures; they're out there for visitors to discover on their own. Doing so preserves a little bit of what Adolph Bandelier must have felt in the 1880s when he explored the area for the first time. How cool would it be to pick your way through a rock outcropping and stumble across a petroglyph knowing that you might be the first person in hundreds of years see it?

Karen and I will have to add this—hiking in the backcountry of Bandelier—to our overflowing wish bucket.

Bandelier was made a national monument in 1916, the same year the National Park Service was established. In the 1930s and 1940s, the Civilian Conservation Corps built roads in the monument, many of the trails, and the building that's now the visitor center. During World War II, the area was closed to visitors while personnel working on the Manhattan Project in nearby Los Alamos lived there.

Rather than driving our rental SUV into the park, John parked at the White Rock Visitor Center eight miles from the park entrance. To reduce traffic, the park service runs shuttles from there into the park. It can be a hassle to take a shuttle, but many parks have gone to shuttle-only access during their busy seasons. Even though I'd rather drive into the parks, I think it's worth the compromise. Once you're in the park, the reduced traffic makes the parks feel more like parks.

Instead of riding the shuttle to the main visitor center, we got off at the first stop inside the park: Juniper Campground. From there, we hiked the 1.5-mile Frey Trail into Frijoles Canyon. It was an easy hike and mostly downhill with great views of the canyon. The trail connected to the Main Loop Trail, which took us past the cliff dwellings and Big Kiva.

The park was crowded with visitors, which we expected it might be on a Saturday in May. After climbing a few ladders and poking our heads inside some of the ruins, we started out on the nature trail that leads back to the Alcove House site. As we walked along Frijoles Creek, we saw debris from the 2013 flood: huge, uprooted trees that looked like scattered matchsticks along the banks. A series of fires in the last couple of decades, including one that was the result of a controlled burn that *got away* from the national park folks, left the area vulnerable to flooding. In September 2013, a heavy rainstorm caused a torrent of water to rush through Frijoles Canyon. The flood threatened to wash the historic visitor center downstream to the Rio Grande, which is the southeast border of the park, but the building survived. The NPS had put up protective barricades and sandbags around the visitor center knowing that a flood of this size was just a matter of time given the effects of the fires upstream.

The first glimpse of Alcove House was spectacular. Nestled into the cliff walls forty feet above the canyon, you can only reach it by climbing a series of four, steep, wooden ladders. A sign at the bottom warns visitors with health problems or a fear of heights that they shouldn't attempt the climb. We made it up the ladders just fine with only a few short waits on the small landing areas while other groups coming up or going down passed by us.

Once we got to the top level, we saw that the alcove was much bigger than it looks from the bottom of the canyon. The NPS estimates that twenty-five people once lived there. A reconstructed kiva, with a ladder you can climb down, sits in the middle of the alcove.

After taking in the incredible views, we descended the ladders, but we weren't ready to call an end to our visit. At the advice of one of the park rangers, we hiked the Upper Falls Trail. We wanted to take it all the way to the Rio Grande, but the park service blocked the trail about two and a half miles from the visitor center because rains had eroded the path, making it too dangerous to hike past that point. We stopped at the overlook to the Upper Falls, took a few selfies, and then hiked back toward the visitor center.

As the shuttle took us back to White Rock, we felt we'd gotten a solid start to our trip. In total, we'd hiked/walked over eight miles. That was enough to burn off some of the ill-advised chicken wings from last night.

Bandelier is about forty miles from Santa Fe. It took us a little less than an hour to drive from White Rock to our hotel. After settling into our rooms, the four of us walked to a nearby brewery to hang out for a while. The place was packed, but Karen scored us a table for four. She has a knack for finding open seats in bars and restaurants. It's remarkable watching her work a room; I would use the analogy of a pig finding truffles, but I know better than speak that comparison out loud.

To my dismay, a band was setting up their instruments in the corner of the tap room. I'd hoped we could sit and have a quiet conversation with John and Lolly about our plans for the rest of the week. When the band started playing, my concerns were gone in an instant. The band—the Santa Fe Revue—was terrific.

When they took a break between sets, we all used our phones to search for a place to go for dinner.

"Hey, there's a Buffalo Wild Wings in town. We could go there," John said.

"No!" the three of us responded in unison.

"Let's try The Shed, if we can get in," Karen said. "We ate there the last time we were in Santa Fe, and the food was great."

The Shed didn't disappoint. The food was fantastic, although the other three thought their meals were almost too spicy to eat. Mine was perfect. We had a leisurely dinner and walked back to our hotel. Tomorrow we don't have much planned. We built a day into our itinerary to see Santa Fe and some local attractions. The gals also mentioned shopping, but I'm hoping the stores aren't open on Sunday.

Your friend,
Matt

From: **Matt Smith**
Subject: **Chimayo**
Date: **May 21 (Sunday)**

Dear Bob and Sue,

Today being Sunday, we went to church—twice as a matter of fact. It was a beautiful, sunny morning. After coffee at our hotel, we walked toward the Santa Fe Plaza with plans on having brunch. On our way, we stopped at the Loretto Chapel. While we were walking, I overheard Karen say to Lolly, "I'm so glad we're going to see the magic staircase. The last time we were here, the chapel was closed."

"The staircase is magic?" I asked.

"I meant miraculous," she said.

In the heart of downtown Santa Fe, the Miraculous Staircase is in the Loretto Chapel. When the chapel was built in the 1870s, there wasn't enough room to build a traditional staircase to the loft, so the sisters prayed to St. Joseph, the patron saint of carpenters, for a solution. On the ninth day of prayer, a man showed up looking for work. Many people who were there at the time believe the stranger was St. Joseph. This is why it's considered miraculous—and because the entire, double-spiral staircase has no external support; it was built with no nails, and the carpenter used only a few primitive woodworking tools. The mysterious worker insisted on total privacy while building the stairs, and then disappeared once it was complete without accepting payment.

The miraculous staircase in the Loretto Chapel

Inside the chapel, we jostled our way through the crowd to get a few unobstructed photos of the staircase. It was an amazing sight. Maybe not magical, but pretty cool. Karen and Lolly were whispering as they looked around the other areas of the chapel. "Why are you whispering?" I asked.

"Because we're in a church," Lolly said.

"Didn't you read the sign in the lobby? This chapel is privately owned. It's a for-profit museum and wedding venue.

You could throw parties in here if you wanted. I could buy this place and hang a big screen TV on the magic staircase."

"Shhh! We're in a church. Geez!" Karen whispered.

"First, we're not in a church, I just said that. And, second, you shouldn't say 'Geez' in a church. I'm pretty sure you can go straight to hell for that," I replied.

"I'm hungry," John said in a normal tone of voice. "Let's go find a place to eat."

Both Lolly and Karen looked appalled. "You're as bad as he is," Lolly whispered while tilting her head toward me.

"What? You can be hungry in a church. There's nothing wrong with that. It's not like I said 'Geez'," he replied.

"We should leave now," Karen suggested.

"Yeah, let's talk outside," Lolly said.

Outside in the brightness of the full sun, it took a few minutes for our eyes to adjust so we could check our phones for directions to Café Pasqual's; our server at The Shed said it's the place to go for Sunday brunch.

There was a crowd outside the café when we got there. That's the deal on most weekends; you put your name in and hang around until they call you. It was a good thing the weather was nice because the café has no room inside to wait. About half an hour later, we were sitting at a window table for four. "Let's just park it here for a couple of hours and eat and drink. And then go back to the hotel and take a nap," I said.

"I'm in," John replied. The second full day of our road trip was turning out to be a low energy day. The wives wouldn't have it.

"Nope, we've got things to do today," Karen said.

"We're. On. Vacation," I replied. "We don't have to do anything we don't want to do."

"That's right. And what we *want* to do today is go to Chimayo," Karen replied.

"Chimayo sounds like something you'd put on a Subway sandwich," I said. "On my foot-long club I'll have lettuce, pickles, and Chimayo, thank you."

"I'll have extra Chimayo on mine," John said.

"We're traveling with morons," Karen said to Lolly.

"You better be careful there; the rental car is in my name and no one else is allowed to drive it," John said. "You need to be nice if you want me to take you somewhere."

"OK, sell us on the idea. What's Chimayo and why is it better than a nap?" I asked.

"First, it's supposed to be one of the most beautiful towns in New Mexico," Karen said.

"And the church there has magic dirt," Lolly added.

"It's only a half an hour away, so let's get the car and go there right after we eat," Karen said.

"Back it up. Chimayo has magic dirt?" asked John. "We'll need a little more information about that. We already fell for the 'magic staircase' story. Two miracles in one day is pushing it."

"It's true," Lolly said. "The guy at the front desk of our hotel told us all about it. The church in Chimayo was built on the site of a miracle that happened two hundred years ago, and now people come from all over to visit. It has a room where people can take dirt from a hole in the floor. There are lots of stories about people being cured by this miraculous dirt. They rub it on their bodies and some even eat it. He also told us that even though thousands of people take dirt every year, it never runs out; it replenishes itself."

"OK," I said. "I'm calling bullshit on the magic, self-replenishing dirt."

"I'm with Matt on this one," John said.

"Why would the guy at the hotel make this up?" Lolly asked.

"It's the most beautiful town in New Mexico; we have to see it. We didn't come all the way from Seattle to take naps," Karen said.

"That's exactly what we came all the way from Seattle to do. We're. On. Vacation," I said.

"That's fine, Lolly and I will go. You guys can stay here," Karen said.

"No, I have to drive. We'll take you to see the magic dirt. Maybe it'll heal my bad back," John said.

"Yeah, I'd like to see the dirt replenish itself. I want to get a video of that," I said.

Chimayo was a charming town, all one block of it, but I'm pretty sure there are more beautiful towns in New Mexico. The church (El Santuario de Chimayó) looked like a place a miracle would happen. It was built in 1816 on the site where a previous small chapel had been. Many stories about miraculous things happening at the site are documented, but the Catholic Church doesn't offer an official stance on the validity of these stories.

Inside the church is a prayer room off to one side. Photos covered the walls; most were of children. Apparently, several hundred thousand people come to the church each year, many in hopes that their visit will help them or their loved ones overcome an illness. During Easter week, tens of thousands make a pilgrimage walk to Chimayo, some from as far away as Santa Fe. After seeing the photos of the kids, I changed my mind; I hope the dirt *is* miraculous.

A large plaque outside the church explains that the dirt in the chapel does *not* replenish itself. The church brings it in and a priest blesses it before placing it in the hole in the floor. For good measure, Lolly scooped a couple of handfuls into a plastic bag before leaving. Maybe John can sleep on her sack of dirt tonight to heal his back. We have a few strenuous hikes planned for later in the week, and he needs all the help he can get.

Another forty minutes in the car driving back to the hotel made for a long day. Before we called it a night, the four of us had dinner in town with Betsy, who was one of the crewmembers on our dory boat trip last year on the Colorado River. Betsy lives in Santa Fe, and we contacted her a few weeks ago to let her know we'd be in town. It was fun catching up and reliving our adventures on the river. She had some great stories to tell us about other river trips she'd been on.

It's good that we're getting to bed early tonight; tomorrow we have a full day. The plan is to hike in Kasha-Katuwe Tent Rocks National Monument and then drive to the town of Alamogordo. I'll give you a full report in my next email.

Your friend,
Matt

~.~.~.~.~.~.~.~

From: **Matt Smith**
Subject: **Kasha-Katuwe and Petroglyphs**
Date: **May 22 (Monday)**

Dear Bob and Sue,

When Karen first told me she wanted to visit a place called Kasha-Katuwe, the way she pronounced it sounded like she sneezed. "Bless you," I said. She looked at me like I was an idiot—something that she does regularly—and repeated the name. I finally figured out she was referring to Kasha-Katuwe Tent Rocks National Monument, and because it's such a mouthful, we agreed it would be easier to call it Tent Rocks. The monument is about forty miles west of Santa Fe and just south of Bandelier. Kasha-Katuwe is a Puebloan phrase meaning *white cliffs*.

Karen is now on board with visiting all the National Monuments. I'm not sure how long it will take us to see every one of them; there are a hundred and twenty-nine. And that's as of today. By the time we see all of those, there will probably be another boatload of new ones to visit. The National Park Service manages the majority of the national monuments, but other agencies manage some as well. The BLM, for instance, manages or co-manages twenty-seven, one of which is Tent Rocks. The access road to the park runs through Pueblo de Cochiti tribal land, and they co-manage the park with the BLM.

When we got to the entrance booth this morning, the ranger asked us what our plans were. We told him that we were hoping to hike the Slot Canyon Trail. He explained how to get to the trailhead and gave us a map.

"You want to start on the Cave Loop Trail and follow that for about a half a mile. Then, you'll pick up the Slot Canyon Trail, which keeps climbing for another mile. The last half of the hike is pretty steep," he said.

"Good, we need a strenuous workout," John said. "We've been eating too much over the last few days."

"It'll be a workout for sure, and you have a good day for it—sunny, but not too hot," the ranger replied.

"Any other suggestions of what to do while we're here?" John asked.

"A lot of people also visit the Veterans' Memorial Scenic Overlook. It's another three and a half miles past the trailhead," he said.

"OK, maybe we'll check that out as well," John said.

"One other thing. Watch out for snakes while you're hiking," the ranger said.

"Got it, thanks," John said as he drove away.

"What was that last thing he said to you?" Lolly asked.

"He said, 'Watch your step while hiking.' We must look old and frail," John replied.

"He said, 'snake,' not 'step,'" Karen said.

"Snake!? John, did he say, 'snake!?'" Lolly asked.

"Hey, don't bother the driver. I'm trying to concentrate on the road," John said.

"Matt?" Lolly said.

"He did *not* say 'snake.' He said 'snakes.' Plural," I replied.

"Thanks a lot," John said to me. "You threw me under the bus without hesitating."

View of the tent rocks,
Kasha-Katuwe Tent Rocks National Monument

The parking lot at the trailhead was more crowded than I thought it would be for a Monday. I guess it's summer break for a lot of people and they're out seeing the sites. The three-mile out-and-back trail was moderately easy for the first half as it took us through a slot canyon. The canyon section was so narrow that in some places we had to walk single file, and our shoulders touched the side walls. A few large boulders blocked the trail, requiring us to scramble over them.

When we came out of the slot, the trail got steep like the ranger said it would. A series of steps took us up to some fantastic views of the Sangre de Cristo and Jemez mountains. Karen got great photos of the tent rocks—pale pink and tan-colored cones, ranging in height from a few feet to ninety feet tall. They were formed by erosion after the Jemez volcanic field erupted six to seven million years ago.

We didn't see any snakes, even though Lolly and Karen were on high-alert lookout duty. Usually when we're hiking together, we have to wait for Karen to catch up because she's stopped to take pictures. On today's hike, all I had to do was holler, "Watch out for snakes," and she was back with us in a flash.

After the hike, we drove the gravel road to the Veteran's Memorial. It sat up on a hill with great views of the mountains, but we had at least four hours of driving ahead of us to get to Alamogordo, so we didn't linger.

On the drive south, we exhausted about every topic of conversation we could think of, plus the wives had time to take at least two naps each. Three hours into the drive we all needed a break.

"I have an idea," Karen said. "About thirty-five minutes before we get to Alamogordo, we could visit another BLM site just off the highway. I looked it up on my phone and they also have restrooms. I'll need a bathroom break by then."

"What's the attraction of the site?" John asked.

"Well, the name is Three Rivers Petroglyph Site, and it says here that they have over twenty-one thousand petroglyphs. There's a half-mile hike out to a boulder field where we can walk amongst them and see them up close."

"Are you sure a bunch of teenagers didn't just carve them last week?" John asked.

"John! We're stopping to see the petroglyphs," Lolly said.

"I was just asking. I'm always up for seeing petroglyphs," he said.

"To answer your question, John, I think they're legit. Their website says that the petroglyphs date back to 'nine hundred AD to fourteen hundred AD.' That's older than last week," Karen replied.

Petroglyphs at Three Rivers Petroglyph Site

What we had planned as a short pit stop turned out to be a ninety-minute visit. Only one other couple was there when we arrived, and they left soon after. We had the place to ourselves. The half a mile hike wasn't "rugged" like the description on the website indicated. You couldn't take a wheelchair or stroller on the trail, but it was a relatively easy hike to the boulder field where the petroglyphs were.

Walking through the strewn boulders looking for markings on the rocks was a blast. Every time we found one it was a small thrill. The number and quality were remarkable. Being there reminded me of when Karen and I went to Petroglyph National Monument outside of Albuquerque years ago. On that trip, when we visited the Piedras Marcadas Canyon section of the monument, we were surprised that the petroglyph area was adjacent to a residential development. While we hunted for petroglyphs, many dog owners walked their dogs past us, seemingly unaware of the cultural treasure right next to where their dogs were pooping and peeing.

When we reached Alamogordo, the sun was still high enough in the west that we could see a raging sandstorm billowing up in the distance. John and I stood in the parking lot of our hotel watching the dust build in the sky. "That looks like it's right over White Sands, doesn't it?" he asked.

"Yep, and it's white."

"We better hope the wind dies down before tomorrow morning or we'll be looking for something else to do."

As I'm writing this email, the wind is still howling outside. Hopefully, it'll calm down overnight. Our plan for tomorrow is to do a hike in White Sands National Monument in the morning and then drive to Ruidoso in the afternoon and spend the night there. Keep your fingers crossed for us.

Your friend,
Matt

~.~.~.~.~.~.~

From: **Matt Smith**
Subject: **White Sands National Monument**
Date: **May 23 (Tuesday)**

Dear Bob and Sue,

Hiking through sand dunes is one of our least favorite things to do, but over the years we've heard from lots of people how incredible White Sands National Monument is, so we figured we should check it out for ourselves.

The skies were clear and the wind was calm this morning when we left our hotel; the dust from last night had settled. It only took us twenty minutes to drive there from Alamogordo; I'd anticipated that the 275 square miles of dunes would be farther away than they were.

We had plans to hike the Alkali Flat Trail, which is a loop through the dunes about five miles long, so we were relieved that the temperature was cool when got to the park. In the car on the drive over, Karen told us about an article she'd read about a couple who died in the park while hiking that same trail.

They were visiting from France two years ago in early August. That day, the temperature was over a hundred degrees. Their nine-year-old son was with them at the time. About a mile into the hike, the wife, who wasn't feeling well, decided to hike back to their truck at the trailhead. She only made it about three hundred feet before collapsing. The father and son had continued along the trail. At about 5:00 pm that afternoon, park employees found her where she'd collapsed; she was dead. They looked at the pictures on her camera and saw photos of the father and son at the park's entrance, so they began searching for them immediately. About a half mile away, they found them. The boy was still alive, but the father had also died. The medical examiner said their deaths appeared to be heat-related. The three of them had only two twenty-ounce bottles of water between them when they began their hike. The park recommends that each person hiking the Alakali Flat Trail take a gallon of water. What a tragedy.

At the visitor center, we talked with a ranger about the hike. He explained to us that several trails wind through the open dunes, and the park marked each of them with five-foot-high plastic signs. Every trail has a unique color and symbol to distinguish it from the others.

"The Alkali Flat Trail signs have a red square with a black diamond in the middle. We've spaced the signs so you can always see the next one when you're on the trail. And by the way, this trail isn't flat like its name. It has ups and downs and is a strenuous hike," the ranger told us.

John asked, "I noticed the sign at the entrance that says there's no alcohol allowed in the park from February through May. That seems like an odd rule. Why just those four months?"

"There are several colleges and universities within a few hundred miles of here," the ranger said. "It used to be that they'd all come here for spring break. The drinking and partying was out of control, so we had to shut it down for those months."

"What you're saying is, we shouldn't pull out our lawn chairs and drink beers in the sand after our hike today," John replied.

"Nope, I wouldn't do that if I were you. Come back in June though, and you're more than welcome to."

White sand covered the road through the park. As John drove slowly, he said, "I keep thinking I'm going to slide off the road if I drive too fast. The sand looks just like snow and ice."

"Is it slick at all?" I asked.

"No. I have perfect traction," he replied.

The sand at the monument is mostly gypsum, the same stuff that's on the inside of drywall. That's why the sand is so much whiter than other sand dunes. It was a stunning sight: waves of snow-white sand, with a backdrop of mountains and a brilliant blue sky above. Because it looked like snow, it seemed odd taking our first few steps onto it in flip-flops. I was relived to find that the sand was more firmly-packed than other dunes we'd hiked. Another difference was the brightness of the sun reflecting off the sand. We all made sure to wear sunglasses, not only to protect our eyes from the glare, but also from the blowing sand.

Karen and Matt hiking through
White Sands National Monument

I have to make myself be patient when I'm hiking through sand. There's no way to hike fast without wearing out quickly. Once I settle into a slow, steady pace, it can be hypnotic. It took us a few attempts to find the red signs that marked our trail, but once we got the hang of it, we could always see the next one, barely.

When we'd hiked about a mile down the trail, I couldn't help but think of the French couple and their son. It was tough to imagine that someone could be so close to the trailhead and not be able to make it back.

At the halfway point of the loop, we were near the western boundary of the park where a sign explained that the area beyond the park border was off limits to visitors. The restricted area was White Sands Missile Range. Another sign along the trail warned hikers not to touch any strange-looking objects they might find in the sand because—I'm paraphrasing—there's an air force base close by and the objects that sometimes fall off the planes as they fly over the dunes could be dangerous.

John and I looked at each other after reading the sign. "That can't be true," I said. "Things don't just fall off military aircraft."

"Then why did they put up the sign?" John asked.

"I don't know," I said, shaking my head.

"Let's go see if we can find a missile in the sand," John said.

"John! Do *not* touch anything that you find," Lolly said.

"If I find a missile, I'm digging it out and carrying it back to the car," John said.

"There are no missiles out here, Lolly," I assured her. "And we're not searching for anything either. We need to stay on the trail, red sign to red sign. It's starting to get hot."

The hike back seemed much longer than the hike out. As I said, it was getting hot, but it was still probably in the eighties, not even close to the level of heat they get in the summer. We had plenty of water and salty snacks, and we knew we were going in the right direction because we could always see the next red sign. Even with all of that going for us, we got a little disoriented toward the end of the hike when we caught a glimpse of the park road to our left.

I can't remember why we did it, but for some reason we thought we should ignore the last couple of red signs and head off in the direction of the road. Once we'd hiked to a point where we could no longer see any signs of any color, we also lost sight of the road. We were in a mild panic for a few minutes. Fortunately, after we climbed the next dune we saw the park road again. Following it to the trailhead parking lot, we realized that we'd only been about a quarter mile off course. Now I understand how people can get lost and disoriented out there in the vast ocean of white sand.

Celebratory beers in the parking lot would typically be in order after a hike like this one, but we settled for peanut butter and jelly sandwiches and water.

"We have to start eating this dried fruit," Lolly insisted.

"What a coincidence, I was craving dried fruit the entire time we were out there, Lolly," I said.

"Then here, have some apricots," she said as she tried to hand me the bag.

"I was *not* serious. No one's going to eat the dried fruit," I said. "It's all yours."

"No, I need something with protein in it. I'm going to have one of these red, plastic-wrapped cheese things we bought," Lolly said.

"Those have been sitting in the back window unrefrigerated for almost a week now," I said. "I'm not sure they're still good."

"They're fine. They don't need to be refrigerated," she replied.

"Well, John's driving so you'll have to let him know when to find a bathroom on our way to Ruidoso this afternoon," I said.

"There's nothing wrong with them! Here, have this one," she said, peeling the wax off the cheese.

I didn't fall for it, and surprisingly, Lolly felt perfectly fine on our two-hour drive to Ruidoso. Instead of taking the most direct route, we drove to the town of Cloudcroft and hiked a few miles in the Trestle Recreation Area. Our afternoon hike was in the mountains, with trees, shade, and cool temps. It was as different as it could be from our morning hike on the sand dunes. We went from 4,300 feet elevation at White Sands to 8,600 feet elevation at Cloudcroft. The diversity of the land and variety of outdoor activities is one of the great things about New Mexico.

"Why are we spending the night in Ruidoso?" I asked the group as we approached the town. No one had an answer. "Karen?" I asked. "Was there something here you wanted to see?"

"Yeah. It's a mountain village in an alpine setting surrounded by a National Forest. You can ski in the winter and hike in the summer. They have outfitter stores and breweries and wineries. I think we might want to move there," she said.

"Did you take a job with the Ruidoso Chamber of Commerce? Because that description sounded a little too well-rehearsed if you ask me," I said,

"No. I read about it. That's my job; I'm Managing Director of Research," she replied.

"Time out. I don't remember you getting a promotion to Managing Director," I said.

After checking into our hotel, we found a delightful Mexican restaurant in town and enjoyed another great meal. It's a good thing we've been doing a lot of hiking on this trip because we've been eating like we're training for the Olympics.

Tomorrow we're driving to Carlsbad. We can make as many stops along the way as the others want; the only thing I care about is seeing the Smokey Bear Museum.

Your friend,
Matt

~.~.~.~.~.~.~.~

From: **Matt Smith**
Subject: **Smokey Bear Museum**
Date: **May 24 (Wednesday)**

Dear Bob and Sue,

Karen was moving slowly this morning, so I went for an early walk by myself. Because of Ruidoso's high elevation, it was still cool at 7:00 am. When I got back to the room, Karen asked, "Did you have a nice walk?"

"Yeah, I saw a moose in the parking lot."

She thought I was joking.

"What's on the plan for today?" she asked, changing the subject.

"Seriously. A moose was in the parking lot. He was a small one, maybe two years old," I said.

Karen went to the window, pulled open the curtains and said, "Where? I don't see a moose."

"He moved on. Moose don't just stand around in parking lots. He crossed the street, went down to the creek, and then moseyed downstream by those cabins over there."

"Hmm," was her reply. I could sense doubt in her *hmm*; she needed visual proof before believing my story.

When we met for coffee in the lobby, I told my moose story to John and Lolly. They didn't believe me either. "Are you sure it wasn't a big dog?" John asked.

"I'm not sharing my wildlife sightings with you anymore," I replied. "You better hope I don't see a mountain lion or Big Foot, because I'm not telling you guys. Everyone is on their own."

"I don't think there are moose here in Nevada," Lolly said.

The three of us responded at the same time, "New Mexico!" All week long Lolly has been saying we're in Nevada.

"New Mexico, that's what I meant," she replied.

Last night I'd read just about every tourist brochure I could find in the lobby of the hotel. I said to the group, "The only thing I want to do today on the way to Carlsbad is visit the Smokey Bear Museum in Capitan."

"We definitely need to do the Smokey Bear Museum," Karen agreed. She has a thing for Smokey.

"That's perfect because I'd like to drive the Billy the Kid Trail, which is on the way to Capitan. I hear it's a scenic drive. Then we can go to Roswell for lunch," Lolly said.

John asked, "What's there to see in Roswell?" None of us had an answer for him, but we all knew the town was famous for something to do with aliens. "Maybe we could visit Area 51 when we're in Roswell," John suggested.

"I don't think Area 51 is by Roswell," I said.

Lolly searched "Area 51" on her phone. She said, "Area 51 is in Lincoln County, and the Smokey thing is in Lincoln County, so yes, we should be able to go there on our way to Roswell."

"I think Area 51 is in Nevada, Lolly," I said.

"It says right here, 'Lincoln County,' Matt," replied Lolly.

"Yeah, Lincoln County, Nevada," I replied.

"Oh wait, you're right, it *is* Lincoln County, Nevada. Well, that's confusing. You'd think they'd put all of the alien stuff in the same place," she replied.

The drive to Capitan along Highway 48 took about a half hour. When we reached the intersection with Smokey Bear Boulevard (Highway 380) in the center of town, Karen said, "There it is! The Smokey Bear Museum."

As we parked, we noticed that there was not *one*, but *two* Smokey attractions: the Smokey Bear Historical Park, which the New Mexico State Forestry manages, and next to it, the Smokey Bear Museum Gift Shop.

Inside the small log cabin museum, every imaginable Smokey poster, placard, and sign covered the walls. Several glass cases in the center of the museum overflowed with Smokey items: stuffed toys, figurines, coins, patches, pins, belt buckles, pennants, storybooks, and rulers. There was a Smokey kite, fly swatter, baseball, canteen, backpack, and alarm clock. My favorite item was a ceramic Smokey head with a hole in the top of his hat designed to extinguish cigarettes.

"We gotta get one of those," I said to Karen. "And look at these collector coins. There's a bunch of them."

"This stuff isn't for sale," she replied.

"We'll look on eBay."

She could see where this was going. "We can't turn our house into a Smokey museum."

I paused for a minute thinking through the ramifications, and then sighed. "You're right, we're committed to making a national park visitor center in our front room. Doing that and trying to create a Smokey museum would put us over the edge, wouldn't it?"

"Maybe we could reserve a corner of our visitor center for Smokey memorabilia," she said.

"Yeah, we could," I said nodding my head tentatively. "Do you think that would be weird, though, having a Smokey section in our national park visitor center? Smokey works for the National Forest Service."

"That would be weird for a lot of reasons," John said.

"Hey, this is a private conversation," I said.

"Maybe you should start small at first," John said. "They sell Smokey posters here. Why don't you get one of those?"

I looked at every item of clothing they had for sale and ended up buying two bandanas and a t-shirt that read *Smokey, Established 1944.*

We wandered next door to the Historical Park. It was a larger, more modern building than the museum and had a small garden area with a walking path. Inside, we watched the Smokey video and read every interpretive display. After taking a picture of Karen next to the larger-than-life-sized Smokey statue, I showed the picture to Lolly. "Is she holding Smokey's hand?" Lolly asked.

"Yep, she always holds his hand," I said. "Even when it's just a cutout of Smokey pointing to the level of fire danger, she holds his hand when I take her picture."

I turned toward Karen, "What is it that you find attractive about Smokey? Is it that he's not wearing a shirt, because I look a lot like him when I'm not wearing a shirt. If you squint your eyes the hair on my chest and back looks like fur. Is it the hat, the belt buckle, the shovel? I need to know."

She smiled, shook her head slowly, and said, "It's the whole package."

"You're not going to beat that, Matt," Lolly said.

I knew Karen had a crush on Smokey before we visited the park, but I learned a few other facts about him on this trip. Did you know that he was a real bear? It's true.

The Forest Service authorized the Smokey Bear Wildfire Prevention campaign in 1944, but it wasn't until six years later that the program had a live bear as its living symbol. In the spring of 1950, the Capitan Gap Fire burned over 17,000 acres close to Capitan. In the smoldering aftermath, firefighters found an orphaned cub in the trees. The fire had burned his paws and hind legs, but a local rancher, who'd been part of the firefighting crew, agreed to take the bear home and care for him. His original name was Hotfoot Teddy.

The story of the rescued bear drew national attention. His popularity continued to grow, and the state game warden offered Hotfoot Teddy to the Forest Service so long as he'd be used to promote the prevention of wildfires. The bear was renamed Smokey Bear and lived at the National Zoo in Washington D.C. until his death in 1976.

I also learned that there's a hot air balloon in the shape of Smokey's head. It's ninety-seven feet tall and owned and operated by Friends of the Smokey Bear Balloon, Inc. The balloon flies at public events, usually in the Southwest. It's actually the second Smokey hot air balloon. The first was destroyed in 2004 when it snagged on a radio tower in Albuquerque. Miraculously, the accident didn't cause any injuries, but the balloon's pilot and the two passengers had to climb down the 700-foot tower to safety.

The intent of the balloon is to draw attention to Smokey and spread his fire prevention message. Yet at least a couple of U.S. senators over the years have proposed eliminating the $31,000 that the federal government contributes each year toward the cost of operating the balloon—which is a fraction of the total annual cost. Given the expense to the public of a single forest fire, I think $31,000 a year is a bargain to promote Smokey's message: Remember… Only You Can Prevent Forest Fires.

I'm keeping my eye on the event calendar on the Friends' website in hopes that someday we'll be able to work into our travels an in-person viewing of the balloon.

I also learned that the National Forest Service considered other spokesanimals for its forest fire prevention effort. A couple of years before the Smokey campaign began, the Forest Service organized the Cooperative Forest Fire Prevention program. The program was intended to increase the public's awareness of the need to prevent forest fires due to human behavior and carelessness. At the time, Disney had just released the movie Bambi, which was a big hit. The movie's woodland theme was a perfect fit for the program, and Disney agreed to loan the use of Bambi's image to the CFFP for one year for its awareness campaign. The Bambi promotion was a success, but Disney wouldn't extend the contract beyond the first year. The CFFP went looking for another spokesanimal.

They considered a squirrel. While I've got nothing against squirrels, I think they made the right decision to move up the food chain and select a bear. A careless camper wouldn't think twice about shooing away a fire prevention squirrel, badge or no badge. Try that with Smokey, and you'll end up with a shovel up your you-know-what. Besides, how big of a shovel could a squirrel carry?

Smokey also has a dedicated zip code. According to one of the interpretive signs in the Historical Park, in 1962, Smokey received more mail than any other resident of Washington D.C., including the President of the United States. In response, the postal service issued Smokey a zip code and the Forest Service assigned a secretary to Smokey. In 1994, the postal service decommissioned 20252, Smokey's zip code. However, there's a happy ending: They reactivated the zip code in 2014 to honor the seventieth anniversary of the Smokey Bear campaign.

For fans who are more into twenty-first century modes of communication, Smokey has his own Facebook page, Twitter account, Instagram account, and YouTube channel. How does he find the time?

The most important thing I learned was that I'm not losing my mind, at least not yet. I'd always thought that Smokey's full name was Smokey *the* Bear, but it isn't—there's no *the* in his name. I learned that I'm not the only one who refers to him as Smokey the Bear. The cause of the confusion is, in part, because Disney published a Little Golden book titled Smokey the Bear in the 1950s, and in it, Smokey refers to himself as Smokey the Bear. A popular kids' song, also from the 1950s, added to the confusion. The songwriters added "the" to his name because it better matched the rhythm of the song. Mystery solved. I think I'll go back to calling him Smokey the Bear, or in the privacy of our home, The Smoke Man.

Our tour of the Historical Park ended with a solemn visit to Smokey's final resting place. In the garden behind their main building, we followed the path to a boulder that had a metal plaque attached explaining that this is where they buried Smokey.

We paused in a moment of silence, and then Lolly said, "They brought Smokey all the way back here to Nevada to bury him?"

The three of us looked at her without saying a word and waited.

"New Mexico! I meant, New Mexico!"

Lunch in Roswell was pleasant but uneventful; we didn't see any aliens except for the plastic ones in the store windows. I'm sure if we hadn't been in such a hurry we would have seen at least a few suspicious lights in the sky, but we wanted to get to Carlsbad by mid-afternoon.

We've now checked into our hotel rooms and are getting ready to drive to Carlsbad Caverns National Park in hopes of seeing the bat flight program. Karen can barely contain her excitement.

Your friend,
Matt

~.~.~.~.~.~.~

From: **Karen Smith**
Subject: **Bat Flight Program**
Date: **May 24 (Wednesday)**

Dear Bob and Sue,

I took one of my wishes out of my wish bucket tonight: seeing the bat flight program at Carlsbad Caverns National Park. After checking into the La Quinta Inn in Carlsbad, we made sure we were at the park by six thirty. There's no set time for when the bats fly out of the cave each night; they usually come out at dusk.

It was the bats that led to the discovery of Carlsbad Caverns in 1898. When Jim White—one of the early explorers of the cave—was sixteen, he was in the area mending fences and saw a dark plume rising from the ground in the distance. At first, he thought it was a brush fire, but when he rode over to investigate, it turned out to be bats leaving the mouth of the cave. A few days later he went back to the entrance, made a ladder, and descended sixty feet holding on to the ladder with one hand and a torch with the other. Jim continued exploring the cave for years and promoted it until his death in 1946.

The NPS built an amphitheater opposite that same large entrance so that visitors can sit and watch the bats fly out of the cave. They estimate that about 200,000 to 500,000 Mexican free-tailed bats live in the cave during the summer, but the population can grow to over a million during migration periods. Sometime in October—the bats don't let anyone know when this will happen—they leave the cave for the winter and migrate south.

If you're traveling to Carlsbad Caverns to watch the bat flight, it's a roll of the dice as to whether you'll get to see it. The bats don't come out every night. Sometimes, hundreds of thousands of bats form a spectacular column as they leave the cave, other times it's just a trickle as only a few come out. There's no guarantee from night to night.

The amphitheater was only about 10 percent full when we got there. We grabbed a spot at the top thinking that would be the best vantage point. I had my phone out hoping to capture video of the bats. Nearly everyone else in the crowd was doing the same. One visitor, sitting close to the bottom, had placed a camera on the front ledge of the amphitheater. It looked like a device that captures 360-degree video.

About thirty minutes before dusk, a ranger walked down the steps and stood at the base of the amphitheater. He looked over at the 360-degree camera and then picked it up. "What the heck is this?" he asked.

The camera's owner stood up, looking concerned, and said, "Uh, that's mine. It's a video camera."

The ranger handed it to the visitor and said, "Sorry, you can't take videos of the bats. I'll explain in a minute."

He called for our attention and started his introduction. The ranger told us that they're never sure exactly when the bats will come out each night, so he'd do his talk about the bats until they started coming out.

"The first thing we need to go over are some basic rules," he said. "It's important that we don't interfere with the bats in any way. If they're frightened or feel threatened by us being here, it could affect their feeding patterns and could even affect whether they come back to this cave each year. So, we have a few rules that I need to enforce. First, we have to keep as quiet as possible. I know that's hard sometimes for families with young ones, but if you have a crying baby or little ones making noise, I suggest you take them to the back. There's a flat area back there away from the cave entrance where you can still see."

After the crying baby warning, one dad stood up and took his fussing toddler to the top of the amphitheater. The other four families with screaming babies just sat there staring at the ranger as if they hadn't heard a word he said.

The ranger paused, and then continued, "Another rule is we *cannot* allow any form of electronic interference while the bats are flying. That means you can't take photos or videos, not even if you turn off the flash. And I'm going to ask you to turn off your cell phones. I mean off, off, not just turn the sound off. Even the vibration of a cell phone could affect the bats."

The ranger paused again. He could see that his "no electronics" warning was being taken as seriously as his "no crying babies" warning. "Now, I don't want to be a meany, I really don't. I want everyone to enjoy their experience here at the park, but I need to enforce these rules. Just about every evening at least one visitor decides these rules don't apply to him or her and starts taking photos or videos anyway. And every now and then, I'll have someone in the crowd tell me that I can't enforce these rules. I need to tell you something: I'm a law enforcement ranger. That's a different type of ranger than an interpretive ranger who conducts tours and answers visitors' questions. I'm a federal officer; that's why I carry a gun. I'm here to protect you and the park. When I ask you to put away your phone, I mean it. If you still refuse, well, let me just put it this way: If I lay my hands on you, you're going to jail."

Matt and John both chuckled. "That's the best line I've ever heard from a ranger," Matt said. "What do you think it takes to become a law enforcement ranger? I want his job."

"They'd never let you have a gun, sweetie," I said.

"Oh yeah they would, and I would enforce the rules," he replied.

"You can't arrest people for having a crying baby," I said.

"Karen, let me put it this way: If I lay my hands on you, you're going to jail."

I couldn't count the number of times Matt and John repeated that line the rest of the night.

"That was worth the price of admission right there," Matt said.

"We didn't pay anything to be here," I replied.

Matt cocked his head, gave me a stern look, and then said, "Karen, if I put my hands on you, you're going to jail."

"John!" Lolly said. "Quit laughing every time he says that, or he'll never stop."

John looked at Lolly and said, "Lolly, if I put my hands on you..."

Matt finished his sentence, "...you're going to jail." Then they both laughed like little kids.

As the crowd put away their electronics and tried to calm their children, the ranger continued his talk. He gave us the history of the park and described how the cave was discovered. Every couple of minutes he looked over his shoulder toward the cave entrance to see if the bats were flying. A young woman sitting close to the ranger yelled, "One just landed on me!"

The ranger laughed. "That's just a moth. It's a big juicy one, though. Did everyone see that?" he asked the crowd. "That's what the bats are looking for. They love to eat those moths."

Minutes ticked by and still no bats. The ranger told every story he could think of while the sky got darker. "Here's another fun fact about bats," he said. "The juveniles don't come out at night to feed. The mothers nurse their babies when they return, because of course, bats are mammals. When the mothers leave at night, they put all of the babies in one area of the cave we call the rookery. And when they return, the mothers know which baby belongs to which mother. We're not entirely sure how they know this, but they can pick out their baby from the thousands of others in the rookery. But, here's the thing, mother bats don't take in orphans, ever. Therefore, if something happens to mama when she's out feeding at night, and she doesn't come back, the baby won't survive."

"How sad," I said. "I'd take care of those baby bats."

Eventually, the bats began emerging from the cave. It wasn't a strong showing for sure, but we could see them. They were coming out in streaks of a dozen or so at a time. After a couple of minutes, we moved down to the front row to see them better. From the top row of the amphitheater, they were nearly impossible to pick out against the dark backdrop of the cave opening. At the front row, we could look up and see them whiz by against the light of the sky.

"There's one!" Matt said. "There's another one!"

John joined in. "There's one!"

It was as if they were trying to outdo each other spotting bats. "You can stop now," I said. "We all see the bats. Remember what the ranger said about being quiet?"

"I just saw another one!" Matt replied.

"Matt," Lolly said. "Let me put it this way: If I put my hands on you, you're going to jail."

We sat spotting bats until it was so dark we could no longer see them. By this time we were nearly the last visitors left; back in the parking lot only a few cars remained. A couple of families were still trying to corral their kids into their minivans. I was sure a kid would get left behind and we'd have to take him or her with us back to the La Quinta.

"Let's hang out here until everyone leaves," I said. "I'd like to see the stars."

An exterior light shining above one of the side entrances to the visitor center was making it difficult to see the night sky, so we piled into our rental car and drove down to the end of the parking lot, as far away from the visitor center as we could. Once our eyes adjusted, we could see the Milky Way. I love seeing the Milky Way. It was very peaceful standing there looking up at the stars. If we'd had lawn chairs with us, I could have stayed for hours.

After a few minutes, our stargazing was interrupted by headlights coming toward us from the other end of the parking lot. We could tell from a distance that it was a ranger. He pulled up to where we were standing, rolled his windows down, and said, "Hey, folks. What are you doing down here?" It was the law enforcement ranger from the bat flight program.

"We're just looking at stars," Matt said.

"No problem. It's my job to close up the park. When I saw your car way down here I needed to come check you out."

"Is it OK for us to stay here awhile?" Matt asked.

"Sure, you can stay here all night if you want. You just can't camp. If you're awake that's fine, but if you fall asleep then you become a camper, and that's not allowed."

Matt and John stood next to the front passenger seat window and chatted with the ranger for a good twenty minutes. I could overhear them laughing about his "you're going to jail" speech. A couple of times, Matt and John stepped back from the ranger's truck and tried to say goodbye, but the ranger would start another story and they'd lean in again and continue their discussion. It seemed like he was having fun talking with them about the park and sharing his stories.

We're back at the La Quinta now, tomorrow we have another big day at the park; it's cave tour day—yay!—and we have to be there bright and early. If we make it out of the Lower Cave, we'll send you a full report tomorrow.

Your friend,
Karen

From: **Matt Smith**
Subject: **Carlsbad Caverns, Again**
Date: **May 25 (Thursday)**

Dear Bob and Sue,

Of course we got to the Carlsbad Caverns Visitor Center this morning much earlier than we needed to. Unfortunately, being early gave Karen and Lolly plenty of time to look through the gift shop before we had to report for our tour. Twenty minutes later, when they joined John and me in the waiting area, they were oohing and aahing over a Native American bear pendant Lolly had just bought.

"This tour is getting expensive," John sighed. "I bet that cost fifty bucks, didn't it?"

Lolly winked at Karen and replied, "Yeah, fifty bucks, that's what it was."

At the designated time, we gathered with the eight other cave-goers in a room right off the main lobby for our orientation with the two rangers leading the tour: Lacey and Jim. Lacey went over the ground rules and told us about what we'd experience in the cave. Then she asked, "Did everyone bring two AA batteries for the headlamps you'll be wearing? It was in the informational email we sent you." Three members of our group looked confused and shook their heads.

"No big deal. We have a few minutes. You can go to the gift shop and buy some," Lacey said.

While the three were off in search of batteries, the rest of us were fitted with hardhats (which had built-in headlamps) and gloves. I asked ranger Jim, "I brought my own gloves. Can I wear them instead?"

"We can't allow you to wear your own gloves," he said. "We have to be very careful about cross-contamination of white-nose disease from outside the cave. I know it's a very small chance that your gloves would have any pathogens on them that would be harmful to the bats, but we have to take every precaution regardless."

When the three battery-less visitors returned, I overheard Lacey say to them, "These are AAA batteries. You need AA batteries." Off they went again to the gift shop while the rest of us got to know each other better. Lacey and Jim spoke about the importance of having redundant sources of light. We'd be leaving the lights of the Big Room behind once we descended into Lower Cave.

"Jim, how many lights do you usually carry with you when you're in the cave?" Lacey asked.

He had a small backpack and several pouches attached to his belt. "Besides my headlamp, I think I have five flashlights. No, six. And extra batteries for several of them."

Lacey told us, "We never go into the cave without multiple flashlights."

All of a sudden, I felt woefully under-prepared. I'm usually not comfortable unless I'm over-prepared. I thought to myself, *I need five flashlights. What happens if...*

Karen could see the worry on my face. "Calm down," she whispered. "I think in a group this size we have enough headlamps and flashlights to share in case yours stops working."

Once everyone had batteries and was outfitted for the tour, we went outside. "Oh yeah," Lacey said. "Today they're doing the annual maintenance on the elevators, so we'll have to walk down into the cave through the natural entrance. It's a mile and a quarter to the start of the tour, but it's all downhill."

One of the members of our group asked, "What about when the tour is finished?"

"Well, you'll have to hike back out also. Maybe if you're lucky, the maintenance folks will be finished by the time the tour is over. But if you have any concerns about being able to hike out, let us know now. The trail has about a seven-hundred-fifty-foot elevation change from top to bottom."

We hiked single-file down from the mouth of the cave, with Lacey in front and Jim bringing up the rear. Karen and I had hiked this before, but it's still a pretty cool descent no matter how many times you do it. The trail ended at the snack shop and restrooms by the bottom of the elevators. Lacey gave us a few minutes for a pit stop and then we walked a short distance through the Big Room to the opening of the Lower Cave. She told us to turn on our headlamps. Jim unhooked a chain that blocked the entrance and led us to a spot where a thick rope had been tied to a boulder. The other end disappeared into the darkness of the cave below.

"This is the first of a couple of tricky spots on the tour," Jim said. "One at a time, we're all going to rappel down the side of this rock and wait at the bottom before we descend the metal ladders into the Lower Cave."

Jim demonstrated to us the proper technique for rappelling. "It's important that only one person is on the rope at a time, so the rule is: When you first grab the rope, you say, 'On rope,' and when you're at the bottom and drop the rope, you say 'Off rope.' You need to say it loud enough so that we can all hear it." Jim grabbed the rope with both hands, said "On rope," turned to face the rock, and began stepping his way down.

"I'll show you a trick," he said. "As the rock begins to slope down, lean back away from it like this." When he reached the bottom, he dropped the rope and said, "Off rope."

Jim made it look like a piece of cake as he eased down the fifteen-foot slope. When it was my turn, though, I found the rappelling more difficult than I'd expected. As you're descending backwards, it's hard to see where you're stepping. It was never dangerous; we probably could have slid down on our butts if needed, but later we'd find out why we were using a rope to descend. As each of us took our turn, Lacey would call out, "Lean back and trust the rope."

Jim chimed in, "That rope isn't going anywhere. We could play tug-of-war with the boulder it's attached to all day and not budge it."

We all made it down without incident. The next challenge was a series of three metal ladders that took us fifty feet into the Lower Cave. "Similar to the rope, we need to let each other know when we're on and off each ladder. Only one person can be on a ladder at a time," Jim said. "When you start down the first ladder, say, 'On ladder one.' That lets everyone know you're on the ladder and it's not safe to start down ladder one until they hear 'Off ladder one.' Everybody got it?"

Jim disappeared down the first ladder into the darkness. When we heard him say, "Off ladder one"—pause—"On ladder two," we all stood there looking at each other. No one wanted to be next. After a few awkward exchanges like, "No, you go next, please. No, you, I insist," we all made it down the three ladders safely. We were now in the Lower Cave, and Karen was in awe.

Lacey and Jim led us through several large rooms, explaining the cave formations we saw. It was dimmer than a dimly-lit basement; the beams coming from our headlamps provided the only light. The floor of the cave was wet, but there was a dry, shoulder-width trail for most of the way.

At one point, Lacey said, "For the next part of the tour, we need to break into two groups because the area we'll be going through is small and we can't all fit inside at the same time. We're going to see the Texas Toothpick, a fragile cave formation."

Maybe she said it to make us feel special, but Lacey told us that not all groups who take this tour get to see the Texas Toothpick. She said, "Part of our job as rangers is to assess the group to make sure they're capable of doing certain parts of the tour. I'm happy to say you guys all passed the test. When we did the rope rappelling at the start of the tour, Jim and I were watching. You guys all looked in control. We can't risk taking visitors back there who might lose their balance and bump into the Toothpick and possibly damage it."

"We all passed?" Karen asked. "Are you sure you were watching when I did the rope thing?"

"You were fine. No baby giraffes in this group," Lacey replied.

"Baby giraffes?" Karen asked.

"Yeah, if anyone goes down the rope with wobbly legs, like a baby giraffe, we just skip the Texas Toothpick part of the tour," Lacey said.

Once we were back in the area of the Toothpick, I understood why they have to be careful who they take back there. The Toothpick was a huge, but delicate, stalactite (hanging from the ceiling of the cave) that was right next to the trail. It took a bit of coordination to pass by without bumping it. The trail was soggy, and I could see how someone might slip and grab the Toothpick to keep from going down. Also back there was a shaft, at least hundred feet tall, that led up to the Big Room. An old, dilapidated rope and wood ladder hung from a point so far above us that we couldn't see what they were attached to. The ladder used to be the only way for visitors to access the Lower Cave. It didn't look like it could hold much weight and I was shocked that anyone would have been willing to brave that way down into the cave.

After seeing the toothpick, we trekked through several more rooms, stopping as Jim pointed out cave pearls growing in pools of water that were a foot or two deep. Cave pearls are small spheres of calcite that sometimes form in pools when there's enough movement in the water to prevent them from turning into stalagmites. He told us that in the early days, visitors would take them as souvenirs.

Drawing our attention to several cave crickets and horsehair worms floating in the pools, Jim began to tell us how the horsehair worms rely on the cave crickets to reproduce. "First," he said, "the cricket swallows the worm larva when it drinks from the pool."

I whispered to Karen, "I bet this story doesn't end well for the cricket."

Jim continued, "Once inside the cricket, the worm begins to grow and essentially takes control of the cricket's nervous system. You see, a horsehair worm can't live out of the water, but crickets avoid the water unless they're thirsty; they can't swim. So the worm excretes chemicals into the cricket's brain directing him to jump into the water. Then the worm bores out of the cricket's body. At that stage, well, it's kind of like the movie *Alien*."

I nudged Karen and said, "I wish I could unhear that last part. Add that to the other reasons I don't like caves."

She shushed me.

"It's a brutal environment down here," Jim said. "For instance, Mexican free-tailed bats can only take flight by letting go of their perch on the ceiling of the cave. If they don't start flying before they hit the ground, there's no way for them to get airborne again."

"Just a hunch, but I bet this doesn't end well for the bat either," I whispered to Karen.

"It takes the cave crickets about three minutes to completely consume a bat that hits the ground. There's nothing left but a small bat skeleton," Jim said.

"Now I don't feel so bad about the horsehair worms killing the cave crickets," I said.

"And that's a perfect segue to our next stop on the tour." Jim led us a short way down a dead-end path and said, "Here we have a cave formation that grew around the skeleton of a bat."

He held a light up to the backside of the column so we could see parts of the bat in the translucent rock.

"How long do you think that bat's been in there?" John asked.

"We don't know for sure. This was a popular site many years ago. You can see how people used to write their name in pen on the side of the rock. We think that graffiti is at least fifty years old, so the bat has been in there at least that long," Jim said.

For the grand finale of the tour, Lacey led us through a narrow passage to a small room where we all sat on the floor close to each other. Once we were all accounted for, she asked us to turn off our headlamps. We did this on the King's Palace tour years ago, and I have to say, the *sitting in complete darkness* part is my favorite.

We sat there in the absolute absence of light for a few minutes. I opened and closed my eyes several times to detect even the smallest hint of light; I couldn't. I had to suppress my urge to ask Jim if I could borrow one of his backup flashlights. Being there in the dark made me realize how risky it was for the early cavers to explore the caves. If anything were to happen to their makeshift lanterns, they might never find their way out. That's probably why Jim White used to string twine throughout the cave—to help him find his way out in case he got lost or his lantern went out. That twine might be the only thing to save his life.

Before we turned our headlamps back on, Lacey had one more thing to say. "I hope you all enjoyed this tour and I hope you now love this cave as much as I do. But if you don't, that's OK. The national parks have something for everyone. There are grasslands, mountains, canyons, historic sites, and wide-open wilderness areas. Find the park that speaks to you." I could tell without seeing her face that Karen was wiping her eyes.

I'm glad she got to take another wish out of her wish bucket. I imagine today's cave tour was not the last one we'll be doing, but I'm still drawing the line at crawling on all fours. Now that I know about horsehair worms, I'm not touching the floor of a cave with anything but the bottom of my shoes.

Tomorrow we're off to Guadalupe Mountains National Park. I'd wanted to hike to the top of Guadalupe Peak the first time we visited that park, but Karen chose McKittrick Canyon instead. Now it's my turn to take a wish out of my bucket.

Your friend,
Matt

~.~.~.~.~.~.~.~

From: **Matt Smith**
Subject: **Guadalupe Peak Trail**
Date: **May 26 (Friday)**

Dear Bob and Sue,

I almost died today. It all unfolded after we detoured into Texas for our last hike of the trip: Guadalupe Peak Trail (or Guad Peak as the locals call it). The peak is the highest point in the state at 8,751 feet. The trail is 4.2 miles to the top, and has an elevation gain of 3,000 feet, so we knew it wouldn't be a cake walk.

As we drove to the park, I said to the group, "We need to keep doing strenuous activities to stay in shape. I want to be able to do hikes like the one we're doing today when I'm in my eighties."

Everyone nodded in agreement. Lolly added, "You also need to exercise your brain. I do the New Year's Times crossword puzzle to keep my mind sharp."

"Did you say New *Year's* Times crossword puzzle?" I asked.

"Yeah, the mini version they have online. I do it every morning."

"Do you think it helps?"

"Definitely!"

"The New Year's Times crossword puzzle. Karen, maybe we should try that."

The drive from Carlsbad to the park along US Highway 180 took about an hour. Other than a few dusty oil wells and a seemingly endless, scrubby desert, we didn't see much along the way.

Our first stop inside the park was the visitor center; I wanted to get a map and talk to a ranger about the hike. Yesterday, we asked one of the rangers at Carlsbad Caverns if he had any advice for us about hiking up Guad Peak. "Yeah, Advil," he said. I was hoping that the Guadalupe rangers had more specific advice.

I waited in line to speak with the ranger working the information desk. When it was my turn, I told him we were planning to hike to the peak. He looked at me carefully. Rangers know to assess visitors, steering people to or away from activities by evaluating their physical fitness. We must have passed the smell test because he didn't discourage us from doing the hike.

"The hike takes about six to eight hours to complete, and you'll need at least a gallon of water each," he said.

I asked, "Will it be cold at the peak?"

"It'll be about ten degrees cooler at the top than down here at the visitor center. Early in the day, the wind can be pretty cold. You should take some kind of windbreaker. There are sections of the trail where the wind can be strong. The trail is wide, so it won't blow you off a cliff, but it's good to have trekking poles to keep your balance. It can move your legs around when it's gusty. And it's always windy at the peak."

"Any other advice?"

"Watch out for mountain lions and snakes."

Mountain lions and snakes? *I'll put Karen in charge of that*, I thought.

From the visitor center, we drove a short distance to the nearby campground and parked. After John set, then reset, his GPS—a few times—we were off. I was first in line. I don't like being the lead hiker, but the group insisted. When I'm leading, I always feel I have to keep track of everyone and make sure I'm not going too fast or too slow. I can never tell if the grunts coming from behind me are intended to prod me to move quicker or to slow the pace. Before starting, we all agreed we'd take our time and go at a relaxed pace. In my opinion, a relaxed pace is when Karen and Lolly are breathing too hard to talk about who posted what on Facebook that morning but not so fast that they rebel and stop. I must have gotten the speed right because I didn't hear a lot of chitchat coming from behind me and no one bailed.

Just like the ranger had warned, the wind was fierce at a couple of spots along the trail. It sucked the warmth right out of us, but it never remained strong for more than a few minutes at a time. About a third of the way up, we met a backpacker coming down. I asked him if it was windy at the top. "Yep, it's windy alright," he said. "Sustained winds of about seventy miles per hour. Didn't get much sleep up there last night." He could have been kidding us or the wind could have died down in the time it took us to reach the peak. Whichever, we were pleasantly surprised to find calm winds with only a few minor gusts when we got to the top.

A stainless steel pyramid marks the peak. Sitting next to the shiny pyramid was a metal ammo can with a register and a few geocache items inside. The ammo can is a good idea. We've been to many hard-to-reach destinations and found a college notebook for a register sitting out in the open with just a rock on top protecting it, thoroughly soaked and with blurred entries.

The sights from the peak were well worth the effort to get there. Directly south, we had a clear view of the top of El Capitan, the farthest south prominence of the Guadalupe Mountains. A hiking trail goes around El Capitan; we'll have to put that on the short list of things to do for our next visit. To the southwest, we could see the brown, flat Chihuahuan

Desert stretching for miles. A few green, irrigated crop circles spotted the desert landscape in the distance.

After we got our packs off and drank water, it was time to take our picture at the pyramid. Fortunately, another couple was there who volunteered to take our photo. "That's perfect, thank you," Karen said to the man when he handed back her phone. I mistakenly thought we were done with the photo shoot, but as I walked toward my pack to have a snack, Karen informed me that we weren't finished.

First, we needed to get a picture of just Karen and me, then John and Lolly, then Karen and Lolly, then Karen and Lolly wearing their matching windbreakers, then Karen and Lolly sitting down next to the pyramid. "We took fewer photos at our wedding," I said as I dug through my pack to find the bag I'd carefully filled with the largest Ruffles potatoes chips I could find.

"Yes! They didn't break," I said as I found a comfortable rock to sit on. My rest was soon interrupted.

"I forgot to take out the sign!" Karen said. Before we left on the trip, she'd printed a sign on our printer with the words "Highest Point in Texas" on it. We had to start the photo shoot over, this time with the sign prominently displayed. I had to retake several shots because the sign was crooked in the photos.

Lolly (left) and Karen posing for a picture
at the top of Guadalupe Peak

Finally I announced, "That's it. I'm calling it."

"Just one more," Karen pleaded. "I want you to get a picture of Lolly and me from behind."

"Behind what?"

"Behind us. I want you to take our picture from the back."

I looked over at my pack. My sandwich bag was fluttering in the stiff breeze. I could imagine the last few Ruffles blowing off the side of the mountain with the next gust. "Really? You want me to take a picture of your behinds?"

"Not of our behinds, from behind us. This is what everyone does these days. We'll be standing at the peak looking toward the view in the distance."

I could have argued. I could have offered my opinion that this was a stupid idea. I could have refused. But those would have taken more time than just taking one more picture. Karen and Lolly stood on opposite sides of the marker with their backs to me. The view in the direction they were facing was spectacular.

"Are you ready?" I asked.

"Yes."

"Are you sure?"

"Yes, just take it! The wind is going to knock us over."

"OK. Smile."

I gave Karen back her phone. She and Lolly shaded their eyes from the bright sunlight and looked at the photo. They both made sour faces. "Well, that looks stupid," Karen said.

"Yep," was all I said as I walked to my pack. This whole time, John was off by himself eating, acting as if he didn't know us.

We'd spent most of our snack time taking pictures. A couple of minutes later another foursome arrived. We felt it would be courteous to let the new group have some time alone on the peak. Slowly, we gathered our stuff, strapped on our packs, and started hiking back. I told the group I wanted to be the sweeper on the way down the trail, but they wouldn't have it. They insisted I lead again.

Soon after we started, it was warm enough to take off our jackets. The wind continued to die down, and the hazy overcast had burned off. By the end of the hike, it was hot.

Despite the ranger's warning to be on the lookout for mountain lions, we didn't see one. Mountain lion sightings are rare, even in areas where they frequently spend time. We've hiked a fair bit in mountain lion habitats, but we've never seen one. We heard one once in Saguaro National Park. And in Canyonlands National Park, we saw mountain lion prints in the wet sand early one morning while hiking. But on our life list of large mammals, the mountain lion box is still unchecked.

After nearly four hours of hiking, I was in a one-foot-in-front-of-the-other trance. We were on the home stretch of the trail, the last mile and a half of mildly steep switchbacks.

On the left side of the trail, the terrain sloped downward and was spotted with gray-green vegetation. On the right was a wall of rock. The path was smooth enough that I didn't need to watch where I placed each step. I continually directed my focus at a spot on the trail about ten feet in front of me. I never saw the rattlesnake until my foot was on top of him.

Both the snake and I were lucky that I caught him with only an inch or so of the toe of my hiking boot. I heard the rattle the instant I felt his body beneath my foot. It was an angry rattle. Later, when I described this to Karen, she asked if there's ever a time when a rattlesnake's rattle isn't angry.

We humans must be born with a database of sounds in our brains, ones that have accumulated over tens of thousands of years based on our collective experience with wild animals. This memory bank is there to tell us which sounds are harmless and which we should be fearful of. When you hear a rattlesnake's rattle, no one has to tell you that you should be afraid. You just are—instantly.

Besides the shock of having just stepped on a rattlesnake, I wondered how he could have appeared out of nowhere. It's possible he'd been sunning himself on the trail and I didn't see him, or he could have darted across the path right as I was passing by. Either way, I had an extremely pissed-off rattlesnake at my feet.

He was about three feet long, dark green with tan markings and the tip of his tail was dark, not what I would have expected a rattlesnake to look like. His rattle was shaking like someone had plugged it into an electrical outlet.

I'd been walking slow enough to stop my stride before I put all of my weight on the foot that was pressing down on the snake. The next couple of seconds were a blur. I danced around like someone who had, well, just stepped on a rattlesnake. I'm happy to say that I didn't scream, shriek or yelp, but not because of my manliness; I was too terrified to make a sound.

While I was dancing, the snake bolted to the edge of the rock wall about four feet away from me. He kept rattling vigorously, rose up and coiled into the S-shaped pose that snakes like to do just before they strike. Quickly, I backed up another couple of feet. As I watched him, a strange dialogue went through my mind. I thought, *He's kind of small. Maybe I should just walk past him.* The other half of my brain snapped back, *It's a rattlesnake dumb-ass. Back up!*"

He must have concluded that I wasn't going to stomp on him again because he stopped rattling and slithered beneath a small plant at the base of the rock wall. Karen caught up to where I was standing. I put my hands up signaling, stop!

"What just happened?" she asked.

"I stepped on a rattlesnake."

"Oh my God, did he bite you!?"

"No, I don't think so, but he scared the shit out of me."

"You don't think so? I'm pretty sure you'd feel it if he'd bitten you. Where is he now?"

"He went under that bush over there. The one right by the trail."

By this time, John and Lolly had reached where we were standing. "I saw you dancing around. What was that all about?" John asked.

I explained what happened and we all stood there looking at the bush. From our vantage point, we couldn't see the snake.

John said, "Let's take a look at him."

"I'd give him some space. He wasn't happy after I stepped on him."

John suddenly became a rattlesnake expert. "It's OK. He's not rattling now. The thing about rattlesnakes is they'll let you know if they're about to strike. If he's not rattling, then he won't strike."

I wasn't convinced, so I kept my eye on the bush as I carefully walked past it. We had no choice; it was the only way to continue down the trail. After we all made it past the bush, John got down on all fours and took a closer look at the rattler. "Yeah, he's in there, coiled up and ready to pounce. He's a little guy."

"Little guy my ass, he's a rattlesnake," I replied.

Another thing that surprised me about my encounter was how difficult it was to see the snake once he went under the bush. The bush was small, and I'd seen exactly where he went, but once in there, the snake was invisible. Whenever we've hiked in areas with snakes, I've felt confident that I'd see one if it were hiding under vegetation. Not anymore. For the rest of the hike, I was on edge; I was sure a snake was under every plant we passed. Even the lizards running across the trail almost made me pee myself.

It took us about another thirty minutes to reach the parking lot. Every time we passed a group of hikers heading up the trail, Karen felt the need to warn them. When we came to the first set of hikers, she stopped and told them the entire story. Then Karen realized the three of us had left her behind. When she grasped the idea that she was alone with the snakes, she ran to catch up. Each time a new group of hikers approached, her story got shorter. By the time we could see the parking lot she'd just say, "Watch out for rattlesnakes, we saw one!" without breaking her stride.

The shaded picnic table in the parking lot was a perfect resting place after our long hike. John's GPS indicated we'd walked for 9.3 miles. We took all of our leftover food out of the back of the car and laid it on the table. We sat there and grazed while we got our strength back.

John said to me, "You're lucky you weren't bitten. I'd have to cut the bite area with my pocket knife, and Karen would have to suck out the venom."

"That's not what you're supposed to do when a rattlesnake bites you," I said.

"Sure it is. That's what they taught me in Boy Scouts."

"That was a long time ago. Back then they also taught you dinosaur safety."

Karen said, "Remember what the ranger in Stehekin told us? Rattlesnakes usually don't use their venom on people because they know you're too big to eat. If that snake had bitten you, he probably wouldn't have used his venom."

"Thank you," I said. "I think when you step on a snake, all bets are off. That one would have used his venom on me. And it was a young snake. Those are the most dangerous!"

"He was a baby!" John laughed.

The area where we were sitting had a strong cell signal, so John searched online for what you're supposed to do if bitten by a rattlesnake. He said, "Well, I guess you're right. It says here you should never cut the bite area. However, it's a good idea to let the wound bleed, which may help some of the venom come out. And it's OK to suck out the venom if you can, but not with your mouth. You should use a device made for that purpose."

"Does it also say that you're never supposed to let John cut any part of your body with his pocket knife? I think that should be our number one rule when we travel together," I said.

John continued, "I hate to say it, but Matt was correct on another point. Immature snakes are often the most dangerous because they aren't as experienced as mature snakes when using their venom and are likely to use more venom on a human."

Karen and Lolly had had enough of the snake talk. "What's our plan for the rest of the day?" Lolly asked.

"I'm just glad to be alive. After my brush with death, I'm happy doing anything," I said.

"Oh, dear Lord, we're going to hear about this for the rest of the trip, aren't we?" Karen asked.

"Yep!" I replied.

After our picnic, we went back to the visitor center. Everyone had to use the restroom before our long drive to Las Cruces, New Mexico, and I wanted to see if there were snake exhibits so I could identify my snake.

John and I looked at all of the stuffed snakes on display. None of them had the same coloring as the one I'd stepped on. I found the ranger we'd talked to before the hike and told him about my encounter.

"I got him with just this part of my boot," I said as I pointed to the exact spot.

"Whoa, that was close! You used up some serious Karma on that one. You're lucky he didn't bite you," the ranger said.

"He didn't look like any of the snakes you have on display. He was green and about that long," I said as I held my hands about three feet apart.

"Oh, yeah. That's a black-tailed rattlesnake. We have those here in the park."

"Yep, you have at least one for sure."

John asked, "What's the treatment for a snake bite?"

The ranger said, "If you don't do anything, you'll die. If you get medical treatment in the first couple of hours, you'll probably live, but you could lose a limb. The treatment is painful, I can tell you that."

"Is the person supposed to stay where they are and have someone else go for help or should they try to hike out and then get treatment?" I asked.

"Depends on how they're feeling. If the snake uses his venom on the person, they should stay put and have help come to them. If they don't keep their heart rate low, they could pass out."

"So, one of you rangers would hike up there and treat the bite?" I asked.

"No, we're not allowed to administer antivenom to snake bite victims; that can only be done by a medical professional. Apparently, some people are severely allergic to snake antivenom, so someone who knows what to watch for must keep an eye on the victim after it's administered."

"Really? Here at the visitor center we're like seventy miles from the nearest medical professional. And if someone is several miles away on a trail and gets bitten, how do they get help within a couple of hours?" I asked.

"That's, uh, a real challenge," the ranger said.

I turned to Karen and said, "I almost died! You have to be nicer to me now."

A group of visitors gathered around us as I explained to the ranger what happened. Lolly rolled her eyes. "By the end of the trip, it'll be a ten-foot snake that Matt had to wrestle to the ground. Get over it, you lived. Can we talk about something else now?"

"Lolly, when one comes so close to dying they have a new perspective on life. I want to share my experience, so others can hike safely in the wilderness," I said.

"For God's sake, let's go. I need a glass of wine," she said.

As we walked back to the car, I said, "Remember that guy we met on the trail who had those black things around his lower legs? Those were snake gaiters. Karen, I'm getting snake gaiters."

Lolly laughed. "Snake gaiters. John, Matt's getting snake gaiters." Then they both laughed.

"You guys can laugh, but I'm the one who almost died."

"Oh, for God's sake," Lolly said.

"Go ahead and laugh. I hope you don't get bitten while hiking with John in the wilderness. After he cuts your leg off with his pocket knife, you'll wish you'd worn snake gaiters."

Lolly laughed again, harder this time. "Snake gaiters. John, Matt's getting snake gaiters."

"Alright," I told Lolly. "Here's a tip for you. Next time you're doing one of your crossword puzzles, if the clue is 'life-saving snakebite preventer,' the answer is G-A-I-T-E-R."

What a day. I crossed Guadalupe Peak off my bucket list while nearly kicking the bucket in the process. Maybe the snake encounter was a sign that we've done enough for one trip and it's time to go home. Tomorrow we have an open day in Albuquerque where we plan on doing a self-guided Breaking Bad tour followed by a brewery tour. Next time we visit Nevada, you should join us. I mean New Mexico.

Your friend,
Matt

From: **Matt Smith**
Subject: **One More Try**
Date: **June 28 (Wednesday)**

Dear Bob and Sue,

This week we're camping no matter what. Unless, of course, we can't find an available campsite. Karen and I are taking the ferry over to the Olympic Peninsula on Friday with plans to camp somewhere in Olympic National Park for a couple of days. We have most of the necessary gear since we prepared to camp in March, but I needed to get a few last items.

"I thought we already have all the camping gear we need," Karen said when she caught me making my shopping list.

"Almost, there are just a few more things to get," I replied.

"A plastic egg holder!? Why do we need a plastic egg holder?" she asked as she looked over my shoulder at my list. "The eggs are already in a holder when you buy them. Besides, I thought we were only doing freeze-dried meals on this trip."

"We should bring some eggs as a backup. I've tried the freeze-dried ones. They're OK, but not the same as the real thing."

"What else is on your list?" she asked while trying to peek at what I was writing.

"Hey, this is private," I said. "You don't need to worry about what I'm buying."

"Honey, we've been married for almost thirty-five years; there's no private *anything* anymore."

"Great. Let me just pull up your Nordstrom account and take a look at your purchase history. I've always wanted to do that," I said. "What's your username and password, honey?"

"Alright. Truce," she said. "But I still don't think we need a plastic egg holder."

"That's fine, you can eat the broken ones floating in the cooler for breakfast when we're camping in the wild. I hope you like your fried eggs on the watery side."

"You mean the 'wild' as in when we cook on the picnic table next to our truck at the campsite while our neighbors twenty feet away watch us?" she replied.

I let my guard down and Karen grabbed my list. "Let's see what else you have here. What's a multi-tool?"

"It's like a Swiss Army knife, only bigger. It has a bunch of tools like pliers and wire cutters and various types of knife blades all together in one tool."

"Do I get one?"

"I'm getting one for *us*. I don't think we need two of them."

"Then I can use it whenever I want?"

"No, you can never touch it."

"That's what I thought. You just like buying gadgets."

"You can touch it, but you need to be careful. The blades on those things are extremely sharp," I said.

"Are you seriously worried that I can't handle a knife?"

"Have you been through knife safety training?"

"No, but I have a knife block full of sharp knives and haven't lost a finger yet," she replied.

"I tell you what, when we're at our campsite, I'll give you a knife safety lesson."

Karen grabbed the soft, white skin on the underside of my arm, pinched it hard, and said, "That's so kind of you. What do you know about knife safety?"

"When Matthew was a Cub Scout, I gave the boys in his pack the knife safety lesson. As a matter of fact, I was the knife safety specialist amongst the Cub Scout parents."

"That was like seventy years ago."

I took out my laptop and asked her, "Is it Nordstrom dot com or Nordstroms dot com? I never know whether to put an "s" on the end." That shoo'd her away for a while.

Anyway, we're making another run at camping. Hopefully, this time it works out for us. If we can't get a campsite, maybe we'll go home and set up the tent in the backyard. I'll have a dozen eggs in a shiny new egg holder just waiting to be fried.

Your friend,
Matt

~.~.~.~.~.~.~.~

From: **Matt Smith**
Subject: **Klahowya Means Welcome**
Date: **July 2 (Sunday)**

Dear Bob and Sue,

We just got back from our Olympic Peninsula trip, and I'm proud to announce we're now officially campers. As I said in my last email, we'd hoped to find a spot in Olympic National Park, but a couple of things worked against us. First, it was the start of the Fourth of July holiday weekend, so we were competing with everyone and their dog for a campsite. And second, nearly all the campgrounds in the area were on a first come, first served basis; therefore, we couldn't make a reservation in advance.

To our advantage, though, we were able to make it to the park early in the day on Friday. Fairholme Campground, adjacent to Lake Crescent, was our first stop. Even though we'd gotten an early start, all eighty-eight sites at Fairholme were taken. The place was full. Karen was getting nervous. "We're not going to find a campsite. I can feel it in my stomach. We'll never get to camp. You'd think by now most campgrounds would take online reservations, so you know you'll have a place to spend the night. What happens if we can't find a spot and all of the hotels around here are sold out?"

"Don't worry; we'll find a spot. Fairholme is prime real estate, so it'll fill up first. The other campgrounds will have spaces left." I'd no basis for my optimism; I was trying to ease her concerns. The memory of Canyonlands in March was fresh in our minds. Karen had convinced herself that it was going to happen again.

Nine miles west of Lake Crescent is Klahowya Campground. The entrance sign says Klahowya is the Chinook word for *welcome*. While not in the national park, the campground is in Olympic National Forest. When we pulled into Klahowya it was still early morning, and few campers were out of their tents. We stopped at the information sign next to the host's campsite and read the instructions for claiming a site. The sign read, "Occupy a vacant site and return here to pay within thirty minutes."

Karen asked, "How do we know if a site is vacant?"

"There's a post at the front of each campsite with a clothes pin attached. You're supposed to write the dates you'll be occupying the site on the flap of the registration envelope, tear it off, and clip it onto the post. Not everyone does that. Some people just spread their stuff out to let the world know they've claimed that spot."

"People just put their stuff out and leave?"

"Yep. See that one over there with a collapsed tent in the middle? Those folks probably got here this morning, claimed their site and are now off hiking."

"And no one will take their stuff? I'm not sure I want to leave our camping gear here while we go off for the day."

"It'll be OK. That's what camping is. No one will take our stuff."

A few yards from where we were standing, right at the entrance to the campground and adjacent to a pit toilet, was an open site. "What about that one right there?" I asked.

Karen couldn't contain herself. "Yes, let's take that one! Matt, we're going to be campers!"

"Quiet. People might still be sleeping. We don't have to take the first vacant site we find."

"No. We have to take that one. What if it's the only one available and someone snatches it from us while we're driving through the campground looking for another one? I'll stay here and hold it while you go see if there are any others available."

Karen grabbed her purse out of the truck, went over to the vacant site and sat on the picnic bench next to the fire pit. I'm not sure why she needed her purse for this. As I drove away, I could see her in my rearview mirror, trying to fight off the chill by rubbing her upper arms with her hands. She was beaming.

I drove through the entire campground and found at least ten vacant sites. When I got back to where Karen was waiting, I rolled down my window and said, "Saddle up partner. There are a bunch of open sites. We can do better than this."

"Are you sure? I kind of like this one," she replied.

"I'm sure. You don't want to sleep that close to the toilet if you don't have to."

We settled on a cozy site under large cedar trees. After we completed the registration and set out a couple of camp chairs next to the fire pit at our site, we left the campground. Karen had always wanted to hike the Ozette Triangle Loop Trail, so we drove to Lake Ozette and did the nine-mile trek: three miles to the ocean on a boardwalk, three miles along the beach, and three miles back on a second boardwalk.

The boardwalk sections were easy but walking along the beach took longer than we expected. It's not like walking on a sandy beach you'd find in California or Florida. The sand is coarse and soft, so you sink as you walk across it. Some areas have no sand at all; you end up picking your way across slick bowling-ball-sized rocks for long stretches. It wasn't physically difficult, just tedious at times.

The trail starts at the Lake Ozette Ranger Station and takes you to the western-most point of the U.S. in the lower forty-eight states: Cape Alava (pronounced like "a lava"). The highlight of the day was finding petroglyphs next to the beach. They're not easy to locate unless you know where to look. We were fortunate to have talked to hikers on the beach who pointed us directly toward the outcropping of rocks where the petroglyphs were.

By the time we got back to the campground, we'd been away for about six hours. Our chairs hadn't moved, and the campground was nearly full. Karen's original campsite by the entrance was still available. "Oh, it looks so lonely. I hope someone camps there tonight," she said. Within another couple of hours, all the sites were occupied.

Since we had plenty of room in our truck, I brought our four-person tent. I suggested to Karen that she set it up. Not only had she never erected a tent before, I'm not sure she'd even seen anyone do it. But without hesitation, she accepted the challenge. I talked her through it and within fifteen minutes we had our home for the next two nights up and ready. We sat inside the empty tent for a few minutes like two kids in the backyard. No one could see us in there; it was our private world.

We thought we'd chosen a site with a little more privacy than the others. On one side of us was a small utility building that must have been the campground's pump house for the running water. On the other was an amphitheater that looked like it hadn't been used in a long time. It was about the size of an average campsite. Having the extra space should have made for a tranquil campsite, but our plan backfired.

A large, old-growth cedar log formed a border between our site and the amphitheater. Every few minutes a small child would pop his or her head over the log and yell, "Look! There's a tent!" And then throw a stick at it. About half the time, the parents would quickly collect their child and use the opportunity to teach them to keep their voices down and to not throw sticks. The other half of the time the parents would come over, glance across the log, and yell, "Look! There's a tent!" These folks would usually then look at us as if we couldn't hear them and continue to talk loudly in our direction. Several times, when they'd linger, I'd get out our two canisters of bear spray and start cleaning them with a rag while pointing the nozzles in their direction, hollering at Karen, "Honey, the trigger on this bear spray is stuck again. Could you bring me the WD-40?"

The amphitheater got a lot of visitors. One guy came in and just sat peacefully on a log for a few minutes then left. I was sure he'd told his wife and kids he was going for a pee, and then instead stole a few minutes of peace sitting under the trees. After him came three camping bros in their mid-twenties who picked the site clean of every stick they could find to use as firewood.

After a while, the constant traffic in and out of the amphitheater became background noise. Karen turned her attention to observing the other sites for camping tips. The guy at the site across the road from us was splitting wood into kindling with an axe. Karen said, "That's what you need, an axe."

"I have an axe. It's in the truck."

"You do? What else do you have in there?"

"Everything we need, sweetie." The bed of my truck has a hard-shell cover. I opened the tailgate so Karen could see inside. Before we left, I'd organized our camping stuff and placed it all in Home Depot bins by category. I labeled each bin: sleeping bags, food, Jetboil, etc.

"Oh, I gotta take a picture of your bins. Sue will die when she sees this," Karen said. "Here, move them so I can see all the labels then stand next to the truck. Better yet, let's stack them in our campsite, and I'll take a picture with you next to them."

"You're not taking a picture of my bins."

"I'm definitely taking a picture of your bins."

"Fine, but I'm not posing with them. By the way, you're lucky I'm organized and brought everything we need. What did you bring?"

"I brought this," she said as she pulled what looked like a knife out of her purse. The words "waiter's friend" were etched into the side of it. It was a corkscrew, foil cutter, and bottle opener—all in one. "This is all I need."

Next, I started a fire. And, as it is with campfires, I restarted it several times until it could keep itself going for more than a minute. I finished setting up camp between fire pokings, while Karen struggled to open a bottle of red wine. Once we were settled, we ate cheese and crackers and marveled at the mobile homestead we'd made for ourselves. The simplicity of it all was relaxing.

We agreed when we made a pact to camp this year that we'd try to keep it simple. To that end, our meals would mostly consist of freeze-dried food. But this is no hardship. At home, we'd practiced using our Jetboil to boil water and had tried several freeze-dried meals. It's amazing how good they taste. While there's nothing better than bacon, steak, eggs, or chili cooked over a campfire, you can't beat the ease of prep and cleanup of the "just add boiling water" meals that are available today.

Dinner that night was Mountain House Chicken Noodle Casserole. My jobs are to boil the water and stir; Karen's the timekeeper. She tells me when to stir and when the meal is ready to eat. It was quick and easy. Karen was finally able to put her Spork to good use, the red one that's been at the bottom of her backpack ever since I bought it for her years ago when we went on our national parks tour.

After dinner, we walked all of the loops of the campground, a couple of times. It was then that camping gear envy began to set in. "Look at that tent," Karen said to me. "Look how big it is. You don't even need to bend over to go inside." She makes comments like this then looks at me as if I'm supposed to respond.

"Our tent is perfect," I replied. "It's just the right size. *And* it was on sale." On sale is the trump card. I don't remember if I got our tent on sale or not.

The topic changed as we went from site to site. "Tarps. Those people have tarps on the ground in front of their tent to keep from tracking dirt inside," she said. Then she saw campers setting up cots inside their tent. "Cots! We should get cots."

"We could get cots. We could also stay at Hampton Inn. At some point you have to draw the line," I replied.

"I agree. I agree. I'll draw the line after cots—and a canopy, just in case it rains—and maybe some sheepskin-lined moccasins." It sounded more like a list than a line, and just the other day she was giving me grief about buying a plastic egg holder.

When we were almost back to our camp, we walked by the host's site. A woman about our age was coming out of an RV, and Karen asked, "Are you the host?"

"Yes, I am. Why? Would you like to be the host? I'm looking for a couple to do the job this summer. I'm only here for a few days."

Karen looked at me as if to say, "How about it?"

I said, "No! No, we don't want to be hosts. We'd be bad hosts. The whole place would fall apart under our management. We just wanted to say hello. Besides, I wouldn't be good dealing with whiners. Do you get a lot of complaints from campers?"

"Not too many. Most people who stay here are pretty easy going. I did have a strange one last week. A woman was camping right across from us, at that site right there. She came over to tell me that the smoke from the campfires was bothering her. She was asthmatic. I told her that I couldn't ask the other campers to put out their fires; it's a campground for goodness sake. Then she said that she was allergic to the dirt around her campsite. Can you believe that? Sometimes I wonder what people think when they come out here. Yes, there's dirt and smoke; that's what camping is."

When we got back to our site, I had to re-start the fire. It was our first night in camp, and I was already running low on wood—rookie mistake. I'd realized this earlier in the day and had thought I could buy wood at the campground, but the shed where they kept the wood was empty. A sign on the shed said, "Firewood will arrive this afternoon." It was 7:00 pm and still no firewood. An RV site a few miles down the road sold firewood, so I drove there and bought several more bundles. My wood run took precisely twenty-eight minutes. As I pulled back into Klahowya, I drove past the woodshed, which, of course, was now stacked to the roof with new firewood.

I made a roaring fire, and Karen and I sat staring at it for a long time. It was very peaceful. We didn't talk much, except every few moments Karen would look at me and say, "Can you believe it? We're campers." I was glad she was enjoying it.

As it started to get dark, I packed all the food and trash into the back of my truck so critters wouldn't get into it. I had a surprise for Karen, but almost forgot to show her before we called it a night. "Stay here and close your eyes," I said. "I'll be right back." With my head lamp on, I fumbled around inside our tent, zipped it back up, and rejoined her by the fire.

"OK, turn toward our tent and open your eyes."

"Wow!" she gasped. Our tent, framed by the branches of the cedar trees draped with moss, was glowing like an orange jewel in the darkness. "It's beautiful. How did you do that?"

"The tent has built-in LED lights on the inside. I just had to flip a switch."

Our tent glowing in our campsite, Olympic National Forest

Once we were settled in our sleeping bags, I realized that the site I'd chosen for our tent wasn't perfectly flat after all. We couldn't help but roll toward the middle of the tent and into each other. It would have been an easy fix to rearrange our sleeping bags, but we were too tired to mess with it. We spent most of the night sleeping face to face.

At 5:00 am, with the precision of an alarm clock, an owl let out a series of hoots that startled me. It sounded like a war cry. A few minutes of silence passed, then he did it again. It wasn't a frightening sound as much as it was impressive: loud, clear, and booming. A moment later, more owls joined him; the back and forth hooting and screeching continued for another thirty minutes or so. I laid awake in my sleeping bag with my eyes wide open. For me, the day had begun; I couldn't go back to sleep after that.

Just as I got our campfire going, I heard the zipper of our tent. Karen emerged wearing almost every piece of clothing she'd brought. She said, "We need a thermostat in our tent."

"You mean a thermometer?" I asked.

She paused for a moment like one does when asked a question before being fully awake. "No, I meant thermostat. You know, the thing that keeps the temperature where you want it. Do they make tents with thermostats?"

"Yes, they're called houses," I replied.

I was curious to see if Karen's attitude about camping had changed during the night. Those first few minutes out of the tent in the morning are when you realize you either enjoy camping or you don't. It's then when you think either, *Why the hell am I here?* or *Isn't this great?* Karen sat next to me by the fire, smiled and said, "Why didn't we do this years ago?"

After I boiled water in the Jetboil for the instant coffee packets we'd brought, we rehydrated the freeze-dried eggs with ham. They were...fair. It's a good thing we brought real eggs. I also splurged and bought a small Teflon skillet that's the perfect size for cooking a single egg. It was easy to flip the metal grate over our small campfire and cook a couple of eggs—one at a time—in our tiny skillet. "This little guy is as cute as can be," Karen said. "But we might want to get a bigger one for our future camping trips."

With a lot on our to-do list for the day, we cleaned up camp and got ready to head out. Karen wanted to see where the dams had been removed on the Elwha River and then go for a hike. I was putting my backpack in the truck when she said, "I need a minute to brush my teeth." I thought she would walk to the bathroom down the road, where there was a sink with running water. Instead, she brushed her teeth at the edge of our campsite and then spat into the weeds. I've never been prouder; she's officially a camper.

Your friend,
Matt

From: **Karen Smith**
Subject: **Elwha River Dams**
Date: **July 2 (Sunday)**

Dear Bob and Sue,

Ever since the Elwha Dam on the Elwha River was removed five years ago, Matt and I have had a running dialogue that goes something like this:

Me: "I really want to go to Olympic National Park and see where they took the dam out."

Matt: "If the dam is gone, what would we be looking at?"

Me: "We'd be looking at where the dam used to be."

Matt: "So we'd be looking at the absence of the dam."

Me: "Yes, exactly, it's very exciting."

Matt: "Maybe I'm missing something here, but doesn't that mean we'd be looking at nothing?"

I knew when we planned our camping trip to Olympic National Park that I'd finally have a chance to see where the dam once stood. They actually took out two dams on the Elwha River: the lower Elwha Dam in 2012 and the upper Glines Canyon Dam in 2014; both had been in place since the early 1900s. Neither dam had been built with any kind of fish passage, which is a violation of current state law. Before the dams were built, all five Pacific salmon species spawned in the river.

The upper reaches of the Elwha River and the Glines Canyon Dam are in Olympic National Park, but the lower part of the river, including the Elwha Dam site, are on the Lower Elwha Klallam Indian reservation. When the Elwha Dam failed to pass safety inspections in 1978, the tribe realized that they faced the possibility of catastrophic flooding should it fail. They joined forces with other partners and lobbied to have the dams taken out. In 1992, Congress passed an act authorizing the removal of both dams and after almost twenty years of planning, the dismantling work began.

The *Seattle Times* and other news outlets ran articles detailing the process, which was the largest dam removal project in history. Already the changes have been dramatic. The newly-freed river has carved new channels and deposited tons of previously blocked sediment where it empties into the Strait of Juan de Fuca, forming a new beach and creating habitat for crab, clams and other sea life. Without sediment muddying its waters upstream, the river is now teal green again. Salmon are returning and so are birds and plants and mammals.

Two years ago, the NPS opened the Glines Canyon Spillway Overlook to visitors, and today we drove up the Elwha Valley on Olympic Hot Springs Road to see where that dam once stood. On our way, we passed the entrance to Altair Campground, which was permanently closed to camping when the river reclaimed a chunk of adjacent land as it charted its new course.

Two viewing platforms are located at the overlook, one on each side of the river. On the west side, eight interpretive exhibits tell the story of the dam.

Walking out onto what remains of the spillway, it was windy, and I was glad to have a metal railing to hold onto. To the south we could see the Elwha River running through a wide valley that used to hold Lake Mills, the reservoir that formed when the dam was built. Park botanists and volunteers have been restoring this area (and the land that was flooded by Lake Aldwell behind the Elwha Dam) with more than 400,000 native plants. Looking down to the north we saw the waters of the Elwha plummeting through the two-hundred-foot deep Glines Canyon. It was an amazing sight. I think Matt was even more impressed than I was.

From there we drove south on the gravel, five-mile Whiskey Bend Road that dead ends at a trailhead. We followed the map the ranger gave us at the pay station booth and did the Humes Ranch Loop Trail, which took us through the forest and then back along the river. We found some big rocks along the bank of the Elwha to park ourselves on and have lunch. The water flowed swiftly and sparkled in the sunlight.

Toward the end of the loop, we saw a sign pointing to a side trail that led to Goblins Gate. We had no idea what it was, but the name sounded intriguing, so we followed the trail which ended at a jumble of massive boulders. At that spot, the river leaves the broad valley and makes a 90-degree turn into Rica Canyon, where huge rocks on both sides jut out like an entry gate. The canyon walls are maybe twenty feet across at this point and the water churns and roars angrily as it's constricted into the narrow gorge.

I loved hiking along the river and seeing how it's thriving once again. Hopefully, the success of the Elwha River dam removal will be the catalyst for dam removal projects on other rivers. In Utah, the Mill Creek Dam has been removed as part of an effort to restore Bonneville cutthroat trout, and in Oregon, the Cline Falls Dam on the Deschutes River has also been taken out. Additionally, several Indian tribes have secured a deal to remove four large dams on the Klamath River in southeast Oregon and Northern California—a project that will surpass even the Elwha in scale.

Maybe one day we'll go on a dam removal tour all across the country and see where dams have been taken out. You guys could join us, and we'll stand and look at nothing together.

Your friend,
Karen

From: **Matt Smith**
Subject: **Preparing to backpack (to Shi Shi)**
Date: **July 7 (Friday)**

Dear Bob and Sue,

One week after camping for the first time, Karen and I have confidence in our ability to boil water and feed ourselves in the wild. We're going to attempt a three-night backpacking trip to Shi Shi Beach (pronounced shy shy). Shi Shi has been in Karen's wish bucket for years. After all the trips we made with you guys to Olympic National Park over the years, I'm surprised we never attempted this hike. Maybe because it's not easy to get to; it's in the remote northwest corner of the Olympic Peninsula. And once you make it to the parking lot, it's a two-mile hike to the beach.

Karen and I quickly learned that preparing for a backpacking trip takes more thoughtful planning than camping at a site we could drive to. When we have our truck with us, we can take anything we want so long as the tailgate closes. But carrying everything on our backs? Nothing goes in the backpack that isn't necessary.

We needed to buy a few essentials before our trip: a water filter, a smaller tent, inflatable pillows (although, I tried to convince Karen that she could put her clothes in a stuff sack and use that as a pillow), lightweight chairs, and of course bigger backpacks.

We both bought new packs big enough to fit all of the extra gear that we needed to bring; mine is seventy liters, Karen's is sixty liters. When we were shopping for them at REI, I tried on a couple of models and was moving toward the checkout counter to buy one when a woman who worked there stopped me and asked, "Are you sure that pack fits you?"

"I tried it on, it felt fine to me," I replied.

"Come back over here and let me take a look."

She measured my torso and adjusted a few straps, then told me I needed a large instead of the medium I was about to buy. I said, "I thought all the seventy-liter packs were the same size: seventy-liters."

"No, each model also comes in several sizes. I backpack a lot and you'd be surprised at how many hikers I see on the trail with the wrong size pack. Your height and weight don't matter; it's all about the length of your torso."

When she was done sizing me I hunted down Karen, who was upstairs in the women's clothing section doing a mini fashion show in front of a mirror. "You need to talk to the woman in the backpack area. She can fit you for a backpack."

"Aren't they all the same size?" she asked.

I explained to her in an expert tone how each model comes in several sizes and how vital it is to get a pack that's appropriately fitted to her torso. I may have also rolled my eyes at her for not knowing this essential bit of information about backpacking.

The woman went through the same fitting routine with Karen. She brought over a pack and showed Karen how to put it on and take it off correctly when it was at full weight. I could tell from Karen's expression that she thought the demonstration was a little too basic.

Then the woman stuffed the pack with thirty pounds of weighted pillows and asked Karen to put it on. Ignoring the technique the woman had shown her, she tried to pick up the pack with one hand. That didn't go so well.

Karen blushed and then asked. "Could you please show me again?"

She smiled and demonstrated again. "You put the pack next to your leg, bend that leg so your thigh makes a nice, flat shelf, then grab the pack here and here, and slide it up your leg so it rests on your thigh. From there you slip one arm into the strap and stand up. Then you can place your other arm through the other strap."

Karen awkwardly hoisted the pack onto her back without either of us helping her. "Whew, that's a little harder than it looks," she said. "This is heavy."

"Now take a hike through the store and see how it feels," the woman said.

Karen marched off, and I watched her climb the stairs to the second floor and then disappear. Five minutes later I had to look for her again. I found her in front of a mirror in the women's clothing section looking at the pack on her back from every angle.

"You're supposed to be walking around to see how well the pack fits. It's not a fashion show," I said.

"It's always a fashion show, sweetie," was all she said.

Thanks to the REI employee, we got the correct packs, but every time we practice packed at home, our backpacks seemed way too heavy, even for a relatively flat hike like Shi Shi. Our bear vaults were partially to blame for the weight problem. The park service requires overnight backpackers to carry all food, and anything with a scent, in a bear-proof container. Unlike the mountainous regions of the park where bears can be a problem, they aren't the main concern on Shi Shi; it's raccoons and rodents.

I had a squatty, seven-liter bear vault, but it wouldn't hold all of our food for three days. We got a second one for Karen's pack and it was still a challenge getting our food into the two of them. Last night, Karen and I dumped all of our freeze-dried pouches on our living room floor so we could plan our meals for the trip.

"What would you like for dinner the first night: pepper beef or black bean chili?" Karen asked.

"Pepper beef," I quickly replied.

"Are you sure you don't want the chili? 'Cause, that sounds pretty good to me."

"I'm sure. I have a rule to never eat anything that looks like bear scat."

Karen rolled her eyes, tossed the pepper beef into my bear vault, and whispered under her breath, "I'm going into the wilderness with a five-year-old."

"You're what?" I asked.

"Nothing," she said. "What about breakfast the next day? Granola with blueberries or biscuits and gravy?"

"Is that a real question?" I asked.

She put the granola in her bear vault and hid the biscuits and gravy under a chair behind her.

We put enough meals and snacks for the three-day trip in our food pile, and then divvied them between the two of us. Karen packed her bear vault and I did the same. The meals barely fit, but there was still a lot of dead space between the pouches. I found that I could slip snack-size Snickers into those remaining air pockets. I was amazed at how many fit; they kept disappearing between the folds of Mylar.

"That's just going to make your pack heavier," Karen said.

"Snickers don't weigh anything," I replied.

"They do once you eat them," she said.

She glanced at some of the other new things I had in my pile on the floor. "Why did you buy two small garden spades?" she asked.

"Those aren't for gardening. They're for digging cat holes," I replied.

"We don't have a cat."

"No, but you may have to poop in the wilderness, and you'll need one of these to bury it."

"They're poop scoops?"

"No, they're sanitary trowels. You dig a hole, do your business in the hole, and then cover it with dirt. You don't scoop the poop; it should never touch the trowel. If it does, then don't bring the trowel back to camp with you."

"Yeah, that's probably never going to happen for me," she said.

"We need to be prepared just in case. By the looks of what you have in your bear vault, I think you should pack a poop scoop. I'm not sharing mine."

I left Karen sitting on the living room floor staring at her bear vault. I'm not sure if the sanitary trowel discussion made an impression on her or not, but I noticed that the black bean chili ended up in the "stay" pile on the floor when she was finished packing her backpack.

On Monday we're off to Shi Shi; John and Lolly are coming with us. If you haven't heard from us by Friday, please call the permit desk at the ranger station in Port Angeles. The ranger there will be expecting your call.

Your friend,
Matt

~.~.~.~.~.~.~.~

From: **Matt Smith**
Subject: **Shi Shi Beach**
Date: **July 13 (Thursday)**

Dear Bob and Sue,

We made it to Shi Shi, and more importantly, we made it back. For two people whose idea of roughing it is sharing a queen-sized bed, we did well.

When we left our house early Monday morning, the heavy traffic almost prevented us from catching the 8:50 am Edmonds/Kingston ferry. Shi Shi seems like a long way from our house, but it isn't. We were strapping on backpacks and hiking down the trail by 2:00 pm. That's not bad; six hours from leaving our driveway we started our hike on the far western edge of the United States.

Getting to the trailhead involves driving to the small town of Neah Bay on the Makah Indian Reservation. In Neah Bay, we stopped at Washburn's General Store and bought a Makah Recreation Use Permit. The permit cost ten dollars and is valid for the entire calendar year. The reason for the permit: Shi Shi Beach is in Olympic National Park, but the trailhead is on the Makah Reservation.

We also needed a National Park Service permit to camp on the beach. The week before, when we were in the park as part of our premier camping adventure, we went to the visitor center on a Sunday—bad idea—to get the permit. The ranger told us we could have gotten it online, but since we were there, he'd do us a favor and process it for us.

Karen asked, "Is there a limit to how many permits you give out for Shi Shi for any specific date?"

"No. What limits the number of campers on the beach is the number of bear vaults we have to lend. Do you have a bear vault?"

"Yes, we have our own," Karen replied.

"Then, you're good. Right now, all seven hundred of our bear vaults are out in the park. Those people over there are hoping one is returned this morning, so they can go backpacking."

"Seven hundred? You have *seven hundred* bear vaults and they're all out in the park right now?" I asked.

"Yep, this being a holiday week, a lot of people are in the backcountry. We require a bear vault when camping in all backcountry areas, not just Shi Shi."

The ranger found the forms we needed to complete for the backcountry permit and asked us a few questions. Then he paused, stammered a bit, and said, "There's no polite way to ask this next question, so I'll just come right out and ask…" (I thought he was going to quiz us to see if we knew the proper way to poop in the wilderness.) "… are either of you close to the age of sixty-two?" We both looked at each other as if to say, "He's talking to you, not me." I paused long enough to let Karen answer, but she wouldn't. It was evident that the ranger was uncomfortable. I kind of enjoyed watching him squirm.

"No, she's not sixty-two yet," I said. Karen punched my arm.

"I just thought I would ask because the National Parks Federal Recreational Lands Senior Pass now sells for ten dollars, but the price is going up soon, and—"

I cut him off in mid-sentence, and said. "She's not sixty-two yet." Karen's second punch was much harder than her first.

For the next few minutes he scribbled on the form and didn't ask us any more questions. I think he was making up answers so he could get us out of there quickly. I figured I would break the tension by changing the subject. "Where do we poop when we're on the beach?" I asked.

"Good question." He was clearly more comfortable with this topic. "There are a few pit toilets in the trees just off the beach. They're a little hard to find, but they're there. You need to be careful where you step when you're in the trees. People aren't supposed to, but sometimes they just *go* wherever, especially when it's crowded. After a holiday week like this, it can be pretty horrific down there."

"Let's go back to talking about how old you think we are," I said.

The ranger printed our permit and grabbed a tide table off a stack sitting next to the printer. He put them in a plastic holder that had a twist-tie at the top. "There you go, you're all set. Make sure you attach the permit to one of your packs at all times."

From Neah Bay we drove south a few miles until we saw the sign for Shi Shi. John and I parked our trucks, and I double-checked that the permit was still attached to my pack. Despite the lessons Karen got at REI, she still needed help lifting her pack off her thigh. The rest of us hoisted our packs and we were ready to go.

From the trailhead, the 2.2-mile trail to the beach runs through the forest; most of it is on the Makah Indian Reservation. The path was muddy for about a third of the way. Hikers had blazed a secondary path through the trees above the muddy sections. The trees and bushes on those higher trails crowded the path and the footing was tricky because of large tree roots. After picking my way through a couple of the detour trails, I found it easier to just walk through the mud.

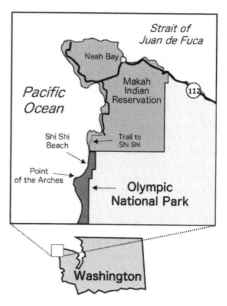

Near the end of the treed part of the trail, a steep section drops two hundred feet to the beach. The park service installed ropes to help hikers descend. We wouldn't have made it down the hill without those ropes, at least not wearing our packs.

I was top heavy; every time I leaned too far downhill it felt like an invisible hand was trying to tip me over. After a few close calls where I almost lost my balance, I began getting the hang of going down the hill with all that weight on my back. The steep part of the trail spooked Karen, so after a few scary moments she sat down and slid the rest of the way on her butt.

Once we were out of the trees, we caught our first glimpse of the crescent-shaped beach. Stretching more than two miles to the south, it was a beautiful sight with the sun reflecting off the smooth sand still wet from the waves. For a moment I thought Karen might cry. I'm not sure if it was the scenery or her sore butt that was making her teary.

The tide was in, but there was still a wide stretch of sand to hike on. It's a magnificent beach for walking, even at high tide, except when you're wearing a backpack with what feels like four bowling balls in it. I don't mean the pink five-pounders that kids use; I'm talking about the big pro model balls.

Our backcountry permit allowed us to camp anywhere on the beach, but John and Lolly had camped on Shi Shi before and they wanted to find the same campsite, which was at the south end of the beach. The additional hike to the far side was a trudge in the soft sand. And it seemed to take forever; we could see our destination the entire time we hiked, but it never felt like we were getting closer. We kept walking by perfectly good campsites, but John never so much as glanced at them or slowed his pace.

Halfway down the beach, we stopped and took off our packs. We'd reached the most reliable water source on the beach: Petroleum Creek. I don't know why it's named Petroleum Creek, and since I drank out of it for a couple of days I don't want to know.

The relief of taking off my pack was indescribable. My first few steps felt like I was floating above the sand. For a brief moment I thought this was our campsite. The jumble of large driftwood logs looked like a perfectly good spot to make camp. But after a couple of minutes, John picked up his pack and continued walking south, and I reluctantly followed.

We hiked until we reached the end of the beach: the Point of the Arches, which consists of several large rocks extending into the ocean about half a mile from the mainland. When I say *rocks*, I mean small islands the size of twenty-story buildings. They made beautiful subjects to photograph at sunset.

Once we'd gone as far south as we could, we started backtracking; John was looking in the trees for his old campsite. A few hundred yards back from the arches, he found it. Just in the trees, and a few feet beyond the natural barricade of sun-bleached logs, was a perfect site: out of the sun, but right on the beach and close to one of the pit toilets—but not too close. There was even a stream of water about a hundred feet south of the site.

View from John and Lolly's campsite on Shi Shi Beach, Olympic National Park

We spent the next couple of hours nesting and making our temporary home in the trees. I chose the perfect spot for our tent and laid out the footprint. John, instead of looking at the ground for a place to put their tent, was looking up at the trees. He'd walk around each one and look at it from several angles. "Are you planning to sleep up there, John?" I asked.

"I'm looking for widow-makers," he replied.

"Spiders?"

"No, branches that might fall on our tent while we're sleeping. If the wind comes up I don't want to be under a dead branch that could skewer me in the middle of the night. You should check the trees by your tent before you set it up."

Looking straight up from our tent site, I scanned the branches. "I think we're fine over here," I said to John. "There's one branch up there, though, that looks a little sketchy. Might be a widow-maker."

"Maybe. If you slide your tent over a couple of feet though, it'll be a widower-maker," he said.

Five minutes after our tent was up and we had our gear laid out where we wanted it, I saw Karen surveying our campsite with hands on hips. I knew what was coming, but I acted like everything was fine and avoided eye contact with her. Then she turned to me and said, "You know, I'd pictured us sleeping on the beach."

"You can still picture us sleeping on the beach. Just close your eyes and picture it."

"I think we should move the tent down to the sand. We can camp in the trees any time; we never get to camp on a beach."

It was a hassle moving everything, but deep down I agreed with her. There are advantages to camping under the trees: it's less windy and you track less sand into your tent. But camping on the beach made for a much softer surface to sleep on.

The park allows campers to collect driftwood for making campfires. Since we were there the week after Fourth of July, the driftwood pickings were slim, but we managed to find enough to burn for our entire stay. It was late afternoon when I had our fire going to the point where I didn't have to poke it every ten seconds to keep it alive. Karen and I sat in our camp chairs watching the tide go out. Other campers would walk by, usually looking for the pit-toilet, but we were surprised at how few people were on the beach. We felt we had the place mostly to ourselves.

Shi Shi is deceptively large. From our campsite, we could easily see to the north end, which looked like a ten-minute walk away, but in reality takes about an hour. A lot of folks can be camping on the beach without it feeling crowded. Earlier in the day, when we were getting ready to start our hike, we spoke with a woman who was just coming off the trail. A ranger told her that three hundred people had camped on Shi Shi the day before. She said she was surprised because it didn't feel like there were that many people there. This is why we try to avoid popular places on weekends, especially in the summer.

Low tide at Shi Shi Beach, Olympic National Park

At about 8:00 pm the tide was near its lowest point. The four of us were able to walk far out amongst the arches and explore the tide pools left by the receding water. Vegetation that looked like phosphorescent seaweed grew at the base of the rocks. It was a stunning sight in the fading sunlight. The starfish were also amazing; some were orange and others were purple. They clung to the rocks in groups of two to five.

Before this trip, we'd heard people say that the tide pooling at Shi Shi was the best they'd ever seen. For us, it was one of the unexpected highlights of the trip.

It was hard not to fall asleep before dark. At 10:00 pm it was still light enough that we could see the ocean from our tent, but we were fading fast. We'd said goodnight to John and Lolly, had our tent zipped tight, and were snuggled in our sleeping bags. That's when I heard small feet skitter across the blue tarp I'd placed in front of our tent. Two seconds later a five-inch-long silhouette appeared less than a foot away from my face. A small critter was on the outside of our tent looking in. I smacked the fabric with the back of my hand, and he instantly disappeared.

The noise woke Karen. She turned halfway toward me and asked in a sleepy voice, "What was that?"

I whispered, "Squirrel."

"Mmm…" was her only response. She must not have heard what I said because she was asleep again in ten seconds. Had she known an energetic rodent was sniffing the outside of our tent, looking for a way to get in, she wouldn't have just rolled over and gone back to sleep. For the sake of full disclosure, it was a chipmunk, not a squirrel. I consider them to be the same; a chipmunk is just a squirrel with more stylish fur.

We slept well that first night listening to the sound of the waves on the beach. If the critters kept trying to get into our tent, we weren't aware of it. At 5:30 am I unzipped the tent and saw two large birds standing on the beach about thirty yards away. Once I put my contacts in I could see they were bald eagles. I'm pretty sure they had a nest in the trees that were growing on the small islands jutting into the ocean just south of our campsite.

It was a little chilly outside the tent that morning, although the temperature was warmer than I'd expected. I started a fire regardless because you always need to have one in the morning when you're camping. I made coffee with my Jetboil; the smell persuaded Karen to get up and join me. She was sitting by the fire looking through her daypack, when she said, "Oh, look at that. I left an opened package of beef jerky in my pack last night."

"Where was your pack?" I asked.

"It was outside on my side of the tent, under the rain flap."

"You're lucky we didn't have a visitor in the middle of the night digging through your pack."

"And smoked salmon! I left smoked salmon in there too."

The ranger who issued our backcountry permit told us the raccoons can be very aggressive on Shi Shi. "The raccoons must be full after snatching food from the Fourth of July crowd," I said. "Can you imagine waking up in the middle of the night and seeing a raccoon six inches away from your face, gnawing on a piece of beef jerky?"

Karen did a shimmy shiver and said definitively, "I. Would. Die. I would simply die right then and there. I hate raccoons almost as much as squirrels."

John had his mind made up that our activity for the day would be a hike along the coast to the mouth of the Ozette River—seven miles south of Shi Shi. He and Lolly had done this hike six years prior, however his memory of how they'd done it had some gaps. That didn't stop us from going in that direction after breakfast.

We rounded the Point of the Arches right at low tide and found ourselves on a narrow gravel beach that soon transitioned to jagged rock. For the first mile and a half south of where we'd camped, the Pacific Coast is a series of small, crescent-shaped coves with rocky points extending into the sea at each end. These are wilderness beaches; there's no way to access them except by foot.

We had to walk carefully over slippery rocks for about a quarter mile to get to the next point. As I was concentrating on where to place my next step, I heard a hissing sound. Without knowing it, we'd scared a raccoon, and he was now about fifty feet up the side of a cliff above us. He looked stuck and afraid, and it was evident that he didn't want us on his beach. The fur on his back was thinner than on the rest of his body; the poor guy didn't look well.

"There's your buddy," I said to Karen. "He's hoping you'll give him a second chance tonight at the beef jerky and smoked salmon." Karen shivered again but kept making her way through the rocks.

"He's staring right at us. Don't make eye contact," she said. "If he thinks we're trapped on this beach, he might climb down here and try to pick us clean."

We made it to the far point and could see around it enough to tell that the next beach would be even harder to walk across than the one we'd just traversed. John kept looking at the cliffs. He said, "I think I remember climbing a rope right about here."

Lolly said, "Yeah, we went up a rope, but I think it was north of here."

"No, it was here, or maybe on the next beach," he replied.

At high tide, several stretches between Shi Shi Beach and the mouth of the Ozette River aren't passable. The hike requires that you climb up a hundred feet or so to the top of the cliff at the back of the beach, hike through the trees, and then climb back down to the beach. At these climb-out spots, ropes are usually affixed to help hikers up and down the cliffs.

I said, "I don't want to be the downer of the group, but we just barely made it around that last point at low tide. The tide won't be that low again for another, I don't know, twenty-four hours. Were we planning on doing a twenty-four-hour hike? Because, if that's the case, I didn't pack enough salty snacks."

"We'll be fine," John said. "As long as we catch the afternoon low tide, we'll make it back. We might have to wade around that point though."

I pulled the tide table out of my permit pouch and looked at the tide forecast. "I don't think the afternoon low tide will be out far enough for us to wade around that corner, John.

It'll be tomorrow morning before we could get past that point again."

I then remembered that I had a Green Trails map of the area in my daypack. "John, maybe we should look at the map," I said.

"Ok. You look at the map; I'll look for the rope." He was still searching the cliffs.

While I got out the map and found where we were, John switched his attention back to the beach. "Maybe we can go all the way along the beach," he said. "Let's round this point and see what's over there."

I said to John, "Well, my map has the words 'Danger Never Round' on the spot where we're now standing. The words are printed in red if that helps."

"What does it say about the next point?"

"It has the words 'Danger Never Round' at the next point also. However, and I think this means something, the word 'Danger' is in bold."

We walked back along the beach as John continued to look for the rope.

"Again, I don't want to be a wet blanket, but I think it's important to point out that the tide is coming in." This didn't elicit a response from any of my fellow hikers. "Maybe I should be clearer. If we can't go farther south from here, and we don't find the rope to climb up the cliff, AND the incoming tide blocks us from going back north—all of which are starting to feel like real possibilities—then we'll be stuck on this slippery, rocky beach for at least the next twelve hours with that mangy, pissed off raccoon. I'm just saying." There was still no response from the group.

I turned to Karen and asked, "Can you hear my voice? Am I speaking out loud or just imagining that I am?"

"Shhhh. John's trying to find the rope."

I glanced at the raccoon who was still on the side of the cliff. He was looking at Karen like a pickpocket looks at a tourist in a train station. I thought to myself, *She's all yours, big guy. She shushed me.*

After a long pause, John said, "Maybe we should go back before the tide traps us on this beach."

"There's a good idea," I said.

We made it back around the Point of the Arches before the water was too deep and returned to our campsite to make a new plan for the day. We decided to explore the other end of Shi Shi, north of where we'd come onto the beach the day before.

More people were camped on the north end, probably because they'd stopped at the first viable spot. Several of the groups had children with them. While we were tide-pooling we heard voices yelling in excitement. Hiking in that direction, we saw whales surfacing a few hundred yards offshore.

It was hard to tell what kind of whales they were; we didn't have binoculars with us. A spout would shoot up and linger in the air and then nothing for a minute or two. The small children squealed every time a whale would appear.

A couple of times, a big one—they're all big, but big for a whale—would poke its head out of the water for a long time, like for two or three minutes. The name for this is "spy hopping." That made me think they were Orcas, but I can't be sure.

Lunch was past due and we were at least a couple of miles from our tents, so we began hiking back in earnest. When we reached Petroleum Creek, Lolly pulled two ten-liter, collapsible water buckets out of her pack. She and I each filled a bucket with water from the creek to filter back at our campsite. John carried one and I took the other. My bucket didn't seem heavy at first, but a mile later I was happy to set it down for good.

"John," I asked. "Why did we carry water for a mile when there's a creek right by our campsite?"

"I didn't like the looks of the dead bird lying next to it."

Good lesson: Always look for dead animals close to your water source.

I set my water bucket down on a long wooden bench next to the bucket Lolly had filled. Her water looked like she'd scooped it off the bottom of the creek bed.

"Lolly, my water looks clearer than yours. Not that it's a competition; I'm just sayin'."

"There's nothing wrong with my water."

"Something is floating in your bucket. I think it moved."

"That's just moss."

"This moss had a mother. Now I see two of them. Now they're chasing each other. It's like the circle of life in there."

She came over and took a look. "That's moss. Quit poking the bucket and it'll stop moving. Your bucket has a bunch of sand in it. It looks like half the beach is in there."

On the way back to camp, Lolly had been scavenging amongst the driftwood that had accumulated along the tree line. Just after a national holiday, an unfortunate amount of stuff (mostly trash) was left on the beach. She was proud as she showed us her haul. "John you're going to love this," she said as she held up a combination spork/hex wrench/bottle opener. "It's a tool."

"I can see that," he said.

"Matt, this is for you." She presented me with an extra-long hotdog skewer. It wasn't an ordinary hotdog skewer; it had two prongs, not just one.

"It's a poker for your fire," she said.

"Thank you, Lolly." It was like Christmas morning.

"And the big score…" She was opening her backpack and fumbling around. "…wait for it. Ta da!" She held up a bottle of whiskey that was about a third full.

"Whaaat? Lolly, what do you think we're going to do with that?" I asked.

John said, "We're gonna drink it."

"Noooo!" Karen said as she squinted her eyes and shook her head.

"You have no idea what's in that bottle, John," I said.

He took the bottle from Lolly and said, "Looks like whiskey to me."

"Or some other brown liquid," I replied.

"There's nothing wrong with it," he said.

"Oh, there's something wrong with it. I guarantee there's something wrong with it."

"Matt, you need to be a little more trusting of the world. No one would leave a tainted bottle of whiskey on the beach."

"Yes, that's exactly what someone would do." I couldn't believe he was going to drink it. "I thought you brought whiskey with you."

"I did. I'm going to drink this as soon as I run out of the stuff I brought."

"Good, there's still time for me to talk you out of it."

The whiskey was Maker's Mark with the words, "Enjoy Shi Shi - Happy Camping," and "Pröst," written in red ink on the label, followed by someone's Instagram username.

"You see here, Matt. It's a gift. Why would a person mess with the bottle and then write their name on it?" John put his treasure on display next to the fire pit, and then rubbed his hands together giving us the universal sign for, "I can't wait."

The entire trip with John and Lolly was a contrast between old school and new school backpacking. We were new school; most of our gear was less than a couple of months old. John and Lolly had been camping for decades, and they had the vintage equipment to prove it. When looking at their stuff, I got the feeling there's a diorama in a camping museum somewhere with a plaque that reads, "Celebrate the Bicentennial in the great outdoors! 1976." It'd be a mock-up of a mid-70s campsite with all of the latest gear of the era displayed. But the scene would be empty because John and Lolly had called the museum last week and said, "Hey, we need our camping stuff back. We're going to Shi Shi with friends. We'll return it when we're done."

The contrast was most apparent at mealtime. We'd agreed the week before that it would be best if each couple was responsible for their own meals. I'm not sure if we decided this because it would genuinely be easier, or John and Lolly got whiff of the fact that all of our meals would require re-hydration.

Our dinner lasted about fifteen minutes each night. That included preparing, eating and cleaning up afterward. I'm pretty sure it took John fifteen minutes to open their canned meat with his Leatherman tool.

After Karen and I finished each meal, I would watch John and Lolly make theirs. John sat in front of his small gas stove while Lolly scurried about opening and chopping and draining and mixing. It looked like a lot of work. Their stove was a metal device attached to a small gas canister with prongs sticking up that allowed a pan or skillet to sit on top.

The first night they stir-fried vegetables, set them aside and then boiled ramen noodles. They added the veggies to the noodles along with a can of cooked beef.

"How are you going to wash all of your pots and pans?" I asked John.

"We're going to boil water and scrub them."

"That seems like a lot of work. You should try these freeze-dried meals. All I have to do to clean up is fold the used pouch, stuff it in a Ziploc bag, and put it in my bear vault."

"I need real food, thank you. I don't mind doing the dishes afterward," he replied.

Don't get me wrong; I'm not poking fun at them or their gear. The new way and the old way of camping each have their advantages and disadvantages. At the end of the trip, we were eyeing each other's gear, both thinking, *It'd kinda be nice to have one of those.* They certainly ate better than we did. Their meals were elaborate compared to our Mountain House: Chicken Fill In the Blank (21grams of protein). And we were fortunate that each night they cooked way more than they could eat. When Lolly cooks for two, I get a second dinner.

Karen was continually admonishing me, "Stop that! Stop eating their food! I'm sorry, Lolly." She said this in the tone you'd apologize for your dog humping a stranger's leg.

"She offered it to me," I snapped back.

"I did. It's fine," Lolly said.

"That's because you stood over them while they were eating, waiting to see if there would be leftovers."

Karen was probably right. I may have hovered. But she wasn't innocent. The next morning while I was making our second cups of coffee down on the beach, I saw her in the trees by their tent with a freshly made breakfast burrito hanging out of her mouth. When she noticed that I was looking her way, she quickly ducked behind a tree.

After John cleaned their pots and pans, we all settled around the campfire. The double wiener was an upgrade from the crooked, skinny branch I'd been using as a fire poker the night before. I could sit farther away and still tend the fire properly. John had found a well-worn piece of plywood with rounded edges on the beach earlier. He placed the board on a stump next to the fire. It made a perfect table for all of our evening accessories: headlamp, bug spray, and booze we found on the beach. This was luxurious camping.

Lolly and Karen were drinking red wine that they'd poured into Mylar pouches and packed in. John and I were each sipping whiskey. I'd brought a small flask with me, as did John. He was drinking slowly, but I could see that he was itching to start on the Maker's Mark. Reaching for the bottle, he studied the label, and then took the top off. He finished the last sip of whiskey in his coffee cup and started pouring in the Maker's Mark.

"Oh, come on, drink it right out of the bottle. That's what a real pirate would do," I said to him.

John ignored my attempt to shame him. "Where's your cup? Aren't you joining me?" he asked.

"No, I'll just watch. Someone has to keep their wits about them so they can flag down the life-flight helicopter."

John sniffed the whiskey in his cup and acted as if he was savoring a rare Scotch. Then he took a sip. Until that moment I thought he was joking about drinking it.

"Tastes like Maker's Mark to me," he announced. "I told you there was nothing wrong with it, Matt. The guys who left this were probably camping just over there a couple of nights ago."

I felt a little foolish for being so mistrusting—just a little. "John, I stand corrected. I think we should send Lolly back out to find more stuff. Maybe there's a half-eaten carton of cottage cheese in the weeds that we could have for breakfast. And hot dogs. Now that I have the double wiener, I need some hot dogs."

Karen was not joining the conversation. She was preoccupied with a splinter in the palm of her hand. Earlier in the day she'd been scavenging as well, but all she brought back with her was a long sliver of wood under the skin of her palm. "Does anyone have tweezers?" she asked. "I can't get a good hold on this splinter to pull it out."

"Let's have a look at that," John replied. Karen held out her hand.

"That's huge!" John said. "Let me get my Leatherman. I'll have that out in no time." John wobbled a bit trying to find his sea legs when he stood up.

Karen had a good reason for not mentioning her splinter earlier; she didn't want help getting it out. More specifically, she didn't want *our* help. "No. No. I can take care of it. I just need tweezers."

"You need a knife," I said. "I've got a knife, a really sharp one."

John and I were now in a race to see who could operate on Karen's hand first.

"Lolly, you need to keep them away from me!" Karen said. "They've been drinking."

John came back with his multi-purpose tool. He held it close to the light of the campfire so he could see to open the pliers. After a few failed attempts he said, "There we go. Now, let's see that splinter."

"I have to cut the skin first, John, then you can pull it out," I said.

"You guys aren't coming near me with those knives. You've had too much whiskey."

"We haven't had too much whiskey," I said. "Well, maybe John has. I've had just the right amount. Maybe you should drink some whiskey before we operate. That's what they did in the olden days. Or maybe we should pour the whiskey on the splinter. The alcohol will sterilize it."

"I'm not wasting my good whiskey on Karen's hand," John said. "She'll be fine. Now, where's that splinter?"

"Nope. I got it. It's out now," Karen said.

"I don't believe you. John, check it out. She won't let me near her."

"I can still see some in there," John said. "You have to get it all out or it will fester. We can't have a member of our group with a festering wound. We're in the wilderness for God's sake."

Lolly, who'd disappeared into the trees a couple of minutes earlier, returned and handed Karen a pair of tweezers.

"Thanks, Lolly," Karen replied. "I can get it out now. You guys can go back to drinking." Karen had been picking at that splinter for hours, but five minutes later it was out. All she needed was a little motivation and a pair of tweezers.

It was time to call it a night. I insisted that we check the area around our camp to make sure all food and trash went into our bear vaults before we went to bed. I didn't want to wake up to the sight of that half-crazed raccoon unzipping our tent. Unfortunately, my bear vault was defective. "Karen, it's broken," I said.

"What's broken?"

"The bear thing. It won't open."

"It's not broken. You're drunk."

"Nope. It's broke. It won't open."

Karen got my bear vault open without any trouble. "How'd you fix it?" I asked.

"You better not snore tonight or you'll be sleeping on the beach with the hairless raccoon," was her reply.

By morning, my bear vault had healed itself, which was good because I felt I needed to at least act like I was making breakfast while waiting for John and Lolly's leftovers. By the way, we realized after we'd had a couple of meals that we brought way too much food.

We had a leisurely morning in camp. Having gotten up at 5:30 am, it was still early when John was finished scrubbing his breakfast pans and stowing them. Since the Ozette River hike was a bust, and we'd planned that to be our activity for one of our days at Shi Shi, we decided to pack it in a day early and try camping inland, closer to the Lake Crescent area of the park. The weather during the previous two days was about as good as it could have been, but it looked like rain might be moving in.

I was hopeful that when I put on my pack for the hike out it would be much lighter than it was on the hike in. I wasn't sure how this would happen. Magic? Maybe. It wasn't lighter, but it did feel a bit more comfortable than before.

John and Lolly came out of the trees with their large, external frame packs already strapped on. They had to carefully balance as they walked across several large driftwood logs piled in front of their campsite. I repeated to myself silently, *please don't fall, please don't fall,* until they made it safely to the beach.

"Alright, are you guys ready to do this again?" John asked.

"Ready!" we said.

It was cloudy when we started our hike north along the beach. I took several good photos of Karen, Lolly, and John wearing their full packs, with the ocean in the background. Walking behind the group, I got a better look at their packs. They were huge. From my vantage point the two of them looked like dark blue refrigerators with legs. I wondered if you could even buy a new external frame pack anymore. When I got home I looked up the answer to that question and learned that a few manufacturers still make them. External frame packs are better for carrying extra heavy loads. I hope I never have to carry so much weight that I need one.

Karen, John, and Lolly hiking out of Shi Shi Beach

"John, do you worry about being struck by lightning when you wear that pack?" I asked.

"Why, because of the metal frame?"

"That, and you're like eight feet tall with that thing on. I bet it makes its own weather up there."

"Well, it's hard to go through the trees wearing this pack," he admitted.

"You need to get one of these," I patted the side of my pack; it had an internal frame and hugged my body. Handy side pockets sat about elbow height. My safety whistle dangled from one of my shoulder straps. John didn't seem amused by my ribbing. "I'll just stick with what I have, thank you," he said.

Back at the trucks, we again felt the sweet relief of taking off our packs. It had only been a couple of nights, but it felt like we'd been away from civilization for weeks. While the others changed out of their hiking boots, I flipped through the photos on my phone. I found the best one of Karen hiking along the beach that morning with her bulging backpack. I showed it to her and said, "We're officially backpackers now." Her face lit up.

Our first try at backpacking was a success, which is good, because while we were sitting around the fire drinking, the four of us decided to do a thirty-mile, three-night backpacking trek in the North Cascades next month. It seemed like a good idea at the time, but the whiskey may have made us a little over-confident. We'll let you know how that goes.

Your friend,
Matt

~.~.~.~.~.~.~

From: **Matt Smith**
Subject: **Newberry National Volcanic Monument**
Date: **July 20 (Thursday)**

Dear Bob and Sue,

Mimi and Papa climbed a volcano the size of Rhode Island today. I don't know why people compare the size of things to Rhode Island. Since I learned this fact on the Deschutes National Forest website I thought I'd share it with you. The Newberry Volcano is part of Newberry National Volcanic Monument, which was given its monument designation in 1990. The monument is entirely within the boundaries of the Deschutes National Forest.

We're here in central Oregon for a week, staying at Sunriver with Rachel (our daughter) and Justin (our son-in-law), and two grandbabies. Newberry is about an hour drive from Sunriver, so yesterday and today Karen and I drove to the monument for a break during the middle of the day to get some exercise and see the area. We'd never been to Newberry before. Karen called it a "pleasant surprise." I asked her if that was higher or lower on her scale than "hidden gem." She said she needed to think about that.

The monument has several attractions: Paulina Lake and its twin sister, East Lake, both have rustic resorts and campgrounds along their shores. They flank the east and west sides of Newberry Volcano, which isn't a volcano but looks like one. It's a collapsed cinder cone. Yesterday, we hiked several miles along the shore of Paulina Lake. Few people were on the trail, and the lake and surrounding forest were stunning against the clear blue sky.

Before our walk along the lake, we did a short, one-mile hike onto the Big Obsidian Flow. The trail took us through the most recent lava flow in Oregon; it's a youthful 1,300 years old. The flow consists of pumice and obsidian, the latter being a hard, black, glass-like rock. You wouldn't want to trip and fall on that trail, many of the rock edges were as sharp as broken glass.

The lava flow hike was interesting, but there wasn't much variety in the scenery. Halfway along the trail, Karen said to me, "Pumice and Obsidian would be good names for dogs. If we had a couple of Jack Russell Terriers, that's what I'd name them. We could call Obsidian 'O.B.' for short." When Karen starts naming our future, imaginary dogs, it's a sign that she's checked out. We headed toward the truck after that.

The hike we did today was the Paulina Peak Trail. The top of the trail is the highest point in the monument at 8,000 feet. For most of the hike, the trail we were on also doubled as the Crater Rim Trail, which is a twenty-mile trek that circumnavigates both lakes, Newberry Volcano, Paulina Peak, and the Big Obsidian Flow. I'd love to come back again and do that entire loop. Today though, we didn't have enough time. The five-mile out and back hike to the peak was a good workout; the elevation gain on the way up was about 1,500 feet.

We were wiped out when we got to the top of the trail and emerged from the forest, surprised to find a parking lot full of sightseers. As we stood next to them taking in the magnificent view, many of them gave us strange looks that seemed to say, *Why are you sweating and out of breath? The parking lot is right there.*

When we got back to our rental house, Hadley (our oldest granddaughter) greeted us at the door. "Mimi! Papa! Where have you been?" She must not have understood that we were leaving for the afternoon. Rachel told us, "The whole time you were gone she tried to find you. She got on her tricycle and started riding down the street. When I asked her where she was going she said, 'To find Mimi and Papa.'"

That made Karen weep. "We're never leaving you again, sweetie," she said.

So much for hiking again tomorrow; I guess I'll be hanging out at the kiddie pee-pool at the family fun center instead. We'll have to go back to the monument another time when we're not with the family. I'd especially like to visit when there's snow on the ground. The ranger at the entrance kiosk told us that they don't snowplow the main road so it's a great place to snowshoe. And the Paulina Lake Lodge stays open in the winter, picking up their guests with a snowcat. That would be cool, to stay in a cabin back by the lake with snow piled high everywhere. We could snowshoe during the day and build big log fires at night. Maybe you could come out west and join us some year.

Your friend,
Matt

From: **Matt Smith**
Subject: **Preparing for North Cascades**
Date: **August 2 (Wednesday)**

Dear Bob and Sue,

Since we survived our inaugural backpacking trip, we decided to follow through on our whiskey-induced plan to backpack for a few days in North Cascades National Park. Years ago, when we were on our quest to visit every national park, we shortchanged our visit to the North Cascades. If you remember, since there are no roads in the park, we hiked several miles on a heavily treed trail just far enough to cross the park boundary so we could say we made it into the park. That was lame. We've since learned about other incredible hikes we could have done to experience the park, although many of them are too long to do in a day. We thought now, early August, would be a perfect time for a proper, alpine North Cascades experience.

Fortunately, John and Lolly were still speaking to us after Shi Shi and up for another adventure, so we planned the details of the trip together. The route was straightforward: drive to the Cascade Pass trailhead, hike up to Sahale Glacier, camp there for one night, then hike east for a couple of days to Stehekin, camping along the way, and then ride the Lady of the Lake ferry from Stehekin to Chelan. We would leave a truck at the ferry terminal in Chelan so we could drive home from there, then the following day we'd go back and pick up the other truck from the trailhead.

Stehekin is the small town we visited years ago when we went to all of the national parks. It sits on the shore of Lake Chelan, and the only way to get there is by ferry, floatplane, horseback, or foot. Near the ferry dock is a lodge with a restaurant and convenience store, a campground, and a visitor center. The land surrounding the town is part of Lake Chelan National Recreation Area, which is an NPS unit.

For backpacking trips in these areas, a permit is required for each campsite. The NPS established an online reservation system for backcountry campsites in the park, which allows visitors to reserve 60 percent of them in advance. The remaining spots are available for walk-ins; you can make a walk-in reservation twenty-four hours in advance at a ranger station. Early this morning, we drove to the North Cascades National Park Wilderness Information Center in Marblemount to get our permits.

From home, the drive to the info center took about two hours. The sky was brilliant blue when we left our house, but halfway to Marblemount a haze appeared. I thought it was morning fog, but it kept getting thicker as we drove east, which seemed unusual; the marine layer coming off the Pacific Ocean typically gets thinner the farther east you go.

John and Lolly drove separately from us. Karen texted Lolly, "Foggy this morning!"

Lolly responded, "I think it's smoke."

"Fires in North Cascades?"

"BC," Lolly texted back.

Up to this point, we'd been oblivious to the forest fires raging in southern British Columbia. By the time we got to Marblemount, the smoke was thick enough we could smell it. Nothing, however, was going to stop us from doing the hike we'd planned, except failing to get permits—which is what happened. The campsite at Sahale Glacier was booked for the entire week and there was no combination of sites we could reserve that would allow us to hike up to the glacier, even as a day-hike from another campsite. We were very disappointed until the ranger mentioned that we probably wouldn't have been able to see Sahale Glacier anyway because of the smoke.

He told us, "If you want to hike into Stehekin, other trails will get you there without as steep of an incline as Cascade Pass. There might be permits still available if you hike McAlester Pass."

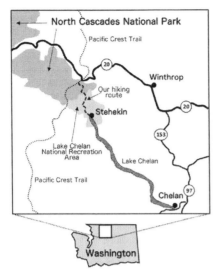

The ranger checked the reservation system and confirmed that we could get the necessary campsites to hike the McAlester Pass route to Stehekin. The new plan was to park at Bridge Creek on Highway 20, hike the first day to McAlester Lake campground, hike the next day to Rainbow Bridge campground, and on the third day hike into Stehekin and camp by the visitor center at Purple Point. The last day we'd take the ferry to Chelan where our truck would be waiting for us. We felt good about saving the trip despite the conditions; in addition to the smoke, an extreme heat warning was in effect. "Even in the mountains, it'll be at least in the nineties during the day, could reach a hundred," the ranger said.

"How are the bugs?" John asked.

"Miserable. They're really bad right now. Some mosquitos but mostly black flies."

"Great. Smoke, extreme heat, and bugs. Let's forget the hiking and go wine tasting instead," Karen said.

"I'm in for the wine tasting!" said Lolly.

I turned toward John and said, "Get the permits before we lose these two."

After our visit to the ranger station, we stopped to have lunch in Winthrop before driving to Lolly's family's cabin where we're spending the night. The sun was orange when we parked the trucks in front of the restaurant. We had just ordered lunch when all of a sudden the electricity went out. Plenty of light was coming in through the front windows, so we weren't concerned until our waitress came back a few minutes later. "Sorry folks, looks like the power isn't likely to come back on anytime soon."

"So we need to order sandwiches instead of burgers?" I asked.

"No, you need to leave. We're closing, for safety reasons." She told us that the outage was widespread throughout the valley due to a fire burning north of town, in the Pasayten Wilderness.

"I just realized," Lolly started. "If the power is off at the cabin the well pump won't work."

"That's OK," I said. "I brought plenty of water for the group. I've got a seven-gallon container that's full. I'll share."

"I'm more concerned about not being able to flush the toilets," she replied.

"We're not using my water for toilet business," I said. "We can go to the bathroom in the sagebrush at the back of your property."

"Rattlesnakes live back there," John said. "You'll have to watch where you squat."

Karen shook her head. "This trip keeps getting better."

We salvaged our stop in town by going to one of the local outdoor gear stores where we bought industrial-strength insect repellent. The woman tending the store was an avid backpacker and she recommended an insect repellent that's made to be sprayed on clothes. "When my husband and I were backpacking last weekend, the flies were thick, but right around us was a bug-free zone. They hovered but didn't land on us." We were sold. Each couple bought a bottle big enough to treat several articles of clothing. The woman had to write our credit card numbers down to process the sales later when the power came back on.

When we got to the cabin this afternoon, we stretched a nylon rope across the front of the woodshed and hung our hiking clothes on it. John sprayed their clothes and I sprayed ours. The instructions said to saturate each item and then let them dry. In the extreme heat, they dried quickly. Afterward,

I said to Karen, "I gave your purple hiking shirt an extra good soaking so the bugs won't bother you."

"The purple shirt is mine," Lolly said.

"I soaked the purple shirt also," said John.

"Then did either of you spray the blue shirt?" Karen asked.

"OK, I'll go spray the blue shirt. There's plenty left in my bottle," I said.

I came back inside the cabin and told Karen, "Not to worry, I sprayed your shirt. I even gave your pants a second coating for good measure."

"Which pants did you spray?" Karen asked.

"The ones next to the blue shirt."

"Those are my pants," said Lolly.

"I'm done with the bug spray," I said. "It's starting to make me dizzy anyhow."

"So, Lolly's pants got sprayed twice by you and once by John and my pants didn't get sprayed at all?" Karen asked.

"I'm lightheaded. I can't be sure," I replied.

"Here you go, Karen." John said handing her his bottle. "Why don't you give your stuff another spray to be sure."

It was getting late in the afternoon and we still had to drop a truck off in Chelan, so we left the clothes hanging on the line and headed out. At the Lady of the Lake ferry terminal it was a relief to learn that tickets were still available for the high-speed ferry from Stehekin to Chelan on the day we wanted. Being the middle of summer we were concerned that it might be sold out; the smoke must have kept the crowds away.

The woman at the ticket desk handed me four tickets. "Who is the most responsible person in the group?" I asked. "Someone needs to be in charge of these and make sure they make it to Stehekin with us four days from now."

Lolly didn't even glance up from her phone and Karen was busy looking at a rack of brochures for the local attractions.

"Hey, let's go to the antique mall on our way out of town," Karen said.

John held out his hand. "I'll be in charge of the tickets. That way I can decide who gets to come home and who we'll leave in Stehekin."

I reluctantly handed him the tickets, but he was a better choice than me. There would be a good chance I'd accidentally use them as fire starter on the trail if they were in my pack. "John being the most responsible person in our group is a *bad* omen," I said.

"Like the smoke, heat, bugs, power outage, and having to pee with rattlesnakes at our ankles weren't bad omens?" Karen asked. She had a point.

Fortunately, by the time we got to the cabin, the power was back on and we enjoyed our last day of civilized comforts. We sat on the back porch and talked while we gazed out over the Methow Valley to the west. A couple of hours before sunset, the sun was fading into the smoke. Before it sank below the horizon it was the color of the brake lights on the back of my truck.

We're still backpacking tomorrow, that is if the womenfolk don't sneak off in the middle of the night to the local spa resort. I think our luck is going to change any minute now.

Your friend,
Matt

From: **Matt Smith**
Subject: **North Cascades Day One**
Date: **August 5 (Saturday)**

Dear Bob and Sue,

We're back a day early, a little smokier and a little wiser than when we left three days ago. It all seems like a strange dream.

Last Thursday morning when we woke up at the cabin, the smoke from the fires was no better than the day before—it might have been worse. I was a little surprised that the wives didn't put up more of a fight about backpacking into the wilderness in the heat and smoke.

With my truck in Chelan, we all had to pile into John's truck for the ride to Bridge Creek, about thirty-five miles west of Winthrop. John and I were loading our gear into the bed of his truck when I asked, "What's this?! John, did you get a new backpack?"

Lying in the bed of his truck was a pristine, internal frame Osprey backpack. "You just want to be like me, don't you?" I asked.

"Not exactly, I thought it was time for a new pack," he replied.

"Did the museum call and ask you to return the one you took to Shi Shi?"

John didn't respond. He went back into the cabin to fetch Lolly's pack. I was expecting to see that she bought a new one also, but a minute later he emerged from the back door with her old external frame pack. It still looked like a blue refrigerator with straps. "I like my pack," Lolly said. "I think it's just fine."

I'd hoped the smoke would thin as we drove west, but it didn't. The trailhead parking lot was only half full. A group of ten or so young women, trail-weary and sitting in the gravel at the edge of the lot, waited for their ride to pick them up. The trail we would start on, across the highway from the parking lot, is part of the Pacific Crest Trail (PCT), so it's common to see hikers coming off who've been hiking it for days, sometimes weeks.

John found a spot to park the truck next to a car that had an Oregon license plate and a "Meat is Murder" sticker on its back window. It took a while for everyone to take care of their last pieces of business and strap on their packs. We were excited to get going but also a bit apprehensive about the strenuous hike ahead of us. From the parking lot, it was about eight miles to our campsite at McAlester Lake.

Scurrying across the highway, we looked like four overgrown kids running away from home. We carried a few days' worth of food and extra underwear on our backs and we were heading out into the trees on an adventure. Fifty yards into the hike—could have been less—we came to a sign announcing that we were on the Pacific Crest Trail. The PCT starts at the border of Mexico in California and runs north to the Canadian border in northern Washington. It's 2,650 miles, 500 of which are in the state of Washington. We were only on it for about three miles, but it's fun to hike sections of the PCT when we get the chance.

The trail marker turned into a photo opportunity. Lolly got a picture of Karen and me by the sign. Karen got a picture of John and Lolly by the sign. I took a selfie of all four of us, so did Lolly, so did Karen. Ten minutes later, satisfied that we'd documented this important moment, we continued hiking. I was in the lead but had to stop fifty yards later when I realized we'd lost Karen. We found her just off the trail taking pictures. We'd been hiking now for about twenty minutes and covered the length of a football field. "We're gonna have to pick it up, folks, if we want to get to our campsite before dark," I said.

"It's not a race," Karen said.

"Correct, we'd have to be moving for it to be a race," I replied.

The group eventually settled into a comfortable pace. According to my map, the trail followed a creek for about three miles, and then made a sharp left at which point we'd start climbing in elevation. We began the hike at 4,400 feet and our campsite by the lake was at 5,500 feet. An 1,100-foot climb isn't too strenuous, but the trail dropped another 700 feet in those first few miles. We then had to hike up 1,800 feet in the last five miles, and much of that was in the final mile and a half. That would be our first serious challenge hiking with heavy packs. The elevation gains at Shi Shi were minimal.

Lolly on the log bridge, North Cascades National Park

Along the first stretch of trail, we crossed over several small creeks. At one of the crossings was a log bridge made out of a single log, hewn flat and about eighteen inches wide.

The log wasn't wet or slick, but it didn't have a handrail and it was just high enough above the creek—about fifteen feet—that we had to pay close attention as we crossed. It's sketchy enough walking across a creek on a balance beam; our heavy packs made it more challenging than usual. We were still getting used to being top-heavy with an extra thirty plus pounds on our backs. I swear I felt that invisible hand again trying to pull me off the log.

I went first and then watched John and Lolly make their way across. Karen went last. Before she took a single step, we heard her shout, "No! Go back! Get away!" Somehow—and none of us know how this happened—a squirrel jumped in line between Lolly and Karen and was now running back and forth across the log. The line jumper squirrel would run toward the three of us who were already across the creek, see us, and then run back the other way—toward Karen. When it got within a few feet of her, it would run toward us again. I was sure that Karen would've fainted or jumped off the log into the creek had that squirrel run between her legs while she was crossing. The little guy finally jumped off the log on our side of the creek and ran off.

Our friends must think I make up these squirrel stories, but honestly, she's a squirrel magnet. On separate occasions in London and New York City, squirrels chased her in the park. It's a mystery why they are so attracted to her.

For about six miles we were in North Cascades National Park, then the trail took us into Lake Chelan National Recreation Area. The path was narrow due to dense vegetation that brushed against our legs. Just as the ranger had said, the bugs, mostly black flies, were thick; they swarmed around my face and arms. I kept shooing them away until I noticed that they were rarely landing on me. The insect repellent we sprayed on our clothes was a life saver. It was annoying having them buzz about, but they weren't biting us. That's about the best you can hope for insect-wise mid-summer in the North Cascades.

Just like on our hike up Guadalupe Peak, the group assigned me the role of lead hiker. Despite their assurances that they wouldn't complain about my pace, ten minutes into the uphill climb to McAlester Lake I heard a flurry of bickering from Lolly and Karen behind me.

"Oh, I know, he won't ever stop for a rest," Karen said.

"Why is he in such a hurry?" Lolly asked.

"I don't know."

"Hey," I hollered. "I can hear you. And you can stop hiking whenever you want. You don't need my permission."

John was reading his GPS. I asked him, "John, am I going too fast?"

He didn't look up. "We still have fifteen hundred feet to climb and about three and a half miles to go before we reach our campsite," he said.

"Thanks for having my back," I replied. Then I reminded the womenfolk that I didn't seek the office of lead hiker and would be happy—no, thrilled—to give up the position.

"Nope," said John. "It's a lifetime appointment."

Karen and Lolly took off their packs, found some salty snacks to eat, and took long drinks of water. I never took my pack off, however, I did lean against a log so that most of the weight was off my shoulders. I knew if I took it off and set it on the ground, I wouldn't want to put it back on. I could see Karen and Lolly were hesitant to get going again. Karen was rubbing her sides just below her waist.

"My muffin tops are sore," she said. "The side straps on my pack are digging into them."

"What are muffin tops?" I asked.

Lolly replied, "They're the areas of fat right above your beltline on the side. Like right here." She pointed to her side.

"Lolly, he knows what muffin tops are, he's just being a dick," Karen said.

"Hey, I like muffins, especially yours, sweetie," I said. All kidding aside, Karen's skin was rubbed raw and bleeding, and we hadn't yet started the difficult part of the hike. We spent the next five minutes offering her advice about how to adjust her pack, but there was no avoiding it; the weight of her pack was resting on her sides the way it was supposed to. She just needed a few backpacking trips to become accustomed to the weight and how it rode on her body.

I was concerned, but at that point it was best to just keep going and deal with it at our campsite. "OK, time to saddle up, partners," I said, and we were off.

For the next hour, I kept the pace slow and steady. Hiking up the switchbacks was a trudge that felt like it would never end. Mercifully, the trail began to level off before any of us reached a state of exhaustion, but it was close. Just before we arrived at McAlester Lake, a wooden post directed us to our campsite. The word "hikers" was carved on one of the four sides of the post with an arrow pointing toward the lake; on the adjacent corner a horseshoe was carved with an arrow pointing to our site. The ranger had given us a permit to camp at the stock campsite because it was the only site available.

We stumbled down the path and found a clearing where we could pitch our tents. It was a nearly flat space with compacted gravel and more than enough room for all of us. The site was set up in a triangle pattern; about twenty yards from the sleeping area was a fire pit and another short distance away was a small clearing in the forest with a long hitching rail in the middle. That's where we were supposed to keep our horses.

Karen studied the horse accommodations, then asked, "Do you think people will show up later with horses and want to share this site with us?"

The site was spacious and we could have easily shared it with another group—and their horses. John had done most of the talking with the ranger when getting the permits. The rest of us had only paid attention to selective snippets of their conversation.

"No," he said, "we have this site to ourselves tonight."

I wasn't as confident as John that we wouldn't be sharing, but I was more focused on getting the tent set up while I still had energy left. We placed our tents about twenty feet away from each other. When you're exhausted, setting up camp seems harder than it should be. John and Lolly had their tent up and Lolly was blowing up her air mattress when she said, "I'm not sure I can blow this up, it's making me lightheaded." I tried to come up with a witty response, and then realized I was having trouble forming sentences. That last section of trail really took it out of us.

I did everything I could to keep the flies and mosquitos out of our tent as I set it up and shoved our sleeping pads and bags inside. Once I had it prepared, I squatted and looked through the thin mesh screen to see if I could spot any insects; two buzzed around inside. I opened the flap and tried to scoop them out, but when I closed the flap again I could see three of the little buggers in there.

As I was crouched down thinking about how to rid our tent of insects, Karen came over and casually unzipped the flap on her side of the tent so she could put her backpack inside. She left the flap open while she looked through it, and a few minutes later wandered off without a word. I went over to her side of the tent and zipped it shut. Now, a half a dozen bugs were in there. I did myself a favor: I gave up and joined the rest of the group at the fire pit.

John was resting on a large, flat rock a few feet from the fire pit. He was looking at his GPS. I sat down across from him and started assembling my Jetboil. He said to me, "Are you ready for our daily stats?"

"Sure," I replied.

"Today we hiked 9.7 miles, our moving time was three hours and forty-eight minutes, we spent forty minutes at rest, and the elevation gain was one thousand eight hundred and fifty feet," he said.

"Great," I replied. I'd stopped messing with my Jetboil and was sitting there looking at him as he read the stats.

"Aren't you going to write these down?" he asked. It was clear that he expected me to keep a record of these invaluable statistics. Plus, he would reset his GPS the next morning and would lose the previous day's data if someone didn't record it somewhere.

"Let me find my pen and notebook." For the rest of the trip I dutifully recorded our daily stats.

Karen, Lolly and John at the McAlester Lake campsite,
Lake Chelan National Recreation Area

Despite the warm temperatures, we all agreed we needed a campfire if for no other reason than to keep the bugs away from our campsite. The ranger at Marblemount told us we could make fires in the fire pits, which surprised us given the dry conditions.

We found a few small logs that were left by the previous campers, but not enough to make a proper fire. Since she was so looking forward to a fire, I enlisted Karen's help in searching for stuff to burn. Dead moss that's fallen off the trees makes an excellent fire starter, so I asked her to help collect some. I picked up a clump off the ground and showed it to her. "See, it looks like this. Go try to find a bunch of this—please."

I held out the moss sample, but she wouldn't touch it. "That looks like a dead rat. Are you sure that's moss? It's not green."

"Yes, I'm positive." I pulled it apart to prove it to her. I must say, the older clumps do look like dead rats.

"OK," she said cautiously. "How can I tell that it's not a dead rat without touching it?"

"If it has teeth, tail, or eyes, you shouldn't pick it up."

Karen went off toward the main trail looking for dead rats. I was sure she'd return empty handed or with a heart-shaped stream stone from McAlester Creek, but she surprised me when she arrived back at the fire pit with an arm full of moss.

"What else do we need?" she asked.

"Uh, you can go find my wife. She was just here a minute ago," I said.

"Very funny. Don't we also need some wood?"

"Yes, we're allowed to gather wood that's dead and down," I told her.

"What does that mean?"

"It means that you can gather a piece of wood if it's dead and lying on the ground."

"I'll go get us some wood," she said and then she was gone again.

John and I also searched for wood and before she got back we'd made a nice little fire thanks to Karen's pile of fire starter. I was poking the fire and tossing more moss on top to keep it going when I saw a tree move in the forest. It was about five feet tall and coming right toward us. Karen was dragging it through the brush and when she reached the fire pit she dropped it at my feet and said, "Here you go."

"That's a Christmas tree, sweetie," I said. "We can't burn that."

"Why not? It was dead and down. I didn't kill it." She sounded defensive.

"I wasn't concerned that you'd killed it. The thing is, usually you want to burn the wood part of a tree; this is all small branches and needles."

"I'm done. I got you the pile of dead rats you asked for and an entire tree to burn. I'm going to find Lolly and drink some wine," she said.

A smoky view of McAlester Lake,
Lake Chelan National Recreation Area

I managed to find enough to burn to keep a reasonable fire going while we hydrated our dinners and played a few hands of gin rummy. Before it got dark we walked through the campground. To our surprise, only two other groups were camping by the lake. Several sites were empty even though the ranger told us the campground was booked to capacity that night.

Since we were a mile above sea level, the temperature mercifully dropped once the sun went down and we were able to get a fair night's sleep. Also a bonus: The bugs Karen had let into our tent didn't bother us. Between the invisible bug spray aura we were giving off and the cold night air, they all seemed to disappear.

That was our first day on the trail. It was a challenge, but we held up well given that we'd hiked a pretty strenuous trail. Compared to day two though, our first day seemed uneventful. I'll send you another email tomorrow about the rest of our trip. Have to go to bed now.

Your friend,
Matt

~.~.~.~.~.~.~.~

From: **Matt Smith**
Subject: **North Cascades Day Two**
Date: **August 6 (Sunday)**

Dear Bob and Sue,

I wake up early each morning. I don't try to, it just happens. Even after the strenuous hike the day before, I was lying in my sleeping bag, eyes wide open at 5:00 am on our second day in North Cascades. The sky was beginning to brighten, yet the sun was still behind the mountains. Staring at the ceiling of our tent entertained me for about four minutes. Then I whispered, "Karen, are you awake?"

She rolled over and sighed, "I am now."

"How did you sleep last night?"

"I didn't. I fell asleep about fifteen minutes ago."

I dozed on and off for the next hour trying not to fidget too much and wake Karen again. Then the sun hit the top of our tent; within a few minutes, half our tent was in direct sunlight. That's when the buzzing began. All of the flying insects that had passed out when the temperature dropped the night before woke up and were looking for breakfast.

"What's that noise?" Karen asked.

"Bugs," I said.

"It sounds like a million little racecars right outside our tent."

"Well, maybe it is. I just assumed it was bugs."

"Why did you wake me up at five o'clock?" she asked.

"I didn't wake you up at five o'clock. I just woke up myself. You must have dreamed it."

"You woke me up just as I'd fallen asleep," she said.

"That does sound like a bad dream. How about some coffee?" I asked as I unzipped my side of the tent.

The four of us slowly went through our morning routines, grunting and groaning every step of the way. Despite moving in slow motion and having a million things to do to break down camp, we were standing on the trail with our packs on our backs at eight thirty.

The trail was flat for about fifty yards, then turned steeply uphill just like the end of the trail the day before.

"I thought we were already at the top of this mountain," I said to John.

"We have five hundred feet more of elevation gain before we reach McAlester Pass," he replied.

That didn't sound like much, especially at the start of the day, yet I was instantly tired as we started up that last hill. I expected to feel fresh for at least a little while, but we were back in death march mode and we'd only been hiking fifteen minutes. Fortunately, we climbed that first rise in the cool of the morning.

As the trail leveled off, we came out of the trees and into a spectacular meadow—*Sound of Music* spectacular. For the first time in several days, the sky turned blue and the sun shone without passing through a thick filter of smoke. The grass and mid-summer flowers were still wet with dew and the trail was flat as a table top. For about a quarter mile we hiked slowly across the green expanse. A couple of times I stopped along the trail for no reason other than to look at the scenery. I never do that. That's how perfect it was that morning.

When we stepped aside to let the von Trapp family pass us, John noticed something on the ground. "Hey, look," he pointed. "That's wolf scat."

"You don't know that a wolf left that," I said.

"That's *wolf scat*," he insisted.

"John, I didn't know you were a wild animal poop expert. How did I not know this before? You'd think it would have come up in conversation..."

"It's wolf, trust me."

A few minutes later, we saw a marmot den ahead of us beside the trail. Two large, adult marmots and a baby marmot were close to the den. It was like a scene from a show on Animal Planet. When they saw us coming, one of the large ones scurried off into the trees. The little one stayed in the middle of the den, and the other large one slunk down on its belly next to the den, getting as low as it could. I wasn't sure if we should stay on the trail and hike past them or make a detour into the meadow and give them some space. I stopped hiking and asked the group, "What should we do?"

"Oh, we can go right up to them. They don't care," John said.

"I don't know. The big one looks like it's protecting the baby. I don't want to spend the next two days with a pissed off mama marmot attached to my neck," I said.

"It'll be fine. You worry too much," he said.

I turned to Lolly. "He's a wild animal poop expert and a marmot expert? Lolly, what else do we not know about John?"

"He's a knucklehead, that's what," she replied.

We made it past the marmot den without being attacked. I hate to say this, but John was right; the marmots seemed unconcerned about how close we passed by them. As the trail started to descend, we went into the trees and hiked the next five miles in the shade. The trail was a steady and relatively steep downhill grade. About noonish, we stopped at the Bench Creek campgrounds for lunch. There was a creek nearby—Bench Creek—where we filtered water and filled all of our bottles.

By the time we reached our lunch spot, we'd hiked six miles that morning. McAlester Pass is at 6,000 feet elevation and Bench Creek is at 3,800. It was a good thing we were hiking down rather than up because everyone in the group was weary.

As John lifted his pack and got ready to continue the hike, he said, "Well, we have a little over three miles until we get to Rainbow Bridge. The good news is, the bridge is at twenty-two hundred feet, so it should be more downhill this afternoon."

"That's good," said Karen. "I don't think I can do much more than that. I'm beat."

"Yeah, me too," said Lolly.

As we left Bench Creek and hiked down the trail, there were two things that we didn't know about the three miles in front of us. First, while it's true that we would descend 1,600 feet by the time we reached our campsite for the evening, the trail wasn't straight down. It went down and back up before it went down again. That meant we were in for a stretch of uphill hiking that kicked our butts. Second, over half of the trail would take us through the 2010 Rainbow Bridge Fire area that was complete burnout, with no shade. We'd be hiking in the direct sunlight.

We struggled mightily on the uphill section in the heat and sun. At least a couple of times we stopped and got out our maps to make sure we were going in the right direction. The burnout really threw us off. Keeping the pace slow but steady, I figured it would be better to keep moving and get to our campground as soon as possible rather than rest in the sun.

At one point along the trail, several large trees were close to the path. They were dead and leafless, but their trunks were close together and provided a few feet of continuous shade. I took off my pack and set it down. John was right behind me and Lolly caught up with us a minute later. The three of us sat in the shade watching Karen hiking toward us. For a moment I didn't think she was going to stop because her eyes were focused on a spot beyond us on the trail.

When she reached us, I asked, "Are you OK?" She didn't answer. Karen was somewhere else.

I helped her off with her pack. "You need to sit down right now."

"I think I'm going to throw up," she replied.

"You have to drink some water. Lolly, can you grab her water bottle?" I asked.

Karen sat there in a daze. We had electrolyte tablets with us so we put one in her water and had her drink it slowly.

"We need to keep an eye on her," John said. "She could be on the verge of heat stroke."

"I'm feeling better now. I just need to sit. We haven't been resting enough this afternoon," Karen said.

"Well, it's the heat and the sun. Who knew we'd be hiking through a burned-out forest? It looks like a war zone," Lolly said.

"I'll be fine, this is embarrassing," Karen kept saying.

I poured a trickle of water from my water bottle over her head and on the back of her neck to cool her down. When she didn't protest or try to move away, I knew she was still somewhat in a daze.

"I'm going to soak your bandana. You should put it around your neck to help cool you down," I said to her.

I turned toward John. "We need to lighten her pack, a lot."

"Let's divvy it up. Between the two of us we can take most of it. I can strap stuff to the outside of my pack," he said.

We took the heaviest items out of her pack and somehow managed to fit it in or strap it on to our packs. Karen didn't try to stop us. She may have been embarrassed, but she knew she was close to having a real meltdown.

"I can carry her wine," said Lolly.

"Don't let Lolly take my wine," Karen said. "I'll never see it again."

We insisted that Karen drink about a quart of water before we even considered resuming the hike. We only had a mile remaining and we could see from our vantage point that the trail was downhill the rest of the way.

"Do you think she'll be able to make it to the campground?" I asked John.

"Yeah, but let's keep a close eye on her. I'll lead, you hike behind her and watch her closely."

"Sweetie, do you feel good enough to keep going?" I asked.

"Yes, I'll be fine," she said.

"Are you sure? What day is it?"

"I don't know. Thursday?"

"Hmm, does anyone know what day it is?" I asked the group.

"Let's go!" Karen said.

"OK, she's getting feisty. I think she's feeling better."

As we continued to hike I kept watching Karen's legs from behind to see if they were wobbly or if she was having any trouble keeping her balance. A couple of times I felt my legs wobble a bit. We made it to Rainbow Bridge Campground without further incident, but we all were on the verge of heat stroke when we finally set our packs down.

The four of us went down to Rainbow Creek, took off our hiking boots and socks and put our feet in the water. That was the smartest thing we did all day. It was so cold it hurt, but we could feel the energy coming back as the water cooled us down. Almost like flipping a switch, the power came back on. We sat there talking about how lucky we were that no one had had a serious problem on the trail; every one of us felt we'd reached our limit.

The rest of the afternoon and early evening was taken up with the usual tasks: setting up the tents, filtering water, preparing dinner. Lolly went back to the creek and took a bath.

"This must have been an incredibly beautiful campground before the fire," Karen said.

"Yeah, now it looks a little spooky, doesn't it?" I replied.

"A lot spooky. And we're the only people in the campground. I wonder why that is?"

The burned-out forest surrounding our campsite at
Rainbow Bridge, Lake Chelan National Recreation Area

The underbrush was starting to recover from the effects of the fire, and close to the creek, small trees were green and healthy. However, as far as we could see, the large trees that were alive when the fire came through were dead, even though they were still standing. No leaves or needles remained on their branches, just bare sticks that reached out from the trunks like skeleton arms.

By about eight o'clock we'd done everything we could think of doing, so we called it a night. Our tents were no more than five feet apart. Both couples left the rain flies off because of the heat; it was like sleeping out in the open, except for the thin mesh of our tents that kept the bugs off us. We laid there staring at the dead trees above us. Ten minutes later, as I was unzipping our tent, John was unzipping theirs. We looked at each other and laughed. "It's way too early to go to bed," I said.

"What do you want to do?" John asked. "It'll still be light for another hour."

"We could go for a hike," Lolly suggested.

"Yeah, let's go for a hike," Karen said.

"Are you serious? Do you even remember this afternoon?" I asked Karen. "You went to la la land and John and I had to carry all of your shit the rest of the way."

"I feel fine now," she said.

John put on his hiking boots. "I'm ready."

"You guys are crazy," I said. "Let me find my boots. I can't believe we're going for a hike."

"Let's hike farther up the trail, to the top of that ridge," John said. "Maybe we can see Stehekin from up there."

I led the group to the top of the ridge; it was only about a quarter mile. We could barely see the Stehekin River through the trees.

"Let's go to the edge of the trees over there; maybe we'll be able to see the town," John said.

The moment I stepped off the trail I knew it was a bad idea, but I went along with the group anyway. We walked to the edge of the burned-out trees and looked over the cliff.

"There's the river. If there wasn't so much smoke I think we could see Stehekin right through there," John said as he pointed to the south.

We stood there trying to make out landmarks for a few minutes, then Karen said, "We should go now. I don't want to have to use my headlamp hiking back."

In unison, the four of us turned to walk back to the trail. My eyes caught something moving on the ground in front of Lolly, and I grabbed her by the arms, pulling her back.

"Matt!? What are you doing?" she cried out.

"Rattlesnake!" I said.

"Where?"

"Right there. Five feet in front of you!"

"Oh! I almost stepped on it!" she gasped.

"Where's the snake?" John asked.

"Yeah, I don't see a snake," Karen added.

"Right there!" Lolly and I said at the same time.

The snake was moving away, and we could see his markings as he slid across the ground.

John asked, "What is it with you and rattlesnakes? How did you spot it?"

"It was the first thing I saw when I turned around."

"It's a good thing you grabbed me. You saved my life!" Lolly said. "I guess I have to be nice to you from now on."

John walked over to it and crouched down. "Yeah, that's a rattler. A Western rattlesnake."

I turned toward Lolly and said, "He's a snake expert, too."

Back at the campsite, we crawled into our tents again at ten o'clock. The nearly-full moon cast an eerie glow across the burned-out landscape as the light filtered through the thick smoke. Karen and Lolly must have found comfortable positions to sleep because I could no longer hear them fidgeting; John was snoring.

The wind began blowing, which I thought was unusual; there hadn't been so much as a gentle breeze all day. Within ten minutes the gusts were surprisingly strong. The rushing sound was making me drowsy and I dozed off, briefly. At 10:32 pm, I woke to a loud bang coming from the ridge where we'd just been hiking. I sat straight up in the tent. Another bang followed about a minute later. The noises sounded like gunshots. Karen sat up with a start, clutching her sleeping bag around her. She was terrified, sure that a deranged killer was on the loose. I was hoping she was wrong, but I couldn't think of another explanation. Why else would someone fire a gun at night in the wilderness?

I called out softly, "John. Lolly. Did you hear that?" John responded with an open-mouth snort, and I didn't hear a peep out of Lolly.

The bear spray was right where I put it, in the corner of the tent next to my pillow; it was our only protection. We laid back down and listened intently for more gunshots, or worse, the sound of someone coming down the trail toward our campsite. For the next two hours, I was wide awake looking up at the swaying, dead trees that surrounded us. At 12:30 am, we heard another bang, much louder and much closer than the ones before. This time the sound was more metallic; the report echoed off the surrounding hills.

Karen bolted upright and grabbed for her shoes. Where she thought she was going was a mystery to me. "Karen, wait! Those weren't gunshots. The wind is blowing down the dead trees!"

Lolly's silhouette appeared against the screen of her tent, and she shouted, "What wuth that!?"

"Lolly, it wuth the tweeth," Karen said.

"The what?"

"The tweeth! The tweeth!"

"Weally!? It thounded like a gunthot."

"You gals need to take out your mouth guards," I said. "You both sound like Sylvester the Cat."

"What are you talking about?" John asked.

"John, good, you're alive. I thought the first gunshots might have gotten you," I said.

"What gunshots?"

"The ones we heard two hours ago."

"I didn't hear gunshots two hours ago. Lolly, did you?"

"No. I wouldn't have been able to sleep if I had."

We all watched the trees above us move in the wind. At least a dozen big ones stood close to our campsite. John and Lolly's tent was directly underneath the biggest one. No matter which direction the trees were from our tent, every time the wind howled it looked like every one of them was about to fall on us.

"What are we going to do?" Karen asked.

"I don't think we have a choice other than to stay right here and ride it out," John said.

"Yeah, we're dead center in the middle of the burned-out area," I said. "Even if we moved our tents, there's nowhere else to put them that's safer. And we're not hiking out of here in the middle of the night."

"I'm not hiking in the dark, there are snakes out there," Lolly said.

"There are snakes everywhere, Lolly," I replied.

"Not helpful," Karen said.

By 3:30 am, I'd made peace with the idea that a tree would fall and kill us all. Too exhausted to stay awake any longer, I passed out.

When the sun rose the next morning and I opened my eyes, I was relieved that our tent was undamaged. As I crawled out, I saw that John and Lolly's survived as well. It was impossible for me to tell which trees had crashed during the night because so many were down already when we arrived yesterday.

John came out of his tent; we started a fire and sat on stumps waiting for the water in our Jetboils to begin to bubble.

"John, do you remember what you taught me when we backpacked to Shi Shi last month?" I asked.

"I taught you so many things, Matt," he replied.

"About widow makers."

He looked in the direction of our sleeping area. "Crap!" Hanging directly above their tent was a huge, dead, pointy branch. "I never saw that when we set up yesterday," he said.

"It's a miracle it didn't come down in the wind last night."

The wives joined us for coffee. As we sat around the fire drinking our first cup, Lolly startled us when she said, "What a crazy day that was yesterday, you guys!" Lolly's default voice volume is 9.5—out of ten.

I coughed up some coffee, and then said, "Yep, a lot happened: we had a marmot sighting, then there was the heat stroke, and Karen tricked us into carrying all her stuff; I saved you from a rattlesnake; we thought a crazy person was shooting at us in the middle of the night; and we almost died in a wind storm."

"We saw wolf scat, don't forget that," John added.

"Yep, the wolf scat," I said, rolling my eyes.

"And here we thought all of those signs before the trip were bad omens. Look at us; we're having a great time," Karen said.

"Uh huh, we need to get back to civilization before we die out here," I said.

The hike into Stehekin was uneventful, thank God. Once we reached the paved road, we followed it to the Stehekin Pastry Company, which was in the direction of the town. We stared open-mouthed at their freshly baked quiche and cinnamon rolls as if we'd never seen food before. After a mere forty-eight hours in the wilderness, we were trail-grizzled.

From the bakery, we walked the remaining two miles to Stehekin under a reddish/orange glow. The smoke was back and the thickest we'd seen all week.

"We still have a few things to learn about backpacking," Karen said as we walked.

"Yes, we do," I replied. "We need to get smarter, faster, or it's going to kill us."

In town we hung around at the ferry dock waiting for the boat to arrive. Our tickets were for the next day, but we were hoping there were four spots left on the return trip to Chelan. The smoke was so thick in Stehekin that we couldn't see across the narrow lake. The incredible snow-capped, 9,000-foot mountains that surround the area had disappeared. We weren't in the mood for another night of camping in the smoke.

Our luck finally changed when we learned that the ferry had room for us. After securing our tickets, we canceled our camping reservations at the park's visitor center. Karen was anxious to tell the ranger on duty about our harrowing experience the night before. "You have to be careful out there in the burned-out area," he said after she told him about the trees going down in the middle of the night. "Did any of them fall in the campground?" he asked.

"It's hard to say," she replied. "It was dark and we never saw any of them fall, we just heard them as they crashed down."

"Well, we check that campground every now and then, and shake the trees. If we see one that seems like it might fall on a campsite, we'll take it down," he said.

"The way they were swaying in the wind last night, they all looked like they were ready to fall," she said.

Once we were on the ferry, the engine noise put me to sleep. I don't know what the rest of them did during the four-hour trip; I zonked. We spent the night at Lolly's cabin, and when we woke to another smoky morning, we decided to drop John and Lolly off at the trailhead where they'd parked their truck and head home.

I'm sure you can't wait to go camping with us after reading all of this. Let us know when you think you'll be back this way and we'll plan something fun. Something without smoke and snakes.

Your friend,
Matt

From: **Matt Smith**
Subject: **Buffalo Shoulder Mount**
Date: **August 14 (Monday)**

Dear Bob and Sue,

Now that we made the decision to turn our living room into a visitor center, I asked Karen, "What's the first thing you think of when you hear the words 'national park visitor center?'"

"Gift shop," she replied.

"I was hoping for 'mounted buffalo head,'" I said.

"We're not hanging a stuffed buffalo head in our house. It will scare the grandkids."

"It'll make for a fond memory from their childhood. They'll say, 'Remember Papa's buffalo head? I loved petting it every time we went over to visit,'" I said.

"No, they'll say, 'Remember that creepy dead animal at Mimi and Papa's house? That thing gave me nightmares.' And I'm not sure it's even legal to buy a buffalo head. Aren't they endangered?" she asked.

"That was a hundred years ago. There are plenty of buffalo today."

"You're not going to kill a buffalo so you can mount it on our wall."

"I'm not planning on killing a buffalo. I'm going to buy one on craigslist," I replied.

And so the hunt was on. I thought that locating the right one would be easy. It wasn't. The biggest challenge I ran into was location. I wasn't up for driving hundreds of miles to Missoula or Boise just to check out a head. It's important to see the thing in person before committing. A well-taken photo can hide a lot of flaws: scratched horns, matted fur, patchy snout skin. I wasn't holding out for perfection, but I also didn't want to hang a bug-eyed animal in our brand-new visitor center. I was a little surprised at how many bug-eyed buffaloes I found online.

I was overjoyed when I finally found a handsome specimen for sale by someone who lived in our town. I sent the owner an email on the first day his listing appeared on craigslist. I got no response. After two weeks and many unanswered messages later, he finally replied, "Sorry for not getting back to you. I've decided not to sell the buffalo. I thought I could, but when it came time, I couldn't part with it."

For several weeks I despaired, but then I got another bite: a fine-looking buffalo, at a fair price, and only thirty miles from our home. I wasn't about to let this one slip through my fingers. I called the guy immediately and left a message. By noon we were talking on the phone. "Why are you selling your buffalo?" I asked him.

"My wife is making me get rid of it. It's a real nice head, but she won't have it in our house," he replied.

I'd never bought anything that expensive on craigslist before. "How does this work? Do I need to bring cash?" I asked.

"Yeah, I'd prefer cash," he said.

"Do you want me to come to your house?" I asked.

"I tell you what, let's meet at the Starbucks by the mall," was his suggestion.

From the moment I pulled into the parking lot I felt like I was involved in a drug deal. I found his red minivan and approached it cautiously. "Mark?" I asked.

"Yep." He got out, and we shook hands. "Pleasure meeting you, Matt."

We went to the back of his van. Mark opened the back door and gently lifted a blue moving blanket from the buffalo. I could tell right away he was a beauty. We both stood there silently looking at the head for an uncomfortable length of time. I didn't know what to say or ask.

"I've never done this before, so I'm not sure how to tell if it's OK. I mean, it looks good to me." My inclination was to hand him the cash and get out of there fast, but that seemed a little cold. "Um, what can you tell me about this old boy?" I'd never referred to anything or anyone as an "old boy" before.

"I'm sorry, but I don't have a lot of information for you. I bought it a few years ago at an estate sale. The person who owned it before me must've had it for a long time. The backboard looks pretty old. It's in good shape, though. I dusted it off before I came over here."

I was at a loss for what to do next. Was I supposed to tug on the fur or make sure the eyes were tight in their sockets? I could see people sitting by the window in Starbucks looking at us. One kid was pointing and yelling to his mom.

I thought to myself, *should I give him some time alone with it to say goodbye?* After another long, awkward pause, I reached into my jacket and pulled out the envelope that the bank teller had put my cash in. It was the size made specifically for cash, so everyone in Starbucks could tell it was a drug deal. I'm sure they thought, *How obvious is that? They're hiding drugs in the buffalo head.* (Now that I think about it, maybe I should look inside.)

As soon as he saw the envelope, Mark became agitated. "Before you give me that, I got to tell you something."

"Yessss?" I asked him while looking over the top of my reading glasses. I'd driven through two rush hour traffic jams to get there; I wasn't about to let this guy get cold feet and tell me he "just couldn't part with it."

"I noticed something as I was putting it in the van. You see here? The left horn is loose."

I touched the horn; it wiggled. I looked back at Mark.

"I'm willing to take $50 off the price because of that," he said.

"Loose horn discount?" I asked.

Mark didn't laugh. "I'm sure you can get some of that epoxy taxidermists use, and put it back on nice and tight."

I reached into the envelope, pulled out a $50 bill and handed the rest to Mark. "I appreciate you telling me, Mark."

He nodded and put the envelope in his back pocket.

"Well, I guess that's it. I'm anxious to get this guy to his new home," I said. "I'm parked over there." It felt strange carrying a massive buffalo head across the parking lot. The kid in Starbucks didn't ease my discomfort when he pounded on the window and screamed, "Mom, look! It's a cooooooow!!!"

The Smith's bison shoulder mount

Karen has been a good sport about the buffalo. She's become quite fond of him and makes sure everyone who visits our house has a good look at "our" buffalo. "You mean bison?" is the response we get half the time. Yes, he's a bison, but I'll always call him a buffalo.

In fact, Karen has become a bit too attached. She now talks about decorating him for the holidays: lights on his horns at Christmas, Leprechaun hat on St. Patrick's Day, American flag between his teeth on national holidays. We're not doing any of that; he's an interpretive mammal exhibit, not a mannequin.

As for our grandchildren? They're not the least bit afraid. They want to pet him every time they come over to visit.

Your friend,
Matt

~.~.~.~.~.~.~

From: **Matt Smith**
Subject: **Going to Glacier National Park**
Date: **August 18 (Friday)**

Dear Bob and Sue,

This is the summer of John and Lolly; in a couple of days we're driving to Montana and spending a few days with them in Glacier National Park. It seems like everyone and their cat is traveling to a place where the sun will be 100 percent covered during the total eclipse. Since we won't be in the path of totality, I'm hoping the crowds will be down. I'm sure it would be cool to see, but we'll settle for the slightly-less-than-one-hundred-percent version in Whitefish, Montana.

Our week of travel will be a mix of luxury and roughing it. For the first two nights, we'll be at the Firebrand Hotel in Whitefish. It's a newer hotel that has a modern yet western style. John and Lolly are going the more traditional route while we're in town; they're staying at a bed and breakfast a few blocks away. After that, we have a night of camping together on the west side of the park, followed by a couple of nights at the Many Glacier Hotel. For our grand finale, we'll be back in a tent at St. Mary Campground. If we have good weather, we might tack on a couple of more nights to the end of the trip.

At least that's the plan for now. We initially had reservations for two nights at the Sperry Chalet, a hundred-plus-year-old backcountry chalet on the west side of the park. In January, when the reservation window opened, we were fortunate to score a room for the four of us at the chalet. Yes, one room, two double beds. When we learned how much one room cost, we figured it wouldn't be too much of a hardship to share.

Getting to the chalet involves hiking a little over six miles on a trail with an elevation gain of about 3,300 feet. I hear the views are magnificent in that part of the park and there's always a good chance to see mountain goats. We've never seen a mountain goat at close range. It's Karen's dream to see a nanny goat with her little ones.

The chalet doesn't have electricity, but somehow they manage to cook breakfast, lunch, and dinner for their guests. The Spartan rooms don't have bathrooms; instead, there's a restroom facility with pit toilets. We read that the toilets smell worse as the summer wears on, so we were jazzed about being there in late August. I was looking forward to doing a couple of day hikes from the chalet to explore the area, but I have to admit, I wasn't sure how well it would go with the four of us sleeping together in a single room.

"It's going to be a snorefest," I told Karen when we planned it.

"Yeah, you guys will have to keep it down," she replied.

"What guys are you referring to?"

"You and John. You snore like truck drivers."

"John snores like a truck driver. You and Lolly snore like lumberjacks," I said.

"We do not!"

"Yeah, you do. Remember when we were all sleeping next to each other at Rainbow Bridge? I was the only one awake all night. It sounded like three chainsaws running in the forest," I said.

"Then why didn't you wake me up so I'd stop?"

"Becauth you were thleeping tho thoundly I didn't want to dithturb you," I said in my best Sylvester the Cat voice.

It's all a moot point now. A week ago, we got an email telling us that the park service closed the chalet. A lightning strike in the park ignited a fire close to the trail that leads to the chalet and the park closed it to hikers as a precaution. After many attempts to find alternative places to stay, I was able to catch a couple of cancellations at the Many Glacier Hotel. That's not a bad alternative; it's beautiful in the Many Glacier area of the park, but Karen had her heart set on staying at Sperry. It's been in her wish bucket for a long time.

About five years ago, when we were visiting all the national parks, Karen had planned a day hike to Sperry Chalet. We weren't able to get a room reservation, so we going to hike up, have lunch at the chalet, and hike back in the same day. That didn't work out either. A pre-Labor Day snowstorm that year forced the chalet to close early for the season. So, we're 0-2. Maybe the third time will be the charm.

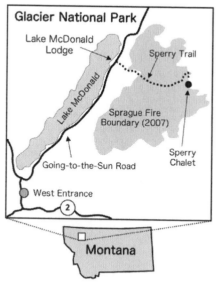

I'm a little concerned about the fires that keep popping up everywhere we go. When we hiked in the North Cascades, I thought the area of fire and smoke was isolated to British Columbia and the north central part of Washington State. Now there are fires in Oregon, California, and Montana. It'll be interesting to see how clear the air is in Glacier National Park. The other day, I saw photos of brilliant orange sunsets over the mountains in the park. No clouds were in the sky, just smoke.

That's the way it goes with travel. Whenever I look at the notes or emails I've written about our past travels, I often only remember the fantastic experiences we had. When I compare many of those trips to our original plans, they're nothing alike. Especially when travel involves outdoor activities that rely on the weather to cooperate, we've come to realize that our plan is only a starting point. It's better to be flexible, embrace the unexpected, and not stress out about last-minute changes to the itinerary. At least that's what Karen keeps reminding me.

Your friend,
Matt

~.~.~.~.~.~.~

From: **Matt Smith**
Subject: **Whitefish, Montana**
Date: **August 20 (Sunday)**

Dear Bob and Sue,

I always think of Montana as a far-away place, but the state line is only six hours from our home, and Whitefish is only nine. Karen and I keep saying we should spend more time here. Every state seems to have a unique vibe; Montana has a wild and wide-open feel. And it's huge: twice the size of New England yet one-thirtieth the population density.

Whitefish has preserved the look and feel of an authentic western town. Founded in 1904 when the Great Northern

Railway was built, it was originally named "Stumptown" because of all the stumps that were left when they cleared the trees. It's a small town—only 7,000 or so residents—but thousands of tourists flock to Whitefish to visit Glacier and Whitefish Lake in the summer, and to ski at Whitefish Mountain Resort in the winter.

We're excited to revisit the park. From our hotel, the west entrance is only thirty minutes away by car. For now, there aren't any driving restrictions that we know of in the park due to fires. On our way here, once we crossed the Columbia River, the skies were smoke-free. The smoke didn't reappear again until we got to Kalispell. Then, we could see it and smell it.

John and Lolly got to Whitefish about the same time we did. After the required stop at the brewery downtown, the four of us had dinner together at a restaurant within walking distance of our hotel. We decided to have a late start tomorrow and then drive over to the area around the park entrance. I've wanted to go back to see if there are still stores that sell animal pelts. Now that we're starting the work to turn our living room into a national park visitor center, I want to have my interpretive pelt collection ready once the room is complete.

As we were walking out of the restaurant, Lolly asked, "Are we getting together tomorrow for the eclipse?"

"We're going pelt shopping tomorrow, remember!?" I said.

"We have time to do both. The eclipse won't last very long. The dead animals will still be there after the sun comes back out."

"You know we can't look directly at it. I'm not sure what there is to see," I said.

"We need a welding helmet," John said. "You can look at an eclipse with a welding helmet."

Karen laughed so hard she had to stop walking to compose herself. "A welding helmet!" she laughed. "Lolly, let's go to the welding store in the morning and get welding helmets."

"John, that's a fine suggestion. Do you have a welding helmet with you?" I asked.

"No, I'm saying that if we had one we could look at the eclipse with it," he replied.

"We need those glasses that let you look at the sun without hurting your eyes. Let's just buy those," Lolly said.

"No, Lolly, we're getting welding helmets," Karen said.

"It's ten o'clock the night before the eclipse. I think we missed our opportunity to buy the special glasses," I said. "Too bad we didn't know sooner that this eclipse was coming. I think they only figured out its exact time and date about seven hundred years ago."

"Yeah, no one has eclipse glasses left for sale. They've been sold out everywhere for the last couple of days," John said.

"Uh, welding helmets. Hello. We're getting welding helmets in the morning," Karen said.

About four blocks before we reached our hotel, a couple approached us at a street corner and said, "Hey, do you guys know anyone who needs eclipse glasses? A friend of ours bought way too many and we're selling the ones we don't need." (I couldn't make this up if I tried.)

I thought to myself, *That's a little creepy. Were they following us and listening to our conversation?*

"Got any welding helmets?" Karen asked.

"Ignore her, she's on strong medication," I said. "Yes, as a matter of fact we do need eclipse glasses."

I think the couple was as surprised that we said, "Yes," as we were that they approached us. We each bought a pair. Karen put on hers and said, "I'm wearing mine now for extra protection. Just in case the eclipse comes early." Then she walked into a tree.

"Sweetie, why don't I hold onto those until the morning. I just gave two complete strangers ten bucks for those glasses, and we don't want to break them before the big event."

I'm so relieved; we're now ready for the eclipse. I can't wait. Not for the eclipse, but for it to be over and to not hear people say the word "eclipse," or the phrase "path of totality," every seven seconds.

While we were getting ready for bed, Karen reminded me that tomorrow is a late start day. You'd think after nearly thirty-five years of marriage we could agree on a simple concept such as late start, but we're still working out some of the details. She said to me, "Late start means I want to be still sitting in bed drinking coffee at 8:00 am."

"Yeah, right. The last time you stayed in bed until eight was after you had your gallbladder removed twenty years ago," I said.

"I'm serious. We need to take our time and relax in the morning. I don't want to see you standing at the door with your backpack on staring at me at six forty-five."

"Sweetie, unless you have a coffee maker in bed with you over there that I don't know about, six forty-five *is* late start for me. By then I'm up, dressed, and out getting coffee for you," I said. Karen still thinks that coffee magically appears each morning when we travel.

"The eclipse isn't until eleven; we don't have to get out of here at the crack of dawn. Where do you think we need to go anyway?" she asked.

"We have to get up and start our day!"

"Let me know how that goes. I'll be in bed enjoying my coffee."

Despite Karen's late start warning, I'll be ready for anything in the morning.

Your friend,
Matt

From: **Matt Smith**
Subject: **Eclipse and Pelt Shopping**
Date: **August 21 (Monday)**

Dear Bob and Sue,

Karen was up early this morning. At 7:00 am, she came out of the shower with a towel wrapped around her wet hair and asked, "What's our plan?"

"What happened to late start day? I'm still drinking my coffee," I said.

"I looked outside. It's nice and sunny. We should go for a walk before the eclipse. Let's go, let's go, let's go!" she said.

"First, calm down," I replied. "Second, I'm going to take a shower, so you'll have to keep yourself busy for a while. Why don't you go outside and walk around with your eclipse glasses on? Try 'em out, but watch out for the trees."

"How embarrassing. That red wine really hit me last night," she said.

"Do you remember saying that you wanted to get welding helmets?" I asked.

"Uh, kind of. Was that before or after I walked into the tree?"

"Right about the same time, sweetie. I'll be ready to go in about twenty minutes. We can walk into town and get something to eat," I said.

Breakfast was slow and relaxing. We rarely have a morning like that when we travel. It was nice, but I felt the day was getting away from us. The eclipse was starting in about fifteen minutes, so we quickly walked from the restaurant to John and Lolly's bed and breakfast. John was in the front room with a map spread open on the coffee table in front of him. One of the bed and breakfast owners was giving him advice on hikes in the park.

"My father was a park ranger for years," he was saying. "I can remember when I was a kid the glaciers were huge. Now there's hardly anything left of them."

John looked at me and said, "I'm getting a lot of great hiking suggestions. Look at this one here." He pointed to a spot on the map.

I didn't look at the map. I wiggled my eclipse glasses at him, mouthed the word "eclipse," and then pointed toward the front door with my head as if to say, "Time to go."

"Hold on, hold on," he said.

The owner didn't pick up on my hint. He sat down next to John and started in again, "If you have time this afternoon, you should go..."

As politely as I could, I said, "I'm going outside now. I'm not a huge eclipse fan, but this is the last one in our lifetime and we paid a million dollars for these glasses last night when we were drunk, so I'm going to take a peek." Neither John nor the owner looked up to acknowledge my comment.

Outside, I found Lolly and Karen a half a block away on a street corner that had a clear view of the sun. Lolly had her glasses on and was looking at the sun. Karen was standing next to a stranger, who was wearing her glasses and also looking at the sun. The two of them were sharing their glasses and making friends with everyone who walked by. I stood on the opposite street corner by myself and watched the moon slowly block the sun. About twenty minutes later, John and the owner came out and joined us.

It didn't take long for the four of us to decide we'd seen enough. Lolly and Karen wanted to walk back into town to visit a few stores. It was a short walk, but about every hundred feet we'd stop, look at the sun, realize it looked the same as two minutes before, and then start walking again. Everyone in town was out in the streets looking up and passing their glasses around.

Since Whitefish was not in the path of the total eclipse, it didn't get much darker at the peak than usual. What surprised us, though, was that the temperature dropped noticeably. I'm not sure by how much, but I'd guess it was ten degrees cooler during the eclipse than before it started.

"I wonder what the animals think when there's an eclipse," Karen said.

"I heard that dogs and cats freak out right before an eclipse," Lolly said. "And I think I read that snakes come out."

"You're thinking of earthquakes, not eclipses," I said.

"Oh, you're right. Well, all of a sudden, it's pitch dark in the middle of the day. They must think it's night," Lolly said.

"If I were an animal, I'd take a nap during an eclipse," I said.

"I bet wolves and coyotes howl during an eclipse," Karen said.

"Maybe they can talk, but only during the eclipse and then they can't speak again until the next one," I said.

"You're thinking of Christmas Eve," Karen said.

"Christmas Eve?" asked Lolly.

"Haven't you heard of that?" Karen said. "We used to tell our kids that animals can talk at the stroke of midnight on Christmas Eve. They'd try to stay awake until midnight to hear if our cat could talk."

"I've never heard of that," Lolly said laughing. "What did they think the cat would say?"

"That's when pets air their grievances with their owners," I said.

"You're thinking of Festivus," John said.

"No, I'm thinking of pelt shopping," I said. "I'm calling it. Eclipse is over."

"Did you say *pet* shopping?" Lolly asked.

"*Pelts.* I said, 'pelt shopping.' That's the exact opposite of pet shopping," I replied.

"What's your fascination with animal pelts?" Lolly asked.

"I have an interest in them. I wouldn't call it a fascination," I replied.

"Then, why are you *interested* in them?" she asked.

"I don't know. That's like asking guys why they like chainsaws or starting fires. It's a guy thing. Right, John? Help me out here," I said.

He shook his head. "Your fascination with pelts seems kind of weird to me."

"Uh, not a fascination, and thank you for supporting a fellow dude," I told him. "You can go with Karen and Lolly to have manicures and pedicures if you'd rather. I'll go search for dead animals by myself."

"Yes! We can all get matching nail polish," Karen said.

"No, we're all going to support our brother Matt. This will be fun. We need to get out and see more of the area," John said.

"And eat," said Lolly. "I'm starving."

Ten miles south of the entrance to the park we came across the Montana Fur Trading Company. The rusted steel bison sculpture next to their building caught my eye, and I asked John, who was driving, to pull into the parking lot so we could check out the store. The instant we walked inside, I knew we'd hit pay dirt. A couple of full-length bear hides, complete with heads mounted in full snarl, rested on a table surrounded by a variety of furs hanging on hooks attached to the wall.

"We're getting this one," I said to Karen as I pointed to a bear that looked like it would take your arm off if you got too close.

"No. Just no," she said, and then walked away.

"We'll discuss it later," I called to her.

"You might want to ease her into the idea of collecting pelts," John said. "You should start small, like with a skunk. That would make a perfect starter pelt." I'm still not sure if John was serious or not. I'm leaning toward believing he was making fun of me with that comment.

The selection of items in the store was impressive. A buffalo robe covered a large area of one wall—robe is another term for hide. A couple of others were bundled up, sitting on the floor beneath it. The woman behind the counter encouraged me to unfold them and take a closer look.

"One of these would look good in our visitor center," I said to John. "But they're so big, I don't know where we'd put it."

"A skunk isn't very big," John said. "You could put it anywhere."

"Talk about fascination. I think you have a skunk fascination, John," I said.

"No, I think if you're going to start a collection, you need to build a foundation first," he argued. "A skunk is a foundational pelt."

"I don't even know what that means," I replied.

Lolly walked up to us and interrupted. "Alright. Buy your pelt. I'm starving."

I settled on two fox pelts and several fur scraps that were fifty cents apiece. When I was paying, I had to tell the nice lady behind the counter that the skunk pelt John put on the counter wasn't mine. "I don't know that guy," I said to her. "He keeps following me around, though. I think you should have him removed from your store. He was talking to that wolf head over there a few minutes ago."

"Why are you buying these fur scraps?" John asked.

"See, ma'am. He's doing it again. Now he's touching my pelts," I said.

"Seriously, what are you going to do with these?" John asked.

"They'll be part of the interpretive exhibits. I can't let people put their dirty hands on my pelts, so I'll have these small pieces of fur that they can handle instead. That way they can experience the feel of the fur without touching my pelts," I said.

"Who's 'they?' Who are all these people you're worried about touching your pelts?" John asked.

"You never know. Friends who come over for dinner, maybe," I said.

"Do you have a lot of friends, Matt?" he asked.

"Fewer recently, John," I replied. "Very recently."

By the time I paid, it was close to 2:00 pm and way past lunchtime. We piled into John's truck and drove north on Highway 2. John found a restaurant by the side of the road and we had lunch. I was hoping to hit one more pelt store before going back to Whitefish. As luck would have it, our waitress told us about a friend of hers, Randy, who had a store just up the road in the town of Hungry Horse.

Randy was sitting out front as we walked toward his storefront. He'd been talking with another gentleman who had a shotgun lying across his lap, but when he saw us get out of the truck he cut off their conversation and stood up to meet us. Right before he stood up, I could swear I read his lips saying, "Fresh meat."

"Hey there folks. Make yourself at home. There's a lot to see here," he said. "If you'd like, I have some just-picked cherries here on this barrel. Help yourself. They're the last of the crop this season. We won't have them again until next year."

"He's already using the scarcity tactic on us," I whispered to Karen.

She shushed me and said, "He's just being friendly."

Randy had some nice animal heads and hides. He also had some stuff that was, well, unusual might be the best way to describe it. A mountain goat head hung underneath the roof of the front porch. I must have stared at it long enough to make Randy think I was interested. He came over and stood next to me. We both looked at the goat for a few seconds, and then I asked, "Is there something odd about that mountain goat?"

"It don't have ears," he said.

"Yep, that's it, no ears," I said.

"You have to look closely at the ears if you're buying a goat head."

"Good advice. You could print that saying on a t-shirt," I said with a chuckle.

Randy cocked his head, closed one eye, and looked at me without saying anything for an uncomfortably long moment. "You looking for anything in particular?"

I wasn't going to show my hand that early, so I said, "No, just looking around. I think the wives are shopping for antiques."

"Let me know if you've got any questions," he said and then went over to continue his conversation with shotgun Joe.

In the end, I decided to get a silver fox and a coyote pelt. Randy also had a stuffed coyote head that John was trying to convince us to buy. The mount went all the way back to the coyote's shoulders and its head was turned. We have the perfect spot for it in our visitor center. I thought it could be our greeter, but Karen vetoed that idea.

The price on the silver fox was $250, and the coyote was $120. I found Randy and led him to where the pelts were hanging. "What's your best deal on the two of these guys?" I asked.

Randy closed one eye tightly and said, "I'll sell you both for four hundred."

I paused, and said, "Randy, that's more than what's on the price tags."

He shook his head as if clearing the cobwebs from his brain. "Alright, final offer, I'll take three hundred for the pair. Cash."

I glanced at Karen, who shrugged her shoulders. "Deal," I said. "But I don't have any money."

"I'll take a check if you got one," Randy replied.

"My wife does. I'll let you two do the paperwork," I said and walked back to take one more look at the coyote head hanging in the back of the store. Randy sighed heavily and walked over to the cash register with Karen in tow. From across the room, I could hear Randy say, "Now, that'll be three fifty for the pair."

Karen looked up from her checkbook and said, "Randy! You just said three hundred."

"Three-hundred, that's right," he replied.

Karen shook her head and wrote out the check.

"What are you two arguing about over there?" I asked.

"Nothing. I'm just helping Randy with his memory," Karen said.

"Now I see why you let the missus hold onto the checkbook," Randy said in my direction.

When I looked over at them, I saw a massive moose head hanging on the wall above the cash register. I don't know why I hadn't noticed it before. It was the most enormous stuffed head of any kind I'd ever seen. From the amount of dust that had accumulated on it I'd guess it had been hanging there for a long time. I walked over to the cash register and said, "How much for the moose?"

"Oh, dear Lord!" Karen said. "We're not getting that moose."

"It's a nice one," Randy said.

"We're not getting that moose," Karen said to Randy as she handed him the check.

That's it for our Whitefish visit. Enough with buying dead animals; tomorrow we hope to see some live ones. The plan is to check into our campsite, get the tents set up, and go for a hike. I'll email you again when we get back into Wi-Fi range on the other side of the park.

Your friend,
Matt

From: **Karen Smith**
Subject: **Pelt Shopping**
Date: **August 21 (Monday)**

Dear Bob and Sue,

In the lower forty-eight states, Montana is the motherlode of animal pelts. Matt's dream of expanding his two-rabbit and one-beaver pelt collection is a step closer to coming true.

The last time we visited Glacier National Park, we saw lots of pelt stores on Highway 2, just south of the park entrance. The vision of turning our living room into a national park visitor center hadn't yet come to Matt at that time, so we weren't in the market for animal hides. Since then, however, he's talked non-stop about doing some pelt shopping on this trip to Glacier.

I've mixed feelings about buying animal hides because there's no way to know how they died. Old age? Road kill? Or were they hunted? I know in some cases animals are killed due to overpopulation, and people subsistence hunt to provide food for their family. What bothers me is when people hunt purely for sport.

Matt looks at it from a more practical perspective. He says these animals are already dead, so why not learn something from them; he keeps using the word "interpretive" in front of "pelt collection," like the dead animals will be an educational tool at our house. Many national parks do have interpretive animal hides, skulls, bones, track casts, and scat. We've seen pelt collections on display in lots of park visitor centers, with tags attached identifying the animals. We attended a ranger conference where the California State Parks had a display table with a huge bearskin (with head), a stuffed wolf and skunk, and many pelts along with molds of the animals' skulls and scat. A sign next to them read "Please Touch." And almost all the historic park lodges that we've been to have animal heads displayed on their walls.

Yesterday was designated "pelt shopping day." John and Lolly wanted to come with us, so after we finished watching the eclipse, our first stop was Montana Fur Trading Company. They sold everything from pelts to jewelry to leather goods. When we walked into the pelt room, the first things we saw were a couple of huge black bears on a table with heads still attached, mouths open and teeth bared.

Matt pelt shopping in Montana

"Nope," I said. "No bears in our house. Nope, no, never."

"How cool are these?" Matt asked as he walked around the table examining them.

"How in the world would you display one, anyway? You can't put those on the floor."

"I don't know," he said as he bent over for a closer look. "Maybe we could drape it over the back of the couch."

"I can see it now," I replied. "When our friends come over, they'll sit on our couch where an inch away from their heads is a giant bear face snarling at them with its huge fangs. They'll never want to leave."

"We can discuss it later," he said as he moved away to the wall of pelts behind him.

I grew bored quickly and wandered off into another room, looking through boxes of beaded moccasins for my size. Lolly found me there. "Where's Matt?" she asked. "John's looking for him. He has a skunk he wants to show him."

"Not sure. Last I saw he was fondling some dead foxes in the corner of the pelt room," I told her.

When we all met up later, Matt had a red fox and a black fox. I was relieved that they were small and didn't have teeth showing. He also had a handful of fur scraps. "Look at these," he said. "They're small pieces of fur that we can put in the visitor center for people to touch, instead of my pelts. That's what the real visitor centers do. They have the animal hides that you're allowed to touch with the back of your hand, and they also have a sample square of fur of the same animal so that you can feel it however you want. Small children only get to handle the fur squares." He paid for his new-found treasures and we left in search of lunch.

As John pulled out of the parking lot, he said. "Let me give you guys a tip on how to find a good restaurant just by driving by."

"We're on the edge of our seats back here," I replied.

"What you do is, look for the number of cars out in front," he said. "If there are a lot of cars in the parking lot, you know that it must be good because so many people are eating there."

"That's brilliant, John. Thank you for enlightening us," I said.

We drove north on Highway 2, and it wasn't long before John was pointing out a place just off the road. "Now look at that place! Packers Roost. See all the cars? It must be really good." He made an abrupt right turn and parked at the end of a row of about eight cars.

When we walked into the restaurant, we were the only people in the entire place. Someone yelled from behind the bar, "Sit wherever you want!"

"Way to pick 'em, John," Matt said. "Hope we can find a table for the four of us."

"John, they parked all those cars out front to sucker us," Lolly said. "Didn't you notice that they all had Montana license plates?"

"It did seem odd that there would be so many locals here at two o'clock on a weekday," he admitted.

We asked our waitress if she knew of any good pelt stores in the area, and she said without hesitation, "Oh you should go to Randy's place in Hungry Horse. He has everything. I don't know the address, but it will be on the left side of the road, and it has all kinds of animal heads out front. You can't miss it."

After we finished our burgers and beers, we piled back into John's truck and headed to Randy's place. Matt found a coyote pelt and a silver fox pelt that he had to have. I watched with pride as he haggled with Randy to get a better price on the two of them. Just before we left, John said, "Come back here, you guys, I want to show you something."

We followed him to the back of the store and he pointed to a stuffed coyote head on the wall.

"This guy is really nice! You should get him, too!"

"He's a beauty!" Matt said.

"Why don't you buy him for yourself, John," I said. "We already have a buffalo head over the fireplace in our visitor center, and Matt wants to find a moose and a mountain goat for the other two walls. I'm going to have to say no to the coyote head."

Lying in bed that night, Matt said to me, "You know, we have coyotes running through our neighborhood all the time. Having a coyote head on our wall would be representative of the fauna whose natural habitat is the area where we live."

"By 'representative fauna of the area where we live,' you mean the animals in our backyard, right? If that were the case, we should put a 'possum and a mole head on our walls too," I replied.

He didn't say anything for a while. I thought he'd fallen asleep when I heard him say softly, "That coyote had a nice face. Did you notice that it looks like he's smiling?"

That was our day yesterday. Matt's interpretive pelt collection got a considerable boost. And as soon as we check out of the hotel this morning, we're going back to Randy's to get the coyote head.

Your friend,
Karen

~.~.~.~.~.~.~.~

From: **Matt Smith**
Subject: **Camping in West Glacier**
Date: **August 23 (Wednesday)**

Dear Bob and Sue,

The Wi-Fi here at Many Glacier Hotel is hit-and-miss, (more miss than hit) so I hope you get this. My email covers two days because we camped last night at Fish Creek Campground on the west side of the park and didn't have a connection.

Yesterday, we had a leisurely start to our day. The check-in time for our campsite wasn't until 1:00 pm, but by 11:00 am we'd done everything there was to do at the Apgar Visitor Center. We went to Fish Creek to see if our site was available early, and it was. Before going for a hike, we wanted to get the bulk of the camp set up, so when we got back we could just sit around and relax.

After the tents went, Lolly zipped herself inside theirs and didn't come out for about twenty minutes. I could hear her struggling in there, so I asked John, "What's with Lolly? Sounds like she's wrestling a bear in your tent." John rolled his eyes, shook his head, and said, "I don't know what her deal is."

Finally, Lolly unzipped their tent and said, "Look, Smiths! Now who has the best tent?"

Karen and I peeked inside and saw that Lolly had set up cots and covered them with nice blankets. She'd been envious of our cots ever since we camped together at Klahowa (after leaving Shi Shi Beach). That night they tossed and turned on the floor of their tent in sleeping bags while we slept soundly. But she hadn't stopped with cots. Against the back wall was a small camp table with a towel on top and a battery-operated lantern sitting on the towel. On the floor, she'd laid a wool rug. She was very proud of her set-up.

"It's not a competition, Lolly," I said.

"Yes it is, and we won," she replied.

"The inside of your tent looks like a hotel room. I can't believe John went along with all of this," I said.

"He thinks I'm crazy, but I did it anyway," she said.

John was busy looking for something in his truck. I hollered over to him, "John, I like your new camping set up."

He came over and said, "We need to call an end to trying to outdo each other every time we camp. It's only been a couple of months and Lolly's already bought all new stuff. At this rate, by the end of summer we'll own one of those bus-sized RVs."

"Yeah, let's buy one," Lolly said.

"Get one that sleeps four," Karen added.

Before the day got away from us, we ate a quick lunch and piled into John's truck to go for a hike. Their bed and breakfast owner suggested we hike to Mineral Creek. The trail began at a site on the park map called Packer's Roost. Yep, same name as the restaurant we ate at yesterday. As we drove north on Going-to-the-Sun Road, the turnoff to Packers Roost was just before the point where the road makes a hairpin turn toward the east and begins to climb toward Logan Pass.

On our way to the trailhead, we saw thick smoke hanging above the trees. We didn't see flames, but a couple of fire crews were parked along the side of the road as we passed Lake McDonald Lodge. I hope they were there just resting. It would be a shame if fire threatened that historic lodge.

John parked at the trailhead and we all put extra water in our packs. The temperature was mild, and the smoke partially blocked the sun, but ever since our heat stroke scare in the North Cascades, we make sure to always carry more than enough water.

The first half mile was mostly in the shade of tall evergreen trees. Soon after, the shade ended, and we were in full sun. The trail took us through a long stretch of burned-out trees. In 2003, the Trapper Fire swept through this area and left behind a forest of dead-standing trees. Most of them were nearly white from being bleached by the sun.

I didn't keep track of how far we hiked. I'd guess it took us about forty-five minutes to reach Mineral Creek. The group wanted to rest, so we climbed down to a spot beneath the bridge over the creek, sat by the water and ate Cheez-Its. Karen and Lolly hadn't been off their feet for more than a minute before the chipmunks found them. They were bold and expected us to share our food with them. It must be a frequent resting stop for hikers because the rodents looked well-fed, and a little hypertensive from all of the salt and sugar in their diet. Our break didn't last long; the wives quickly had enough of the chipmunks.

Just past the bridge, the trail began to climb in elevation. We were getting a workout, which was nice since we hadn't done anything strenuous in several days, but the trail wasn't very interesting due to the burnout. We reached a waterfall farther up the trail before turning back to the truck. We couldn't figure out why the B&B owner recommended this hike, unless he hadn't been there since the fire came through and burned everything. Looking at the park map, the next interesting landmark on that trail was nearly at the Canadian border.

Back at our campsite, we had a relaxing dinner. When we finished, there was still plenty of daylight left for us to walk through the campground and check out all the other setups. This is an essential part of camping, looking at other people's stuff. It's where you get ideas about all the things you need to buy.

The couple at the site next to ours had a teardrop trailer that looked new. The back of the teardrop was open, and we could see their outdoor kitchen. A twelve-by-twelve canopy covered the kitchen area behind their trailer. They'd laid out a large, outdoor floor mat under the canopy. Next to the small side door was a tent large enough to fit a couple of lawn chairs and a small table. The edge of the tent overlapped the door so if it was raining, they could get in and out without getting wet. The tent also gave them a place to get dressed in private.

When Karen and Lolly saw this set-up, their jaws dropped.

"John! That's what we need," Lolly said.

"See, I told you," he said to me. "Every time we camp with you, Lolly wants to buy something else."

"It *is* a sweet set up," Karen said. "We should go talk to them. I wonder if they're home."

The couple who owned the trailer must have heard us talking because just then they came around the corner and invited us over.

"This is so cool," Karen said to the man. "How long have you had it?"

"We got it about a year ago. We've taken it out maybe a half dozen times," he replied.

"How do you like it?" she asked.

"We love it. It's perfect for us," he said.

The couple was very generous to let us look around, even in their sleeping area, which was big enough to fit a queen-size mattress, a few storage cabinets, and a flat-screen TV. If a salesperson had been there at that moment, he or she would have sold two units, without a doubt. Both Karen and Lolly were ready to write checks on the spot.

"We should move along so these nice people can get back to their dinner," John said to Lolly.

"Oh, we've already eaten," the man said.

"Then, we should move along so these nice people don't talk you into spending twenty-thousand dollars on a trailer," John said.

"We're getting one of those," Karen said as we walked away. I was almost as ready as she was to buy one, but we have a lot more to learn about camping before we make a big purchase like that.

This morning, as we were breaking down camp, the skies looked less smoky than yesterday. The smoke came and went by the hour, depending on which way the wind was blowing. Traffic was light as we drove to the east side of the park on Going-to-the-Sun Road. We were going to stop halfway between Logan Pass and the St. Mary Visitor Center and hike to Siyeh Pass, but every parking lot and pull out along the road was full, which is typical in the summer. The ranger at the Apgar Visitor Center had warned us that if we didn't get to the trailhead by at least 8:00 am, we probably wouldn't find a place to park.

The new plan was to grab lunch at Two Sisters Café in Babb, drive to Many Glacier Hotel, and then find a hike by the hotel. On our way, we swung through St. Mary Campground and took a look at the campsite where we'll be staying in a couple nights.

The parking at Many Glacier Hotel was no better than along the Going-to-the-Sun Road. John and I circled the parking lot above the hotel for about a half an hour before we found spots. It wasn't even close to check-in time, but I tried to get our rooms early anyway. No dice; they told us to come back at 4:00, so we had a couple of hours to hike. It was a lovely afternoon even though the haze from the fires came back—the heaviest we'd seen since we've been here.

The hotel sits on the eastern shore of Swiftcurrent Lake. It's a beautiful setting, with the lake in front of it and Grinnell Point directly opposite. Several trails start from the hotel, including the one that dead-ends at Grinnell Glacier, the hike we're doing tomorrow. Today we hiked the two-and-a-half-mile trail that circles Swiftcurrent Lake. It mostly followed the shore of the lake, so the trail was relatively flat and easy.

Back at the front desk of the hotel, I waited in line to check in while the others sat around the large fireplace in the center of the lodge. I'd made the reservation for both rooms, so there was no need for the others to stand in line with me. Only one person was in front of me, but she took forever to finish her business, repeatedly pounding her fist on the counter and saying, "This is unacceptable!"

After about ten minutes, Karen came over and asked me, "What seems to be the problem?"

I pointed to the woman, who'd now produced several printed documents to make her case to the front desk clerk. "Something seems to be unacceptable," I said.

"Those front desk clerks take a lot of shit from guests, don't they?" Karen said.

"Too much," I replied. "What they need is a trap door that you have to stand on when you check in, and if you're too difficult, the desk clerk can push a button and make you disappear, never to be seen again."

"Yeah, you should write that on a comment card and put it in the suggestion box," Karen said.

When it was my turn, I asked the clerk, "Does that happen very often?"

"All the time," she said with a smile, as if she was having a perfectly pleasant day.

"Well, you're a lot more patient than I would have been. Next time that happens you should look over their shoulder and shout, 'Next!'"

The clerk looked over my shoulder to the person behind me in line. "I mean, you should try the 'next' thing later, like after you've checked me in," I said quickly.

Fortunately, the clerk had a sense of humor and didn't give us the two guest rooms in the basement, the ones where they store the insecticides that have been banned in this country for years. She handed me two sets of keys and said, "Here are your rooms, but they aren't exactly the same. One has a view of the lake and the other looks out over the parking lot in the back."

"Great, we'll take 'em," I said. After my lame attempt at humor, I was a little worried the trap door would open if I complained about the one room not having a view.

"It's about time," Karen said when I joined the group.

"You're welcome," I replied. "You know that trap door idea? They should have that for ungrateful spouses also."

"Oh, honey, you'd be down in the dungeon with all the check-in whiners long before me," she said.

I put my finger on the back of the couch where Karen was sitting and pushed an imaginary button several times. "Why isn't anything happening?" I asked.

"Just tell us if you got the rooms," Karen said.

"Yes. The good news is we have two rooms. The not-so-good news is, one has a view of the lake and the other does not. John and Lolly, you can have your choice. The view room is thirty dollars more, though," I said.

"You guys take the room with a view. You booked the rooms," John said.

"Yeah, we don't care," Lolly agreed.

It was settled; Karen and I took the room with a view, and it was spectacular. The windows of the room framed the magnificent view of the lake, the boat dock below with the

American flag waving in the sunlight, and the mountains in the distance. I took photos so we'd remember how great it was.

View of Swiftcurrent Lake and Grinnell Point

Twenty minutes later, we met them on the back deck to have a drink before dinner. A small crowd had gathered at the north end; they were looking toward the mountainside about a quarter mile farther to the north. Many of them had binoculars. Wandering over, we could make out a brown shape moving slowly. "It's a grizzly bear," Lolly said.

John and I went back to our rooms and got our binoculars. The four of us stood on the deck for half an hour watching the bear. Lolly could see him with her bare eyes. "You're our wildlife spotter, Lolly," Karen said. "You're always the first to see something."

"I do have a knack for finding wildlife," she said.

"You haven't traveled with her as much as I have," John said. "On the drive out here to Montana, she made me stop the truck because she thought she saw wild turkeys by the side of the road. They were tree stumps."

"There's another one!" Lolly interrupted. Sure enough, through the binoculars we could see a second brown bear making its way across an open stretch of the hillside.

"I don't know, John. She's picking out bears right and left. Maybe those stumps *were* wild turkeys," I said.

"No, they were stumps. It was a rare mistake," Lolly said.

"Look at those people on the trail below that big grizzly," John said as he pointed to a trail at the base of the hill. Three hikers who couldn't have been more than a hundred yards below the bear were hiking along the path.

"Do you think they have any idea there's a bear that close to them?" Karen asked.

"I doubt that they'd be hiking right there if they knew," I said.

"Isn't that the trail we're planning to hike the day after tomorrow?" John asked.

"No, I think our trail is more to the west. It's over there about a half mile," Karen said as she pointed down the road.

"Oh, so not where the bear is right now, but where it will be in about ten minutes?" he replied.

"Yeah," Karen said slowly.

That's Glacier National Park for you; there are big bears here and they're used to being around hikers. I'll have that in the back of my mind tomorrow when we hike to Grinnell Glacier. Grizzly bears have attacked several people on that trail. We'll definitely take our bear spray.

Your friend,
Matt

From: **Matt Smith**
Subject: **Grinnell Glacier**
Date: **August 24 (Thursday)**

Dear Bob and Sue,

Before we could hit the trail this morning, the four of us had to pack and check out of our rooms. Since I'd gotten the rooms due to a cancellation, we only had the luxury of completely separate rooms for one night. Tonight, we're sharing a two-room family unit with a common bathroom. Party!

It wasn't an ideal morning to be without a home base; we woke up to wind, clouds, and drizzle. After storing our luggage with the bellmen, we met at the snack bar on the lower floor of the hotel for coffee and a quick breakfast. The plan was to get an early start on our hike so we could take our time on the trail and still get back by mid-afternoon.

At the last minute, I suggested we buy a couple of inexpensive ponchos in the gift shop just in case the drizzle turned to rain. It never crossed our minds to pack our raincoats for this trip; forest fires and heat stroke were our primary concerns. We should have known better; the weather can turn quickly in the mountains, and you need to be prepared for it.

From the hotel, the hike to the glacier and back is about eleven miles with an elevation gain of about 2,000 feet; not too strenuous of an elevation change when spread across that many miles.

For the first hour, the rain held off, but it was chilly. As we hiked above Lake Josephine, we saw a tour boat crossing the lake. If you take this boat, and the one that ferries hikers across Swiftcurrent Lake, it cuts out about four miles of hiking from the roundtrip. The third lake we passed on the trail is Lower Grinnell Lake, which is a stunning turquoise color due to the silt coming off the glacier above it.

When we reached the spot on the trail where Karen and I ran into the huge bighorn sheep a few years ago, I expected to see them again. So did John and Lolly. "Where are the mountain sheep you always talk about?" asked John as we stood on the trail with high vegetation on both sides.

"They're wild animals, John, and that was six years ago. Who knows where they might be," I said.

"You owe me at least one wildlife sighting on this hike," he said. "That's the only reason we're out here on a day like this."

"Lolly is the animal spotter. Lolly, do you see any?" I asked.

"I've been looking, but none so far," she said.

A little bit farther up the trail, Karen and I stopped to put on our ponchos. John said, "You don't need your ponchos for this. It's just drizzle."

"John, you may be right, but we have the waterfall coming up," I said.

"You need a poncho to see a waterfall?" he asked.

"No, you need one to walk under it," I told him. "The water falls onto the trail." He and Lolly put on their ponchos.

The waterfall section of the trail is a series of rock steps, with a drop off on one side and a wall of rock on the other. Several streams of water cascade down the wall hitting the inside two feet of the trail. At that point, the path was wide enough for us to hike on the outside edge without water hitting us directly from above. The spray and splash, however, got us pretty good, but it didn't matter; it was just a matter of time before we'd get soaked. The drizzle soon turned to rain, and the closer we got to the glacier the harder it came down.

Grinnell Glacier is much smaller than it used to be; it lost 45 percent of its footprint from 1966 to 2015. Photos from a hundred years ago show it covering a huge area. Today, we stood at the edge of Upper Grinnell Lake; the lake that formed as the glacier retreated. Now what remains of the glacier sits at the far side of the lake and clings to the mountain that marks the Continental Divide. Despite it being smaller than in the past, the white glacier against the dark mountain and the turquoise lake made an incredible sight.

Grinnell Glacier, Glacier National Park

We hiked along the edge of the lake for as long as we could withstand the cold, which was only about a quarter mile. The wind began to howl, and it was all I could do to hold the open sides of my thin poncho together to keep it from blowing over my head. Just as we turned to head back, the rain became chunky. Drops of slush started falling out of the sky and we heard thunder in the distance. Mercifully, the rain stopped as we descended the trail just below the glacier.

It wasn't long afterward that we ran into several groups hiking toward the glacier. The clouds overhead were still threatening, yet hiker after hiker passed us wearing nothing but shorts and t-shirts. One woman was wearing flip-flops. *They're in for a cold afternoon,* I thought.

A couple of miles from the hotel, a hiker on his way up smiled at us and held up his hands signaling us to stop. He was with another man, neither of whom spoke English. They were insistent on telling us something as they pointed up the mountainside toward a clearing in the trees, but we couldn't understand what they were saying. Finally, I heard one of them say, "Bar."

"Bear? Did you see a bear?" I asked.

They smiled, nodding their heads in agreement, and said, "Bar, bar."

We stood with them for several minutes scanning the mountain, but the bear was elusive. Even so, it was a good opportunity to rib Lolly.

"You're going to lose your job as our wildlife spotter," I said as we continued down the trail.

"I don't think they saw a bear. I'd have seen it also," she said. Lolly's pretty competitive.

A maintenance crew had closed the quarter mile of trail closest to the hotel while we'd been hiking, so we followed a detour along a gravel road the rest of the way back. John was in the lead, I was ten yards behind him, and the wives were maybe another thirty yards behind me. John was rounding a bend in the road when he jumped to the side and yelled, "Bear! There's a bear running toward us!"

I kept walking calmly down the middle of the road. "What are you doing!?" he yelled. "Get off the road a bear is coming!"

"I'm not falling for it, John," I said as I walked past him. He didn't follow me. When I looked back at him, he was tentatively peeking around the bend in my direction.

"Why didn't you stop?" he called out. "A big black bear was running up the road right where you're standing. He would have run right over you."

"I thought you were joking. You're always joking," I said.

"No! Why would I joke about that?"

"I don't know. Why would you joke about half the stuff you joke about? Just yesterday you told Karen you saw a snake crawl into our tent," I said.

"What are you guys doing?" Karen asked when she and Lolly and she caught up with us.

"John thinks he saw a bear," I said.

"It was a huge black bear and it was running straight down the middle of the road," he said.

"Oh, that's scary. I hope he doesn't crawl into our tent like the snake did," Karen said.

"I'm serious!" John said.

"John, I believe you," said Lolly rubbing the side of his arm.

"Do you?" I asked.

"Not really," she said.

"I know what I saw. You guys are lucky. I must have scared him back into the forest," John said.

"That's good then, that counts as your wildlife sighting for the day. I'm off the hook," I said.

Back at the hotel, we got our new rooms and moved in. One had two twin beds and the other had a double bed and a cot. Each had a door that accessed the bathroom in the middle. The rooms were on the top floor and the ceiling sloped with the roofline. The hotel had placed the cot against the wall under the slope; it looked like the perfect spot for a small child to sleep. Karen laid down on the cot, which wasn't much longer than she was. "This is cozy; I call the cot," she said.

"I don't think you'll have any competition, sweetie," I said.

"There's one bathroom and all four of us have to take showers before dinner," Lolly said. "How's that going to work?"

"I don't know what you had in mind, Lolly, but I suggest we take showers one at a time," I said.

"No! I meant, what will be our sign for when someone's in the bathroom? We need a sign otherwise we'll be walking in on each other."

"How about when you're in the bathroom you shut the door? I think that's usually the 'sign' people use," I said.

"That's not going to work because when we're finished, we'll open the door to our bedroom, but we wouldn't then open the door to your bedroom. And if your door is shut you won't know if ours is open or not."

"Then, when I want to use the bathroom, I'll open the door enough to peek inside, and if I see you in there, I'll shut the door quietly and you'll never know," I said.

"That's what I'm trying to avoid," Lolly said.

"I know," John said. "When you're in the bathroom, hang a necktie on the doorknob and everyone will know not to come in."

"That's a stupid idea for at least three reasons I can think of off the top of my head," I said.

"What do you suggest?" John asked.

"I suggest that everyone stay out of the bathroom for the next couple of minutes because I have to pee like a racehorse," I said.

Despite our bathroom dilemma, everyone took a shower without being spied on. Although I thought I heard a door open and close while I was shampooing. Maybe that's why Lolly and Karen were giggling all through dinner. Anyway, I need to sign off for the day. Tomorrow we have to check-out early so we can get on the trail again first thing. We're planning on hiking the Ptarmigan Tunnel Trail and then driving back to St. Mary Campground where we'll camp for two nights.

Your friend,
Matt

From: **Matt Smith**
Subject: **Ptarmigan Tunnel and Iceberg Lake**
Date: **August 25 (Friday)**

Dear Bob and Sue,

Brilliant blue skies greeted us this morning when we woke up. By the intensity of the sunshine, you'd think we'd imagined the rainstorms and forest fires from earlier in the week.

Our big activity for the day was an ambitious seventeen-mile hike. After we checked out of the hotel, we didn't have far to go to get to the trailhead, which was right behind the Swiftcurrent Motor Inn. Because we got there early, we were able to park right next to where the Ptarmigan Tunnel/Iceberg Lake Trails begin.

Looking at a map, you see that the trails form a Y pointing toward the northwest; each arm of the Y leads you to either the tunnel or the lake. Regardless of which destination you're going to, the first three-plus miles of the trail are the same. We hiked to Ptarmigan Tunnel first, which in hindsight was the right decision because it was the more difficult trail. From the trailhead, the tunnel is a six-mile hike with an elevation gain of 2,400 feet, and there wasn't a single tree to shade us for the last mile or so before the tunnel. The sun would have been brutal later in the day in the wide open.

Soon after we started out, we met several hikers who'd stopped and were looking at the trees about a hundred yards below the trail. Without binoculars we could see our first wildlife sighting of the day: a large moose lying in the tall grass. It occurred to us that we were at about the same elevation as the grizzlies we had seen a couple of days ago.

Farther up the trail, about two-thirds of the way to the tunnel, we stopped for a water and snack break. With his binoculars, John saw a mama moose and her calf on an opposing slope about a quarter mile away. It was encouraging to see several moose so early in the hike. I read last week that moose populations in some parts of Montana have been struggling for the past couple of decades and the state isn't sure what's causing the decrease. One possible factor could be warming temperatures. Moose are cold-weather animals, and because they don't have sweat glands, they're at risk of overheating when the temperature is above eighty degrees.

The last section of trail before the tunnel is a series of switchbacks on a steep slope with nothing but bare rock above and below. A couple hundred yards before we got to the tunnel, we spotted a large family of mountain sheep just above us. Most of them were lying down, and we didn't stop long. We figured they'd still be there when we came back through on our return. At that point, all we wanted to do was make it to the top and get through the tunnel.

Ptarmigan Tunnel was built in 1930 to make it easier for hikers and horses to get over the mountain ridge. In 1975, the park service installed iron gates at both ends, which they close in the winter. They used to leave the tunnel open all year, but bears would hibernate inside. Nothing wrong with that, unless you're a hiker who startles a half-comatose bear in the pitch dark as you're walking through.

The views on the other side of the tunnel were spectacular. All the better that the skies were clear. I'm sure if we knew all the landmarks we could have identified the Canadian border from where we stood. Looking over the waist-high stone wall, I could see that we were standing at the top of a sheer cliff with nothing below us for at least two hundred feet. Karen told us she read a story about a woman who, in 1998, was standing at that same stone wall next to her horse when the horse stumbled and fell over the wall. In the process, the horse fell on top of her and caused her to fall over the edge as well. They both died. What a sad and bizarre story. As I stood there, it was hard to imagine how that could have happened.

We didn't linger at the top. Since the weather was so beautiful, we were determined to do the Iceberg Lake leg of the trail. Once we'd hiked back down to the point where we were again surrounded by dense forest, Karen called for a pee break. One of the ways Karen is different now, compared to when we first started traveling to the national parks, is she's more comfortable peeing outdoors. Heck, now she'll go anywhere. A minute after Karen disappeared into the woods, another couple about our age reached the spot on the trail where the three of us were waiting. They'd already hiked to Iceberg Lake and asked us questions about what was ahead for them on the Ptarmigan Tunnel Trail. We must have talked with them for at least ten minutes. I think they were looking for an excuse to stop and rest; they were both grumbling about the steepness of the hike.

When the couple bid us farewell and continued on, Karen reappeared. "Hey, thanks a lot, guys. Did you remember that I was peeing right there in the trees? I was ten feet away from you the whole time you were talking, literally caught with my pants down. How embarrassing."

"I wasn't embarrassed," said John. "Were you?" he asked me.

"No, not at all," I replied.

"I can't believe you," Karen said. "No whippoorwill, no nothing."

"What do you mean 'no whippoorwill?'" Lolly asked.

"It's our secret code," I explained. "Whenever one of us has to pee close to the trail, it's the other person's job to be on the lookout for hikers. If someone is coming, the lookout is supposed to call out 'Whippoorwill, whippoorwill,' so the person peeing can wrap up their business before anyone sees them."

"Yeah, where was my whippoorwill?" Karen asked.

"Technically, the whippoorwill only applies to situations where you can't find a private spot," I said. "You could have easily gone another fifty feet into the trees where no one would have seen you. In my defense, I didn't think this was a whippoorwill situation."

"I had to stay close to the trail," Karen said. "There are wild animals in there."

Once we started hiking again, every time people approached us from the opposite direction, John and I would holler back to Karen, "Whippoorwill!" She never laughed.

The trail to Iceberg Lake took longer than I thought it would. Fortunately, the elevation gain was less than the hike to the tunnel. About a half mile before we reached the lake, we saw another moose through the trees below us. Several hikers who had stopped on the side of the trail to watch him told us that the moose had just crossed in front of them.

Matt on the trail to Iceberg Lake, Glacier National Park

Iceberg Lake was more spectacular than I'd anticipated. The turquoise-colored lake sits at the base of a bowl that I presumed had been carved by glaciers. Only a few patches of ice and snow were on the rocky hillside at the back of the lake. A few shy, small icebergs floated in the water on the far side of the lake, as if they didn't want their picture taken. People crowded the shoreline, which you should expect to see in August. Hiking season is short here, and everyone wants to get their hikes in before the weather turns. Even though it felt like the middle of summer today, snow will be falling in this part of the park in about three or four weeks.

On our hike back to the trailhead, we stopped to talk to a ranger on the trail who had just completed a guided tour with a group of visitors. We each had a couple of questions for her, and finally I said, "I'm sorry that we're keeping you."

"No problem, that's what I'm here for," she said. "Besides, on my way back to the ranger station, I have to clean the backcountry pit toilets, so I'd rather talk to you instead."

After she'd hiked ahead of us, I said to Karen, "I think she liked me. Did you see how interested she was in my questions?"

"Her other choice was to clean the pit toilets, so I think the bar was pretty low, sweetie," Karen replied.

"I didn't say she liked me a lot."

The last several miles of the hike approached "death march" status. By the time we got back to our trucks, John's GPS said we'd hiked 17.1 miles. Not quite a record number of miles in a day for us, but enough that we were spent. None of us were looking forward to driving to St. Mary Campground or setting up camp once we got there.

"Before we drive to the campsite, let's just see if they have any vacancies here at the Swiftcurrent," I said to the group.

"There's no way they have rooms available," Karen said. "I called them a dozen times over the last couple of weeks."

"Well, we have to go to the lobby anyway to use the restrooms, so John and I will check for the heck of it," I said.

When we got to the front desk, the young woman working behind the counter asked me, "Are you here to check in?"

"Yes, the name is Smith," I said.

She looked at the reservations for tonight and couldn't find "Smith," which was a little surprising. "Are you sure you have a reservation?" she asked.

"Oh no, we don't have a reservation. We were hoping you might have a vacancy, though. In fact, we need two rooms," I said.

She typed on her keyboard without saying a word for what seemed like a very long time. The longer she typed, the more encouraged I became. Then she said, "I have two rooms available."

John and I looked at each other in shock. What luck! Lolly and Karen came out of the restroom and wandered over to the front desk where we were standing. "No rooms?" Lolly asked.

"What? Of course we got rooms," John said.

"I had to pull some strings and tell them how important I am, and then two rooms immediately opened up," I said.

The woman behind the front desk leaned over the counter with the registration cards, looked at Lolly and shook her head as if to say, *Don't listen to these goofballs.*

"No, we just got two cancellations right before they walked up. That usually never happens," she said.

"We got our party back!" Karen said.

"Let's meet back here at Nell's for dinner in about an hour," Lolly said. "I need a shower."

Sixty minutes later, all clean and relaxed, the four of us were sitting in a booth by the front window of the restaurant. "I'm so glad we don't have to sleep in a tent tonight," Karen said.

"Oh, me too," Lolly agreed.

"Sleeping in a tent is voluntary," I said. "No one is making you do it."

"You two were both ready to buy teardrop trailers a couple of days ago, and now you're celebrating because you don't have to camp," John said.

"What's your point?" Lolly asked.

"It's not worth going down that path, John," I said.

The waiter took our drink orders and when he came back with them, we were ready to order food. When it was John's turn, he had at least a couple of questions about every item on the menu. After he and the waiter had fully discussed the pros and cons of every entree, John paused and then asked a question about the very first item on the menu. I wasn't about to let this go into round two. "John, pick one!" I said. "My beer is going to be gone before I even have a chance to order."

Both John and the waiter looked at me as if I was terribly rude for wanting to eat while I still had teeth. "I guess I need to make a decision," John said. "I'll have the roast turkey."

"Excellent choice," the waiter said. "They serve it like a Thanksgiving meal. It has sausage stuffing and gravy and cranberry sauce."

I felt like saying, *We know it has cranberry sauce! You've already told him that three times, and then a fourth time after he asked you if it comes with cranberry sauce!*

The waiter looked at me expectantly. "I'll have the spaghetti and meatballs," I said to him. "We did a long hike today and I'm in the mood for comfort food."

He didn't write my order on his pad. He just shook his head at me and said, "No."

"No?"

"No, you're not having the spaghetti and meatballs," he said.

"Are you out?" I asked.

"Oh, we have them. But you want the turkey, trust me."

"OK, turkey it is," I said as I handed him my menu.

When the waiter walked away, John said, "Even after you were rude to him, he was looking out for you."

"I was not rude to *him*, I was rude to *you*. I'm surprised you didn't ask if you could see the turkeys before they kill them, so you could pick out the best one," I said.

"Lolly and Karen didn't think I was taking too long," John said.

"They just hiked seventeen miles and then chugged a glass of wine. They don't even know where they are right now," I said.

"Are you talking about us?" Lolly asked.

"No, we were discussing how long it took John to order his dinner," I said.

"Did we order already?" Karen asked.

I need another beer, I thought.

Here's a tip for you if you ever dine at Nell's: Get the roast turkey. There's no way the spaghetti and meatballs could have been as good. The waiter was indeed looking out for me.

Karen mentioned that she was worried about what might happen when we didn't show up to our campsite. This area of the park doesn't have cell service, so we had no way to call the campground and let them know we weren't coming. "I hope when we get there tomorrow they haven't canceled our entire reservation," she said. "We could end up being homeless." I didn't share Karen's concern; I had a Thanksgiving dinner and a cold beer in front of me and a warm bed to sleep in tonight. I'll worry about tomorrow, tomorrow.

Your friend,
Matt

~.~.~.~.~.~.~

From: **Karen Smith**
Subject: **Going Home**
Date: **August 27 (Sunday)**

Dear Bob and Sue,

When we met John and Lolly at Nell's for breakfast, we were all moving slowly. John seemed to be limping. The sky was overcast and the smoke had returned. Over a second cup of coffee, we decided to pack up and head home. The prospect of setting up camp for one night seemed daunting.

After loading the car and saying our goodbyes to John and Lolly, Matt and I drove to St. Mary Campground to let them know that we wouldn't need our campsite after all. We figured that on a busy Saturday in August, someone else might be able to use it. When we pulled up to the entrance kiosk of the campground, Matt found a place to park and I ran over to speak to the ranger. I apologized to her for not canceling the previous night's reservation and she said, "It's a good thing you didn't show up. We tried calling you yesterday to let you know that you wouldn't be able to tent camp here. Bears have been frequenting the campground, so we're restricting the camping to hard-shell campers only. I guess it all worked out."

"What do you do with all the tent campers who have a reservation?" I asked.

"We have to find other places for them to camp. Last night we probably would have sent you over to Fish Camp," she said.

I thanked her and ran back to the car. "You're not going to believe this," I told Matt. "The ranger said we wouldn't have been able to tent camp here because of bears, and they would have sent us to a campground on the other side of the park."

"Wow," Matt replied. "So, last night, after our seventeen-mile hike, we would've had to drive over Going-to-the-Sun Road to get to the campground and then start setting up camp? We dodged a bullet."

The rangers at Glacier have every reason to be cautious when it comes to bears mixing with campers. Fifty years ago—almost to this very week—two young women were killed by bears in the middle of the night while camping. One of the most bizarre aspects of this tragedy is that the two nineteen-year-old women, who were both working at the park for the summer (but didn't know each other), were camping in different areas and were killed by two different grizzly bears on the same night.

The attacks happened in the early hours of August 13, 1967, and they were the first grizzly-related deaths in the park since it was established in 1910. Julie Helgeson was asleep at the Granite Park Chalet Campground when a grizzly started attacking her and her male companion. Her friend survived the attack, but she died from massive blood loss on a makeshift emergency table at the chalet a few hours later. At almost the same time, a grizzly attacked Michele Koons while she was in her sleeping bag at Trout Lake. Michele's friends were able to escape, but she couldn't unzip her sleeping bag fast enough and the grizzly carried her away.

That night radically changed the bear management practices at Glacier. Before the two women's deaths, grizzly bears in the park relied heavily on human garbage for their food. Granite Park Chalet had so many visitors in 1967 that its incinerator couldn't burn all the trash, so they threw it into a gully. Tourists used to watch the bears come out at night and forage through the garbage. And at Trout Lake, bears used to rummage through garbage cans and harass hikers. It's hard to believe now, but during those years, visitors would leave their trash wherever they wanted. Because of this, bears lost their fear of humans and associated them with food.

Over the next few months following the tragedy, the management at Glacier developed new bear policies and regulations: they installed bear-proof garbage cans, they hung cables from trees so campers could suspend their food, and they set up a backcountry permit process. They also started a bear education program for visitors.

According to an article I read titled *The Parks Where You're Most Likely to be Killed by a Bear*, since 1967 ten additional deaths from bear attacks have occurred in Glacier. In that timeframe, Yellowstone came in second with eight reported bear deaths. Taking into account the millions of people who visit these parks, those seem like pretty low numbers. You're much more likely to die from drowning than you are from a bear attack.

I'm happy we headed home with our bear spray canisters still unused. I hope if I ever need to use one, I can figure out how to get the safety off.

Your friend,
Karen

~.~.~.~.~.~.~.~

From: **Matt Smith**
Subject: **Sperry Chalet**
Date: **September 1 (Friday)**

Dear Bob and Sue,

This afternoon I walked into our family room where Karen was sitting on the couch with her iPad on her lap.

"Hey, did you take the blue tape out of my workshop?" I asked her. "I had four rolls in there and now I can't find any of them." She looked up at me with tears in her eyes.

"Something terrible happened to my blue tape, didn't it?" I asked, trying to lighten the mood.

"I'm not crying about your blue tape," she said. "I just saw a post on Facebook about the Sperry Chalet." She paused for a moment trying to compose herself.

"And?"

"It burned. The Sperry Chalet burned down last night. It's gone."

I sat next to her. "I can't believe that. They've been saying for weeks that the chalet wasn't in danger."

"I know. It happened very quickly. An ember shower from the approaching fire fell on the structure, and the building was engulfed in flames before the firefighters could put it out."

"Was anyone hurt?"

"No, thank goodness."

"Wow. We were just there, only a few miles away."

"It's such a loss," she said, her voice faltering. "For the park, for the employees, for all the people who've been there, and for those of us who never got the chance."

Neither of us said anything for a while.

"We just missed it," she said softly. "We missed it by a week. If only we'd booked our trip for the week before or the month before or the year before. Now we'll never get the chance."

"They'll rebuild it, of course they'll rebuild it. People will donate money and..."

"Maybe. But that'll take years. And they can't rebuild the forest. It will be burned-out for a long, long time. You saw how devastated the area was at Rainbow Bridge. That fire was seven years ago and it looked like it happened last month. We won't live long enough to see it look like a forest again."

"Hold on now, let's not put us in the grave just yet. I think we've got quite a few good years left; decades I'd bet. We've seen the forests in Yellowstone that burned in 1988 coming back, way back. It's been thirty years since those trees burned; we have thirty good years left in us, maybe even forty," I said.

"You think you'll be hiking six miles up to the newly built Sperry Chalet when you're ninety-five?" she asked with a hint of a smile.

"Yes, and you'll be right behind me, complaining that your walker is rubbing against your muffin tops," I said.

She burst out laughing.

"You have to promise me. We're going up there no matter how old we are or how long it takes us to hike up that trail," she said.

"I promise."

So, Bob, I'm giving you fair warning. In forty years when we're in our nineties—and you're over a hundred—you guys are coming with us to Sperry Chalet. You might want to start preparing now by doing extra squats or lunges or whatever it is you do for exercise.

Your friend,
Matt

~.~.~.~.~.~.~

From: **Matt Smith**
Subject: **Greetings from California**
Date: **September 3rd (Sunday)**

Dear Bob and Sue,

Months ago, before the western third of the United States caught fire, we planned a trip to California to do some camping. Yesterday, on our drive to southern Oregon, the smoke was dense, and it was no better this morning when we left our motel and drove toward Redding. Since we'd gotten an early start, we had time today to swing by Lassen Volcanic National Park and do a hike before checking into our hotel in Redding.

The last time we were in Lassen, it was late September, and we saw very few people in the park. Today, being a holiday weekend, the park was jam-packed and the traffic slow. Another reason for the crowds could have been that smoke from the Helena Fire had enveloped both Whiskeytown Lake and Lake Shasta, and Lassen was a refuge from the haze. Despite the smoke-free skies, just as we were finishing our two-hour hike, a thunderstorm rolled in and soaked the area. For a while, hail pelted us so hard I was concerned that it would dent my truck, but it didn't.

Here in Redding, the temperature is over one hundred and the sky is thick with smoke. It's like being in an oven.

Tomorrow morning we're doing a book signing at Whiskeytown National Recreation Area. They were the first national park visitor center to sell *Dear Bob and Sue* in their bookstore.

A few months ago, when we were emailing back and forth with the park store coordinator, Pauline, she mentioned that if we were ever in the area, they'd love to have us do a book signing at the visitor center. She didn't have to ask us twice, we were honored to do it.

During the days leading up to our visit, I kept seeing Whiskeytown's posts on social media talking about the nearby fire and how it was affecting park operations. Due to unhealthy air quality caused by the smoke, all outdoor programs were canceled, and water-based activities were strongly discouraged because of low visibility. I expected the park to cancel our book signing as well, but they didn't. We'll keep our fingers crossed and hope a few people show up tomorrow.

When we finish at Whiskeytown, we'll start driving toward Sequoia National Park. We probably won't make it there by tomorrow night, so we'll stay somewhere along the road. In Sequoia, we'll spend one night at the Wuksachi Lodge and then camp in Kings Canyon National Park.

Ever since we visited Kings Canyon during our trip to all the parks, we've wanted to go back and camp back in the canyon. We have a campsite reservation there for two nights and then another two nights at the Wawona Campground in Yosemite. If all goes well, we'll also camp one night at Crater Lake on our way home. That's the schedule, for now. Karen's been keeping her eye on the fire reports. We may have to change our plans this week if the fire and smoke conditions worsen.

Your friend,
Matt

From: **Karen Smith**
Subject: **Sequoia and Kings Canyon**
Date: **September 10 (Sunday)**

Dear Bob and Sue,

As I was packing my bag to leave the Wuksachi Lodge Wednesday morning, Matt took a load of stuff down to the truck. When he came back, he announced, "We have a stowaway. I saw a mouse in the back of the truck."

I dropped my hair straightener. "Define 'back of the truck.'"

"The way back; in the bed," Matt replied.

"How in the world would a mouse get back there?" I asked. "With your cover, it's completely enclosed."

"Drain holes. He probably squeezed through one of those."

"How did you get him out?" I asked.

"I didn't. He's still in there somewhere."

"Well, that's just great," I said. "When you unload the camping stuff later, I'll make sure to stand twenty feet away."

Then I had an unsettling thought. "Is there any possible way he could get from the bed into the backseat of the truck?" I asked.

"Not unless he can open one of the doors."

"Why did you tell me this anyway?" I asked, as I shoved my flip flops in the pocket of my suitcase. "Now I'm going to be worried that he'll make his way into my sleeping bag."

"Oh, he probably already did. It was cold last night. I bet he had the best night's sleep ever, cozied up in your down bag. You might want to check to see if he left you any gifts."

"Thanks for the tip. That's very helpful."

It was fun to be back in Sequoia—one of my favorite parks—and stay at the Wuksachi again. Tuesday afternoon, when we got to the park, we hiked the Giant Forest Loop Trail: a combination of trails that took us seven miles through a forest of giant trees (hence the name). We parked in the main parking lot on Wolverton Road and then walked to the General Sherman Tree with lots of other people who wanted to see the world's largest tree. As we hiked farther into the park, the crowd thinned, and we wandered through the rest of the forest loop pretty much by ourselves. It was a great way to see the sequoias in their natural setting instead of surrounded by pavement, fences, and hordes of people with their selfie sticks.

Karen dwarfed by a sequoia tree, Sequoia National Park

I wanted to do one more thing Wednesday morning before we left for Kings Canyon: climb Moro Rock, one of the most popular hikes in Sequoia. Although, it's more like a set of stairs than a hike. Moro Rock is a granite dome that rises 6,725 feet above sea level. To get to the top, we had to climb three hundred and fifty steps, which was a three hundred foot elevation gain from the parking lot. We were surprised how few people were there when we started our climb. A hand rail lines the steps the entire way, so I never felt as if I might slip and plunge to my death. When we got to the top, huffing and puffing, the smoke from the fires obscured our view in every direction.

"Well, that was fun," Matt said. "What else do you have planned for us today? Maybe we could find a fire we can walk through so we get the full effect. That's about the only fire experience we haven't had this summer."

We stopped at the Kings Canyon Visitor Center at Grant Grove Village to use the restroom and get hiking information from a ranger. We did neither. Busloads of tourists swarmed the parking lot and formed long lines waiting for the restrooms. It was crazy time. We knew the busses would be going to see the General Grant tree, so we skipped that and headed toward Cedar Grove Village in the canyon.

Many people who visit Kings Canyon National Park never make it to the Kings Canyon section of the park; most don't get farther than the General Grant Grove. There are two sections to the park: Grant Grove is a tiny piece, and from there the main road, Kings Canyon Scenic Byway (Highway 180) continues north, leaves the park, and enters Giant Sequoia National Monument. Turning east, it finally takes you back into the boundaries of Kings Canyon National Park, where it winds down into Kings Canyon. The road dead-ends just past Cedar Grove Village. The bulk of the land within the park boundary is wilderness.

One reason why many visitors don't make it back to the Cedar Grove area is that Highway 180 closes from November

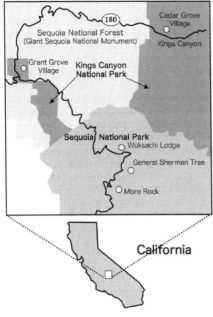

to April, six miles northeast of Grant Grove Village. Once the temperature gets below freezing at night, it's a common occurrence for rocks to fall from the cliffs onto the road. Plus, the thirty-five miles of highway has a lot of twists and turns, and toward the end, some precarious, sheer drop-offs down to the Kings River. It would be a hazardous road with even the slightest bit of ice or snow on top.

Over the last month, Matt and I have been following the tragic story of two foreign exchange students from Thailand whose car plummeted five hundred feet after plowing through a guardrail on this highway. It happened in late July, and even though the wreckage of the smashed car could be seen perched on rocks in the middle of the Kings River, the river was flowing too fast for recovery teams to safely retrieve the car and the bodies inside. On the Friday before we got there, a recovery team finally pulled the car to the riverbank using a helicopter and a winch.

This story has a bizarre twist. A few weeks ago, a Fresno County Sheriff's deputy was watching the local television coverage of an attempted recovery of the car and happened to notice on the video a California license plate in the bushes. The deputy knew that the license plate didn't belong to the Thai students' car, and when he ran the plate, records showed that it belonged to a car that *another* missing couple had been driving. A search of the area led to their white Ford Focus, completely submerged in the river not far from where the students had died. Two couples smashed through the guardrail within fifty feet and ten days of each other, and authorities have no idea what caused either accident.

As Highway 180 enters Kings Canyon, the first glimpse is stunning, with the towering canyon walls rising above both sides of the tree-covered valley. When we were here six years ago, we couldn't believe how incredible it was. It looked like Yosemite Valley, but without all the development and crowds. On that trip we drove through and checked out the campgrounds just off the main road. They were heavily forested and beautiful. I told Matt that this was someplace I could see myself camping, even though at the time I wasn't a camper. Now that we've gotten the hang of camping, I couldn't wait to come back.

It was overcast when we pulled into Sentinel Campground and started looking for our site. I reserved it a couple months ago on Recreation.gov. It's hard to get a sense of what a campsite looks like from the tiny thumbnail photo on the Internet. Using the online map, I chose an available site with the river behind it (we like to sleep with the sound of rushing water) and a bathroom close by (due to the sound of the rushing water).

When we found our site, campers had already set up on either side of us, but there were enough trees to provide some privacy for everyone. Our campsite was long and narrow, and we could get to the river by climbing over a few large, downed trees. As Matt unloaded the truck, it began raining, hard. Just like in Glacier National Park, the last thing we planned for on this trip was rain. All of the extended forecasts we looked at before the trip showed no chance of precipitation this week. We sat in the front seat of the truck and waited for the rain to subside. When it finally let up, we continued unloading, and again, it began raining. Back in the truck. It took a few tries before we got everything unpacked and the tent set up.

We walked to a ranger station adjacent to the campground to ask the ranger about hikes for the following day. He suggested the Mist Falls Trail, which follows the South Fork Canyon four miles to one of the largest waterfalls in Sequoia and Kings Canyon.

I also asked about bear sightings in the campground, so I'd know if I should be worried all night about a bear attack. Several hundred black bears live within the 865,000 acres of Kings Canyon and Sequoia (no grizzlies). He said they hadn't seen a bear in the campground all summer, but if we hiked on the other side of the Kings River on our way back from Mist Falls, we might see one. Then he reminded us to put all our food in the metal bear-proof container at our campsite.

I picked up a pamphlet with a list of suggestions about what you should and shouldn't do if you encounter a bear. Most of them made complete sense, although good luck with the "never run from a bear" tip. We ran like hell in Katmai when the grizzly chased us. I showed Matt the list and said, "Look at this one. It says, 'If a bear does obtain your food, never try to take it back.' Who would ever try to take food from a bear?"

"I might. Depends on what the bear has taken," he replied.

"What foods would you try to get back?"

"Oreos, good whiskey, bacon; those are the ones I can think of off the top of my head."

"What about Cheez-Its?" I asked. "You seem to be protective of them whenever I stick my hand in the box."

"Depends if it's an unopened box. If a bear is going for an unopened box of Cheez-Its, I'm definitely throwing your yogurt, bananas, and granola at him."

"You think that would do it?"

"No, a bear isn't going to eat that stuff, but a man has to try. I'm not willing to give up my place on the food chain just yet."

Before we settled in for the evening, we drove to the nearby general store and bought firewood and snacks. One thing we've learned about camping is that campgrounds don't want you to bring in wood from outside the general region of the park. They stress the importance of buying local to protect the area from non-native insects and diseases that might hitchhike on the firewood you brought from home. Invasive species can lie dormant on firewood for up to two years. A "buy it where you burn it" campaign was started to educate people like us who had no clue that the firewood in the back of our truck could be infested with pests.

Back at camp, Matt started a fire in the fire pit. But being a manly-man, one fire was not enough. He was excited to break out his new tiny portable wood-burning stove, called a Solo Stove. It's about the size of a coffee can, which seemed too small to be useful, but I didn't want to rain on his parade. He set it up on the picnic table on top of a silicone trivet and asked me to help look for twigs about the size of my thumb. When he lit the stove, the fire got going quickly and—I have to admit—it was amazing how much heat and ambiance it added to our dinner.

"Are you sure this thing won't burn the picnic table?" I asked.

"Surprisingly, the bottom doesn't get super-hot," he said. "I could probably set it right on the picnic table without the trivet, but since I have one with me I might as well use it."

We've now tried most of the freeze-dried packaged dinners on the market—at least the ones that don't have beans, lentils or quinoa—and our favorite is still Mountain House Chicken Noodle Casserole. At this point we're ready to start cooking real food when we camp, but with all the fires burning in the west, we didn't know if campfires would be banned in Kings Canyon while we were there. Matt has been spending a lot of time in our back yard practicing recipes in a Dutch oven he bought last month. All my measuring cups and measuring spoons have gone missing, but as long as someone else besides me is cooking dinner, I'm fine with it.

It was a peaceful evening at camp. We sat at the table and played cards by the light of the Solo Stove until it was time to go to bed. And in case you were worried, my breakfast foods were still intact in the morning. Matt didn't have to barter with any bears in the middle of the night.

It was still early when we drove to the end of Highway 180, cleverly named Road's End, where we found the trailhead for Mist Falls. Groups of hikers were strapping on large backpacks; this is the jumping off point for other hikes, several of which connect to the Pacific Crest Trail.

The first two miles of the hike were through forest, and the black flies were horrible. After rummaging around in his pack, Matt realized that he had forgotten his head net, so I gave him mine. As bad as the bugs were, they weren't biting us, and I don't like to wear a head net unless it's absolutely necessary.

After two miles, we turned left and followed the south fork of the Kings River. Unfortunately, the flies also made the turn and continued to harass us. It was a beautiful hike, though, and we saw few people on the way to the falls. The trail started climbing up and over slickrock, and we came to a spot with steep drop-offs where the views of the canyon were incredible.

Karen on the Mist Falls Trail looking into Kings Canyon,
Kings Canyon National Park

When we got to the falls, we left the trail and climbed down onto some rocks so we could have an unobstructed view. The cascading water flowing across the smooth rock was a spectacular sight, but we found out why they named it Mist Falls. So much spray was coming off the falls that we were quickly getting soaked. We hiked farther up the trail for another fifteen minutes, hoping to find some dry boulders to sit on and have lunch, but along that section of the trail there are steep drop-offs to the river and no safe places to sit.

We turned around and ate our sandwiches as we hiked back. Many more people were heading in the direction of the falls by this time, and everyone we passed was waving their arms, trying to swat the bugs away. They all looked at Matt's head net with envy. Many of them made comments to him, most of which were along the lines of how smart he was to bring a head net! One guy said it was "genius." Another guy high-fived him. HELLO! Matt accepted all the compliments, nodding and smiling, never once acknowledging that his wife gave him her head net. I tried to sell it off his head for a hundred dollars, but I guess the bugs weren't bad enough to warrant that kind of money.

When we were halfway back, we took the ranger's advice and crossed a bridge that took us to the trail on the opposite side of the river. For two miles we never saw another person—or a bear. Loud party music greeted us as we got within a quarter mile of our truck, and we came upon a bunch of guys sitting in lawn chairs next to the river with their boom box blaring. I don't remember when I went from being the person partying with the loud music to being the person complaining about it, but it ruined the solitude of our peaceful hike. Matt was muttering under his breath, and I was glad we were still on the other side of the river or he probably would have had a conversation with the guys.

Our last night in the campground was quiet and uneventful. In the morning after we'd packed our gear and loaded the truck, we drove the couple of miles to Zumwalt Meadows and did the short mile-and-a-half loop hike. There's a boardwalk that follows the edge of the meadow, with a viewing platform to stand on. Signs are posted that warn visitors not to hike through the meadow; they don't want humans to disturb the wildlife that lives there. With the river running along one side of the boardwalk, the meadow on the other, and the canyon walls rising up as a backdrop, it was one of the prettiest settings I've seen. The meadow was wet with dew and the heat from the morning sun was causing steam to rise. It was magical. We sat on one of the benches and took it all in.

I was sad to leave Kings Canyon, but the thought of seeing Yosemite again made me anxious to get going. Just outside the park entrance we got back into cell service range, and our emails and text messages from the past two days came through with a chorus of chimes and bings.

As I scrolled through my emails, one caught my eye. It was from Recreation.gov.

"Uh oh," I said.

"What's the matter?" asked Matt.

"There's a fire in Yosemite over by Wawona and they closed the campground because of the heavy smoke. We have no place to stay in Yosemite for the next two nights."

"And it's Friday," Matt said. "I'm sure finding lodging at the last minute on a weekend in September will be a piece of cake."

"Oh man," I groaned. "I can't believe this. Maybe we're a jinx. Everywhere we've been the last couple of months seems to be on fire."

"What do you want to do?"

"I've been looking forward to this for forever. Why don't we stop in Fresno and start calling around for a hotel room? If there's nothing available in the park, then we could try finding a hotel in El Portal."

"Sounds good," he said.

I pulled up the map on my iPad and noticed red X's on Highway 41 into the park. I checked Yosemite's website and found several alerts. A big section of Highway 41 had been closed due to the fire, and they warned that the other entrance, Highway 140, would be experiencing long delays.

"Never mind," I sighed, closing my iPad. "Highway 41 is closed. If we go up to Merced and take 140, we're likely to get stuck in horrible traffic."

Given the fires up and down the West Coast and in central Oregon, we decided our best bet was to start heading for home. It took us a couple of days and we arrived last night. When Matt finished unloading his truck this morning, he came in and said, "You're not going to believe what I found."

"I'm afraid to ask."

"Your mouse friend was still in the back of the truck. There must have been enough potato chip and Cheez-It crumbs back there that he decided to hang with us for the rest of the trip. When I pulled out the camp chairs, he jumped off the tailgate and ran away. The last I saw of him he was scurrying toward the large tree in the corner of our yard."

"No way!"

"Yep. He traveled over a thousand miles from Sequoia to Seattle."

"Now I feel kind of bad for him. He might have had a family in Sequoia."

"I hate to tell you," Matt said, "but I don't think he's going to find his way back."

So, it was kind of an unexpected week. Whiskeytown was smoked in, Yosemite was on fire, and we came home with a live souvenir. How does that saying go, something about the best-laid plans of mice and men often going awry? Now we know what that means.

Your friend,
Karen

~.~.~.~.~.~.~.~

From: **Matt Smith**
Subject: **Going to Alaska**
Date: **September 25 (Monday)**

Dear Bob and Sue,

Karen has Klondike fever. A couple of summers ago, on a rare afternoon when we had nothing planned, we went on a date to downtown Seattle. One of our stops was the Klondike Gold Rush National Historic Park in Pioneer Square. I can guess what you're thinking, *What a romantic idea for a date.* We also went to two bookstores. Hot, huh? The museum is a small national park site, which has a sister site in Skagway, Alaska. According to the park's website, the Seattle unit "preserves the story of the stampede to the Yukon gold fields in the late 1890s and Seattle's crucial role in this event."

We did a thorough visit of the museum in about an hour, including watching a movie about the gold rush. The story of the miners' and prospectors' long journey to the gold fields was fascinating. After arriving in Alaska on ships from Seattle and San Francisco, many of them hiked thirty-three miles on the Chilkoot Trail to Lake Bennett, built boats using timber they'd cut from the surrounding forest, and then sailed five hundred miles to Dawson City on the Yukon River.

"We need to hike the Chilkoot Trail," Karen said as we left the museum.

"Is that a thing? Do people still do that?" I asked.

"They do. I was talking to the ranger about it while you were in the restroom. The trail starts in the U.S. close to the town of Skagway and crosses into Canada. We should go to Alaska and hike it someday—and get the passport stamp," she said.

"Alright, add it to the list," I said.

Coincidentally she's also had it in her mind for the past decade that we should take the car ferry from Seattle to southeastern Alaska along the Inside Passage—just for fun. You can ride it as a passenger only, without a car. The state of Alaska runs the ferry as part of the Alaska Marine Highway (AMH). In Washington, the only port it calls at is Bellingham (an hour and a half north of Seattle), and then it stops at seven other towns as it makes its way up the Inside Passage, before turning back. The round trip takes a week.

These two ideas came crashing together when she learned that the ferry takes the same route that many people took from Seattle to Dyea over a hundred years ago. Today the ferry doesn't call at Dyea, because the town no longer exists, but it stops at Skagway, which is a few miles from the old Dyea townsite.

"It would be like tracing the steps of the gold rushers," she said.

"Then we need to choose a date and get it on the calendar or it will never happen," I suggested.

For the past year, we've both been reading everything we can find about the Klondike Gold Rush. We've tentatively slated our trip to Alaska for next summer. Tentative because the camping permits for sites along the Chilkoot Trail are limited and we won't know until next January if we can get the reservations we want. Today, however, Karen learned some concerning news.

She said to me, "You're not going to believe this. I read that the Alaska State Legislature made a mistake and failed to fully fund the AMH for next year. It said if the funding error isn't fixed, the system will run out of money by next April and the state-managed ferries would stop running."

"The ferries won't shut down. Surely they won't let that happen," I replied.

"You mean as in, the Sperry Chalet won't burn down, surely that won't happen?"

She had a point. "Then let's plan the trip for next April," I suggested.

"The trail will be under ten feet of snow in April."

All day Karen stewed. It felt like Sperry Chalet all over again; the ferry trip was something she'd wanted to do for years but we put if off and now it seemed to be slipping away from her. I got on the Internet and did some poking around. I read the same articles that Karen had about the budget snafu and looked at the AMH website. The website didn't mention possibly shutting down in April, but when I looked at the sailing schedule, April was the last month the schedule was available.

"I think I have a solution," I said to her. "Let's go now."

"What do you mean now?"

"I looked at the AMH reservation system and there are berths still available two weeks from now."

"It's October. There's already snow on the Chilkoot Trail," she replied.

"Let's just do the ferry. If we hike the trail next summer, we'll fly up to Juneau and then take a ferry to Skagway. We don't have to do both parts of the trip at the same time."

"Two weeks? That's crazy. We have too much going on."

"If I can get all of the travel arrangements done, we should do it."

We both got busy with other tasks and didn't discuss the trip for the rest of the day. I'd resolved myself to the fact that it wasn't going to happen. I was in my office when she came in, slapped her open palm on my desk, and said, "I'm in. Let's do it!"

This is why I married her. We're going to Alaska.

Your friend,
Matt

~.~.~.~.~.~.~.~

From: **Matt Smith**
Subject: **Alaska, Ho!**
Date: **October 12 (Thursday)**

Dear Bob and Sue,

Tomorrow is the big day; we shove off for Alaska. I'm ignoring that it will be Friday the 13th and that no one in their right mind would voluntarily take a ferry to Alaska this time of year just for the heck of it. "It'll be an adventure," Karen said to me this morning. That's the attitude we're going with.

We'd hoped to finish the final edits of our new book *Dories, Ho!* before the trip. That's not going to happen. Karen has read the latest draft no fewer than eight times this week and keeps making changes. She said to me this afternoon, "I think a single quote is supposed to go before the period at the end of the sentence when the person we're quoting is quoting someone else."

I stared at her blankly after she said this since I hadn't detected a question.

"We need to search for all single quotes in the manuscript and check to make sure they're correct," she said.

"We're OK," I replied. "I'm sure all of the single quotes are on the correct side of the period."

"And we need to make sure we don't have any en-dashes where we should have em-dashes," she said.

It's a good thing Karen pointed these out to me before the trip; it reminds me to buy extra beer for the ferry ride. I don't think we should try to do the final edits of our new book sober.

Besides scrubbing the book, we intend to do a lot of laying around on the boat and staring out the window at the passing scenery for the next few days. We might even get crazy and do a puzzle.

Our original plan was to take the ferry up to and back from Alaska, making it a round-trip. But if we did that, we wouldn't have much time to get off the boat and see the towns along the way. Instead, we're disembarking in Skagway. The ferry leaves Bellingham at 6:00 pm and is scheduled to arrive in Skagway at 2:45 pm on Monday. We'll spend one night there, which will give us a chance to check out the town and go to the national park visitor center. The next day—Tuesday—we'll take a six-hour ferry from Skagway to Juneau, and then spend a day and a half in Juneau before flying home to Seattle. Karen will have to drive me back to Bellingham next week, so I can get my truck.

Being that we booked the trip so close to the departure date, only four-bed berths were left. We had to pay a little extra, but that's what we get for booking so late. Karen said, "That's fine, it'll give us more room to stretch out."

"Yep, we'll have plenty of space to spread out—and stretch out—in our room. And there's a bonus. Our berth has a porthole," I said. This pleased Karen way more than it should have.

"We'll have a porthole! How exciting! I can't wait!"

It's usually at this stage of our trip preparation that just about anything animates her. I could have said, "Guess what, the door to our room has a doorknob," and she would have replied, "A doorknob! How exciting! I can't wait!"

Your friend,
Matt

~.~.~.~.~.~.~

From: **Matt Smith**
Subject: **Ahoy!**
Date: **October 14 (Saturday)**

Dear Bob and Sue,

I hope this email gets to you soon. There's no Wi-Fi on the *Kennecott*, so I'm trying to catch a sporadic burst of cell service while we're sailing through the Inside Passage just east of Vancouver Island.

Yesterday the weather was perfect in Bellingham when we got to the port. Of course, we arrived about two hours earlier than we needed to, because that's what we do. Once we realized the process for checking into the ferry took all of three minutes, we looked at each other and wondered what we'd do for the next hour and a half. We only had two choices: sit in the terminal and read every brochure in the tourist information rack or go buy snacks.

About six blocks away we found a grocery store. Karen suggested we get some cheese and crackers to go with the bottle of wine she'd squirreled away in her backpack. As we entered the store, I stopped and picked up a basket. "We don't need that for cheese and crackers," Karen said to me. "I don't want to miss the boat because we were messing around in the grocery store."

"The boat doesn't leave for over an hour, and I can see it from the parking lot. I think we have a few minutes to browse."

When we had so many items that we seriously considered getting a shopping cart to carry them, we simultaneously reached the same conclusion. "We gotta go!" I said.

"Yep, I'm going to put this Seahawks umbrella back and you find the shortest checkout line," Karen replied.

We still made it back to port in time to find the long-term parking lot, shove enough dollar bills into the teeny pay slot to cover parking for a week, and get in line to board the ship. We just made it; we were second in line. I'll admit I get anxious when it comes to boarding. If I'm not the first in line or within an arm's reach of the person who is, I'm convinced the plane, train, or boat will leave without me.

"Have you ever truly missed a flight?" Karen asked as I paced back and forth behind the gentleman who was in front of us.

"Yes, as a matter of fact, I've missed connecting flights when my original flight was delayed. More than once I've seen the gate door close as I'm running toward it. I know that feeling, and I don't want to feel it again."

"And amazingly, you lived to tell this story. You know, all that worrying isn't good for you," she said.

Fortunately, we made it onto the ship and had time to settle into our berth before the *Kennecott* pulled away from the dock. Our room was small but had everything we'd need for a comfortable trip: two sets of bunk beds, a sink, and a closet-sized bathroom with a toilet and shower. We even had enough time to take several selfies on the bow of the ship with the sun shining on us and the deckhouse in the background. "This is a nice one," Karen said, holding her phone out for me to see.

"Yep, that's the one CNN will post when they put the pictures of the missing passengers on their website."

"Remember what I just said about worrying?"

Six o'clock, our scheduled departure time, came and went yet our ship hadn't left the dock. We stood outside on the main deck and looked across the bow. A man in a tiny sailboat had dropped anchor about a hundred yards directly in front of the *Kennecott*. Two crewmembers were on the deck below us. I heard one of them say to the other, "What does he think he's doing there? We told him earlier to move, but he's still in the same place." We could see the guy on the deck of his boat fiddling with something and then putting things into the hatch, but he never gave any indication he was going to move. The *Kennecott* shoved off anyway and barely slipped past him. For a moment I thought we'd bump his little boat and toss him into the water. It was a close call.

The *Kennecott* docked at Ketchikan

As the *Kennecott* slowly chugged across Bellingham Bay, we tried to figure out which direction the captain would take us through the maze of islands. Would we go east of Lummi Island or curve around its southern point and go between Orcas Island and Lummi? Other small islands crowded the horizon: Portage, Sinclair, Vendovi, Eliza. Once we were away from the dock and our ship made a couple of steering maneuvers, they all looked the same to me. And I didn't have a clue which direction the boat was sailing. The sun had set and it was getting chilly on deck, so we ducked inside for the night.

From visiting with the purser, we learned that the *Kennecott*—officially named *MV Kennecott*, but we're on a first name basis—was built to accommodate 499 passengers. When we left Bellingham, 118 passengers were aboard.

Back in our room it was time for happy hour. We were allowed to bring alcohol on board, but we could only drink it in our berth. The unused lower bunk had been folded up to make a bench; its upper mate was pushed flat and secured against the wall opposite our beds. Karen moved the grocery bags aside and placed an arrangement of cheese and crackers on the bench between us. We had our own little sendoff party, just the two of us.

Karen drank her wine and I had an IPA. It was comfortable in our room, and she could have easily talked me into calling it a night at seven o'clock. But we've gone down that path before, which leads to us looking at each other wide-awake at 4:00 am wondering what to do for the next few hours. Plus, we were feeling cut off from the rest of the passengers. I finished my beer and said, "Let's go look around. We need to familiarize ourselves with the boat, just in case."

"Just in case it capsizes like in the *Poseidon Adventure* and we have to make our way to the engine room to escape?" she asked.

"Not the engine room! I've been to the engine room, it's underwater! You're all going to die!" I said in my best Gene Hackman impression.

Karen shook her head while putting the leftover cheese in a sandwich bag. "I think it's time to retire the whole 'I've been to the engine room' thing, don't you?"

"You brought it up."

We wandered the halls and read every informational sign on the boat. A couple of areas were clearly labeled "Muster Station." There was station A and station B. "Muster Station A is ours," Karen said to me.

"I don't understand anything you just said," I replied.

"It's where we're supposed to go in case of an emergency."

"You're making that up. It's where people muster. See, there's a picture of a family standing together. They're mustering."

"I'm not making it up. I read about it on the back of the door in our berth. We're supposed to go to station A, got it?"

"If there's an emergency, I'm going straight to the nearest lifeboat," I told her. "You can muster with all of the families at station A, then meet me on shore—if you don't go down with the ship."

We also walked the length of each deck—or at least the areas we could access. The first deck is where the vehicles are stowed. The doors to the car deck are locked except for a couple of times each day, when an announcement over the loudspeaker lets passengers know they can access their vehicles. This is when they're allowed to go down and let their pets out to roam around the deck and do their business. Pets aren't allowed above the car deck.

The second deck is where our stateroom is and the purser's office. Above that is the boat deck with a food court, dining room, and forward observation lounge. On the fourth deck are more staterooms and above that is a solarium. The solarium is covered and heated, which might not seem like a big deal, but it is for those who'd planned to camp on the ship.

There were two solariums in fact, one of each side of the ship. Karen and I climbed the stairs, expecting to find them both empty. We were surprised to see a tent in both areas. In one of the tents, I could see that whoever was in there had taken a plastic chaise lounge, placed it inside their tent, and covered themselves with a blanket. That'll be their home until they get to their destination.

The solariums looked dark and dismal; the only light came from a couple of bare yellow lightbulbs. Not the party atmosphere the purser had told us that it typically is during the summer. In the high-season, when the ship is near capacity, real estate in the solarium is at a premium. It's filled wall-to-wall with campers; a small tent city on the top deck. People play guitars, party, and have a grand ol' time. "Do you still want to camp on a ferry?" I asked Karen. She'd read about the camping on deck while researching the trip and suggested maybe we try it instead of getting a berth.

"I might if more people were up here and it was during the summer. I think it would be kinda creepy up here now with only one other tent."

Despite the heat, it was a little chilly in the solariums, so I can only imagine how cold it would be on the other ships in the Alaska Marine Highway fleet whose solariums are uncovered or three-sided. Not only would it be cold, but the wind would also be relentlessly trying to toss your tent into the ocean. The purser said to us, "If you're thinking about camping on deck in the future, make sure you bring lots of duct tape. You have to tape your tent to the deck or it will blow away. We've had tents blow off a ship before. Some people bring weights to hold down the corners of their tent, but you should still tape it down."

Our tour of the ship had taken enough time that we didn't feel too lame for going back to our room and getting ready for bed. I offered to take the top bunk, but Karen insisted. I'd like to think she was doing this out of the kindness of her heart, but more likely she was trying to avoid me stepping on her in the middle of the night when I had to use the restroom. The thought of having a foot come down on her face at 2:00 am would have kept her up all night, so I slept on the bottom bunk.

It was one of the best nights of sleep I've had in a long time. My lower bunk was warm and cozy. Between the sound and vibration of the engines and the slight rocking of the ship in the waves, I zonked. I never heard a peep out of Karen in the upper bunk either. Although, I saw the light from her iPad reflecting off the ceiling once in the middle of the night. I think she was trying to see if she could get cell service; she doesn't like being out of reach of our kids for more than an hour.

It was a restful night, but the gentle rocking that lulled us to sleep became less gentle as the night wore on. We woke up to a stormy sea. Right now I'm looking out the front windows of the observation lounge at large waves ahead of us. Every few minutes, water comes up over the bow of the ship and splashes the windows. That's a long way for water to be splashing! I think I'll go put on my lifejacket and hang out at Muster Station A until the sea calms down. Tomorrow morning we arrive at Ketchikan. I'll send you another update then.

Your friend,
Matt

From: **Matt Smith**
Subject: **Made it to Ketchikan**
Date: **October 15 (Sunday)**

Dear Bob and Sue,

Yesterday was a rough day at sea yet we made it to Ketchikan this morning at our scheduled time of 7:00 am. We only have four hours here and then we shove off again. Our next stop will be tonight at Wrangell.

Since we'd gone to bed so early Friday night, we were up at the crack of dawn Saturday morning, way before the cafeteria opened. We read and otherwise killed time in our room. When the cafeteria finally opened, we were the first passengers through the doors. The food choices were simple, but they served a hot breakfast, which was great. Karen got a veggie omelet and I ordered pancakes and bacon, even though she tried to convince me not to eat like a caveman. "The sea is angry today," I told her. "I need to eat something that will stay down." I was joking, of course, though later in the day I'd find out how true those words were.

Cookie handed us our breakfast plates through the window to the kitchen where we'd shouted our orders five minutes earlier. We paid and went to the dining room to find a place to sit. Karen stood next to an open booth and waited for me to consider all of our seating options. She knows it's easier to let my OC spin for a few minutes while I choose the table, rather than to have to get up and move a couple of times.

I walked through the dining room eyeing the booths. "They're all the same," she called out from across the room; she's never understood why it takes me so long to choose a place to sit in an empty restaurant. Neither have I.

"Nope, this is the one," I replied, and waved her over.

"What's so special about this booth?" she asked as she slid in.

"It's the mammal table," I replied.

She looked down and laughed. The tables in the dining room had laminated tops with illustrations and descriptions of animals. Each table's animals had a theme: birds, crustaceans, mammals, etc.

"I can't eat breakfast looking at crustaceans," I said.

"Of course you can't," she said, nodding her head in agreement.

For the next twenty minutes, we ate and talked about each of the mammals represented on the table: moose, bear (two kinds), wolverine, otter, Dall sheep. During our mammal talk, I became distracted trying to coax nearly-solid pancake syrup out of its small plastic container. "Karen, I hate to interrupt your fascinating story about caribou migration patterns, but this is the last time I can do this."

The mammal table in the dining room on the *Kennecott*

"What, have a stupid conversation about wildlife during breakfast?"

"No, this," I said holding the syrup container upside down. The syrup was solid. "My pancakes will be ice cold by the time the syrup comes out."

"You could try putting something healthier on your pancakes, like strawberry jam," she suggested.

"Strawberry jam on pancakes? Did this ship just cross into a new dimension or something?" I asked. "Who puts strawberry jam on their pancakes?"

"Or fresh fruit. I saw they had fruit cups," she continued. "That would be even healthier than jam."

"Who are you and what have you done with my wife?"

She shrugged. "Worse things could happen to you than not getting to eat pancakes this morning."

The syrup never came out. I ate the dry pancakes anyway. Now I know why we put syrup on them.

After breakfast, we went to the observation lounge and claimed a prime table to park ourselves for the day. From where we sat, we had a 180-degree view of the open water in front of us. It was cloudy and rainy and the dark green shorelines in the distance didn't change much throughout the day.

Karen and I agreed that we'd do one last read-through of the *Dories, Ho!* manuscript, make our final edits, and be done. We figured that the next couple of days would be a perfect time to do this as there wasn't much else to occupy our time on the boat. I held the table while Karen went back to our room and got both of our laptops. We sat across from each other; Karen would read her copy on her laptop, stopping when she had a question or suggested edit and we'd discuss each one.

As tedious as it was to do the final scrubbing of the manuscript, I enjoyed the process because it gave us a chance to work together closely. We settled into our routine and made good progress. Even though it looked like almost all 118 passengers were with us in the observation lounge, it didn't feel crowded. It was too wet and cold to go outside onto the deck of the boat, and we didn't feel like we were missing anything by sitting inside.

Having never taken a ferry through the Inside Passage before, I didn't know what to expect, but I was still surprised at how much the ship was rocking back and forth. At about 10:00 am the captain came onto the public-address speakers and said that the winds were blowing at forty-plus knots and we'd be entering open water in about thirty minutes. I didn't understand the significance of this information until he closed by saying, "If you're prone to seasickness, now would be a good time to take Dramamine."

Karen and I looked at each other and said at the same time, "What's a knot?"

Now, we're not complete idiots, we know the concept of a knot, but we didn't know how many miles to a knot or vice versa. We later learned that the wind was blowing at a speed of forty-five to fifty miles per hour and the open water he was referring to was Queen Charlotte Sound.

As soon as we got into the sound and away from the protection of Vancouver Island to the west, the ship began to buck noticeably harder. Being a manly man, I hadn't taken Dramamine when the captain suggested doing so. Karen asked, "Are you sure you don't want to take any seasickness medicine? Because that stuff can take thirty minutes or more to start working."

I was reading a document on my laptop when she asked me that question and I was about to answer, "No, I'm fine," when a wave of nausea came over me. I knew enough to quickly look up and find the horizon through the windows at the front of the ship. In an instant, I went green.

I shut my laptop and breathed deeply through my mouth. "I'm going to go back to the room to lie down." I stood up and left without waiting for Karen to acknowledge what I'd said.

I took a Dramamine and sat on the edge of my bunk for ten or fifteen tense minutes. Mercifully, I began feeling better. I never lost it, but it was close. Back at the observation lounge, Karen was working, unaffected by the occasional waves crashing over the bow of the ship.

"Are you OK?" I asked her.

"Yeah, I never get seasick," she said. "But I still don't think we have these single quotes in the right spot. See here," she said as she turned her laptop toward me.

"Sweetie, I *cannot* read anything right now or I might lose it all over your single quotes. We'll have to discuss it later."

As I sat there looking out over the water, I wondered what it must have been like for the thousands of people who took boats from Seattle to Skagway in 1898 during the Klondike Gold Rush. Surely some of those voyages experienced similar storms. Imagine a smaller boat, crammed with people and animals, tossing about in the rough seas. I don't know if they even had seasickness medicine back then. Some of the stories I've read describe horrific conditions where people were sick for a good part of the journey. Nope, not me. I wouldn't have made it to the gold fields back then. I'd have gotten off the boat at the first port of call along the way and walked back home to Seattle.

The medicine I'd taken made me feel much better and also sleepy. It wasn't yet noon and I already needed a nap. "I'm going back to the room to rest for a little bit," I said to Karen.

"I'll go with you," she said as she stretched her arms over her head and yawned.

"Why are you so tired? You didn't take Dramamine."

"Yeah, but the rain and clouds and the rocking boat are making me drowsy. And I'm on vacation."

The walk back to our room was tricky. Had I taken a video of it you'd think we were drunk. Even in the wide hallways, we'd both body slam the right wall, try to correct our path, and then body slam the left wall. I had to time my steps to keep from falling into one of the open doorways along the hall. The storm was pitching the ship side-to-side. It felt like we were in a bouncy-house.

Once I laid down in my bunk, the rocking motion didn't bother me as much. The waves lulled me to sleep quickly, and I slept for a solid couple of hours.

When we woke up from our naps, the sea had calmed considerably. I think it had more to do with the fact that we were sailing once again through the Inside Passage, than an improvement of the weather. It was calm enough for us to get back to editing the manuscript without me turning green again.

Dinner in the cafeteria was burgers and fries. We sat at the mammal table again. Karen said to me over her salmon burger, "We're going to sit at this same table for every meal, aren't we?"

"Yep," I replied. Gazing around the dining room, I noticed that most of the other passengers were sitting at the same tables they'd sat at when we were there for breakfast. "You see, you have to stake out your spot early in the trip. If I'd let you choose the table this morning, we'd be looking at crustaceans at every meal."

"I'm so lucky I married you," she said. She didn't sound convincing.

It was another early-to-bed evening. We would have called it a night at 7:00 pm had there not been a movie scheduled at that time about the history of Ketchikan. "Are you going to join me?" Karen asked as she tilted her head toward the movie lounge.

"No, I did a book report about Ketchikan in the sixth grade. I think I'll just stay out here in the observation lounge."

"You're going to stare out the window at the darkness, aren't you?"

"Yep. I'm on vacation too," I replied.

Your friend,
Matt

From: **Matt Smith**
Subject: **Still Northward Bound**
Date: **October 16 (Monday)**

Dear Bob and Sue,

It's 6:00 am and we just arrived in Juneau where it's dark and rainy. I didn't realize that the ferry dock is a few miles north of downtown Juneau at Auke Bay. There's really nothing to see here at the dock, and we're shoving off again in ninety minutes, so we're staying on board while in port.

When I sent you the email yesterday, we'd just arrived at Ketchikan. It felt good to get off the boat and stretch our legs there. The rain had mostly stopped, although we got caught in a brief shower or two as we walked along the road.

A few blocks from the ferry terminal, we came upon a cluster of totem poles. They looked to be new, as in a decade or two old: The carving was clean and the paint fresh. I'd read that Ketchikan has one of—if not the—largest collection of totem poles in the world. We'd love to come back in the future and spend time visiting the totem sites and photographing them. The boat was leaving again at 11:00 am, so we didn't venture far from the terminal.

Totem in Ketchikan

Yesterday the seas were calmer than on Saturday. The *Kennecott* sailed slowly through a maze of islands as it snaked its way to Wrangell (5:50 pm) and then on to Petersburg (9:15 pm).

Karen and I finished our edits of *Dories, Ho!*, so we could officially relax and veg out on the scenery. The landscape—trees, mountains and rocky shoreline—was beautiful, what we could see of it. The sky was overcast, and the clouds hid whatever was above 1,000 feet in elevation.

Many times during the day, the ferry sailed close to the coast. Now and then we'd see a house built amongst the trees, with stairs leading down to a small pier jutting out into the water. "Wouldn't you love to have a cabin in the woods like that?" Karen asked.

"I think it would be nice for a day or two, but you'd be completely on your own," I replied. "You might see a ferry each day, and maybe a freight ship or barge, but other than that, you wouldn't have much contact with the rest of the world."

"I'd be OK with that for a couple of weeks at a time," Karen said.

"Really? You think you could do without your phone and iPad being connected to the Internet for two weeks? Because you seem to get a little edgy after two hours at sea without a connection."

"We'd have to get a satellite dish. And lots of bear spray."

"I think the bear spray they use up here is the kind that has big fat forty-five caliber bullets," I said. Karen shuddered.

Seeing those houses made me wonder how much of Alaska is privately owned. I did a quick search and learned that other than Native land holdings, which equals about eleven percent, only about one percent is privately owned. The rest is owned by the federal government or the state. Most of the scenery we were seeing was public land.

That's my report for yesterday (Sunday). Today we'll make it to Skagway after a brief stop in Haines.

Your friend,
Matt

From: **Matt Smith**
Subject: **Breakfast in Skagway**
Date: **October 17 (Tuesday)**

Dear Bob and Sue,

Good morning from Skagway! It's a ghost town here, as we expected it would be. Once the last cruise ship makes its final stop for the season, most of the locals bug out of here for the winter. I don't blame them; right now I can see flurries outside the window of our room at the bed and breakfast.

I'll back up and start my update from where I left off the last email; it was yesterday (Monday) and we were sitting at the ferry dock at Auke Bay in Juneau. The *Kennecott* was only docked for a couple of hours, and by 8:00 am we were underway again sailing north toward Haines.

Sitting in the observation lounge after breakfast, I noticed a dozen or so new passengers had come aboard. By their dress, several of them looked as if they were going to Haines for business. It was then I realized it was Monday morning. *What a fantastic commute,* I thought.

The rain had stopped and there was little wind, but the clouds remained. We stepped outside onto the observation deck to get a clear view of the passing scenery. It was chilly yet comfortable enough to stay outside for ten minutes or so at a time.

I went back to our stateroom to do some packing; we had to check out by mid-afternoon and I wanted to be ready to go ashore when we reached Skagway. On my way to the room I stopped outside the purser's office. On the wall across the hall was a flat screen TV monitor, displaying a large a map of the ship's location, speed, and directional heading. I studied it and then asked the purser, who was sitting at his desk, "When will we be at the spot where the *Princess Sophia* went down?"

He came out of his office and looked at the map with me. "We're definitely in Lynn Canal now, although I don't think we're at the site of the sinking yet. Vanderbilt Reef is where she went down. I don't see it on the map here, but we're very close." I went back to the observation deck and stood on the west side of the ship hoping to catch a glimpse of the reef. At low tide it's only a few feet out of the water, but there's a fixed beacon attached to it, so I figured I should be able to pick it out.

Karen had found the story about the sinking when she was doing research for this trip. Many boats have sunk in the Inside Passage, but none of them were on the scale of the disaster that struck the *Princess Sophia*.

The ship left Skagway on October 23, 1918 (almost ninety-nine years ago to the day) at 10:00 pm, three hours later than scheduled. It had been snowing most of that day, and by the time the *Princess Sophia* was an hour into her voyage the winds were gusting up to fifty miles per hour. A few hours later, at 2:10 am, in the midst of a raging snowstorm, the *Princess Sophia* ran aground on Vanderbilt Reef in Lynn Canal about forty-five miles north of Juneau. The reef was marked by a buoy, but the buoy wasn't lit, so seeing it at night would have been difficult if not impossible. It's likely that the storm blew the ship off course, and coupled with the low visibility, the captain wasn't able to keep the ship away from the reef.

Princess Sophia, equipped with wireless communication equipment, sent a distress call a mere five minutes after the grounding. At that point, the ship was resting on the reef, high out of the water and still had heat and electricity. For the time being, the passengers were safe and unharmed.

Several large ships sailed to her rescue, and one report said that as many as fifteen fishing vessels were circling the *Princess Sophia* ready to help. Despite several attempts the next day (October 24), the passengers and crew were still not evacuated. The captain felt the sea was too rough to try a transfer of passengers and crew to another ship and decided to wait in hopes that soon the conditions would be safe enough.

By October 25, the weather had worsened. Late that afternoon, even the largest ships attempting to aid the *Princess Sophia* abandoned their efforts so they could seek cover from the storm. The snow was so heavy that at one point, the *Cedar*, a lighthouse tender large enough to take on board all of *Princess Sophia's* passengers and crew, was essentially navigating blind as it tried to reach the *Princess Sophia*. The captain of the *Cedar* quickly became concerned that they might run aground as well, or worse, collide with the *Princess Sophia* in the whiteout. The *Cedar* turned around and sought shelter in the lee of a nearby island. That was around 2:00 pm on the afternoon of October 25.

Sometime in the next few hours, the *Princess Sophia* was pushed off the reef by the storm and quickly sank.

The *Cedar* returned to the reef at 8:30 am the next day, October 26. Only the foremast of the *Princess Sophia* was above water. No one survived; all 343 persons aboard perished. Most of the watches recovered from the wreckage, some still attached to the bodies of the victims, read 5:50 pm, the presumed time the ship went down.

Dubbed "the *Titanic* of the West Coast," the sinking of the *Princess Sophia* is the worse maritime accident in the history of Alaska and British Columbia in terms of loss of life. It's one thing to read about an incident like this in a history book, but to stand on the deck of a ship and look out over the spot where it happened makes it seem very real. As if it could have happened yesterday.

On a less somber note, I'm happy to report that we had an uneventful remainder of our voyage through Lynn Canal up to Haines. Eerily though, the wind picked up quite a bit as we approached Haines. It was coming out of the north just as it had in October 1918. For a short time on our approach to Haines, it seemed the *Kennecott's* engines were churning away, yet we made almost no progress against the stiff wind.

Our ship sat at port in Haines for an hour and a half. We were there long enough that I watched two over-sized forklifts unload an entire barge filled with shipping containers. Nearly everything that arrives or leaves the towns in southeastern Alaska does so by boat. Many of the towns don't have roads connecting them to anywhere else. Even the roads in Juneau, the state capital, don't connect to the outside world.

Haines and Skagway are two exceptions; they both have roads that lead out of town and connect with major highways. As the crow flies, there's less than twenty miles separating the two towns. The car ferry takes an hour and a half to travel between them, but the overland route is a 350-mile drive that requires crossing the US/Canadian border twice. For our visit to Skagway, we'd originally considered staying in Haines when we had difficulty finding a place to stay in town, and then taking the ferry back and forth between them. Now that we're here, we're glad we persevered and found a bed and breakfast in town. It wouldn't have been practical to spend ninety minutes each way on a ferry for such a short visit to Skagway.

When we arrived yesterday at 3:00 pm, we dragged our pull-behind suitcases through town and across the wooden boardwalks to find Mile Zero, our home for the night. After checking in, we went right back out, hoping to find a ranger at the Klondike Gold Rush Visitor Center before they closed the office for the day.

Several streets run northeast-by-southwest through town, but the majority of the shops and restaurants are clustered together along one of them: Broadway. The center of town lies within a National Historic District, and the NPS works with private land owners as well as the city, state, and the federal government to preserve the 1890s look and feel of the buildings within the district.

Skagway's deserted Broadway Street
on a cold, drizzly day in October

About a thousand people live in Skagway, which is far fewer than in the year 1900 when it became the first city to incorporate in the Alaska Territory. By the look of the deserted sidewalks and closed businesses, we'd guess that most of those thousand residents were probably off in Hawaii or some other warm place.

Karen had called the visitor center last week to find out if it's open in the off-season. She spoke with a ranger who said the office is open all year, but most of the sites are closed. The ranger told Karen, "If you don't find a ranger in the museum, walk up the stairs to the second floor and come into our offices." That's exactly what we did when we got to the visitor center, which is located in the historic White Pass and Yukon Route depot. We talked at length with a ranger who was happy to give us a ton of helpful information about hiking the Chilkoot Trail and how to obtain the necessary permits for the campsites. She told us that the ideal way to hike the Chilkoot is to camp four nights along the trail and on the fifth day when we reach Lake Bennett, take the White Pass Railroad train back to Skagway. Hopefully, that's exactly the plan we'll follow next summer—if we can secure the permits.

"Are you in town for the night?" the ranger asked.

"Yeah, just one night though. We're taking the ferry back to Juneau tomorrow," Karen said.

"Do you know where you're going for dinner?" the ranger asked in a concerned tone.

"We thought about going to the brewery," Karen said.

"Good, so you know about Skagway Brewing," the ranger said, obviously relieved. "That may be the only place in town that's open this time of the year. I didn't want you to wander around in a panic thinking that there was no place to eat."

Of course, we got to the brewery right when it opened. Karen insisted we walk another couple of loops around the block before going in. She hates it when we get to a bar right before they're ready to open and I rattle the front doors while they're still locked. I've been forbidden to peer inside the windows and yell, "Hey, you guys open or what?" Fortunately for Karen, the doors were unlocked when we got there and the restaurant was open for business. The food was great, beer was great, service was great. We'll definitely eat there again when we come back to hike the Chilkoot.

Gotta go catch the six-hour ferry to Juneau; I'll write again tomorrow.

Your friend,
Matt

From: **Matt Smith**
Subject: **Back in Juneau**
Date: **October 18 (Wednesday)**

Dear Bob and Sue,

Happy Alaska Day! We had no idea until this morning that we'd be in the state capital for Alaska Day. To tell the truth, we didn't know until this morning that there was such a thing as Alaska Day. Whoo, whoo!

When I went down to the lobby of the hotel this morning to get coffee, I asked the manager at the front desk, "Does the city do a big celebration for Alaska Day?"

"The what?" he replied. I began to think Karen was playing a trick on me. She'd said she learned about it on the Internet this morning.

"Uh, Alaska Day? Someone told me that today is the hundred and fiftieth anniversary of Alaska becoming part of the United States." I wanted to add, "Help me out here, does any of this ring a bell?"

"Yeah, not sure," he replied.

Karen's dicking with me, I thought as I rode the elevator back up to our floor.

"Are you sure about the whole Alaska Day thing?" I asked as I handed her a cup of coffee.

"Uh, yeah, I saw it on CNN," she replied. A minute later she continued, "It says right here on the Alaska Day Festival website, 'Alaska Day Festival annually commemorates the Transfer of Russian claim of Alaska to the United States of America at Sitka on October 18, 1867.' Is today October 18th?" she asked.

"Yep, all day," I replied.

"Well then, this is a big deal. It's the one hundred and fiftieth anniversary of Alaska becoming part of the United States. 2017 would be a hundred and fifty years wouldn't it?" she asked, and then started counting on her fingers.

I'm not sure what she was counting, but it took her longer than I expected. Common courtesy would suggest that counting on your fingers while in the middle of a conversation is kind of like calling a time out. You're holding your place in the conversation until you have deciphered this critical piece of information after which you rejoin the conversation where you left off. But the other person is only obliged to wait for so long, and then they're free to start talking again or walk away.

"Are you counting to a hundred and fifty on your fingers?" I asked.

"No! I'm trying to figure out if this is really the one hundred and fiftieth anniversary."

"Yeah, 1867 to 2017, that's a hundred and fifty years."

"Well then, we need to get ready for a party," Karen said with renewed energy. I love that she's always ready to get ready for a party.

"The guy at the front desk didn't seem to know what Alaska Day was," I said. "I'm not sure it's a big deal here."

"It has to be a big deal here, Juneau is the state capital," Karen replied. "I hope there's a parade."

"You might want to control your expectations. Isn't it odd that we didn't see any banners or signs about Alaska Day on our way here from the ferry terminal last night? And we've been in the state for almost a week, but this is the first we've heard of it?"

"If it's the hundred and fiftieth anniversary, then it's a big deal." This time when she started counting on her fingers, her lips were moving. That's when I left to take a shower.

I'll email you another update tomorrow, that is if we aren't still out partying. Happy Alaska Day!

Your friend,
Matt

From: **Matt Smith**
Subject: **Last Day in Alaska**
Date: **October 19 (Thursday)**

Dear Bob and Sue,

Apparently, Alaska Day isn't a big deal in Juneau. We enjoyed our time here, but the town was pretty quiet. Because of the rain, we decided not to visit the Mendenhall Glacier, which is supposed to be spectacular. We'll save that for another trip, maybe next year on our way to or from Skagway.

A few short blocks away from our hotel was a coffeehouse where we had a leisurely breakfast. "What's the plan for the day?" I asked Karen. I always need to know what the plan is, otherwise I'm ready to take a nap after breakfast.

"I wanted to visit the Sealaska Heritage Institute that we walked past on the way here, but the sign out front said it's closed for the winter. I'd still like to go inside the lobby and look at their carved cedar panels.

"That sounds like ten minutes of activity," I said.

"Since it's raining, I thought we might also go to the Alaska State Museum. It's a five-minute walk from here," Karen said.

I wasn't super-excited about spending the morning in a museum, but that sounded better than taking a taxi to the glacier, standing in the rain looking at it for five minutes, and then taking the taxi back to our hotel.

The Alaska State Museum was a pleasant surprise. The layout of the exhibits and the items on display were impressive; there were extraordinary pieces of historic native art, which we particularly enjoy. Normally I try to move Karen along through museums as quickly as I can, but several times I looked up to see Karen staring at me with an, *Are you ready to move on now?* expression on her face. We both stood for a long time looking at the items on display that were recovered from the *Princess Sophia*; seeing them made the tragic story seem more real.

The museum shop had several books about the Klondike Gold Rush that I had to buy. I want to do as much reading about it as I can before we hike the Chilkoot Trail next year. Museum bookstores usually have books that are hard to find elsewhere. The young man who checked us out was chatty. We were the only ones in the store, and by the looks of the sparse crowd in the museum, we might be his only customers for a while. "Do you have big plans for the day?" he asked.

When I get this question from a stranger, I'm inclined to say, "Yep, I'm on my way to get a colonoscopy, and by the way, where's your bathroom?" but Karen has convinced me that this is rude, so I let her respond.

"Not sure, we just have one day here in town. We thought we'd check out some of the stores downtown and then have dinner at the Red Door Saloon tonight," Karen replied.

"I think you mean the Red Dog Saloon," he replied.

"Yes, that's right. The Red Door Saloon is in Seattle."

"Something you might want to check out before you leave is the Alaska State Archives upstairs."

Karen looked at me after he said this, and I furrowed my brow. "What's in the archives?" she asked.

"I believe they have a few special displays today because it's Alaska Day. You should check it out. It's open to the public," he said.

As we walked out of the store, Karen said, "We should take a look upstairs. We have all day, and it's only eleven."

I was fine with taking a spin through the archives, hoping they might have some interesting Klondike Gold Rush documents on display.

The archive space was spotless and looked like a library that had rarely been used; we were the only people up there besides the workers. A couple of interesting documents were on display, but they weren't about the Klondike. I figured we'd be there for a total of four minutes as I drifted closer to the exit in hopes Karen would follow. She shot me a look that said, *Cool your jets, I want to look around.*

With a few minutes to kill, I went up to the woman who was sitting at what looked like the reception desk. "Do you have any documents on display related to the Klondike Gold Rush?" I asked.

"No, I don't think so," she said. "But you can do a search of the archives, and if you find something you'd like to look at, we could bring it out for you."

At one of the computer terminals in the center of the room, she showed me how to search the archives. "See this number here," she said pointing to the screen. "That's the number of the box and file where this item is stored. If you write down the box numbers of the items you want to look at and take them to that area in the back, they can pull those boxes for you.

By this time Karen was looking at me from across the room wondering what I was up to. I searched the archives for the term "Klondike" and a long list of items came up—too many for me to look through. I then searched "Klondike diary," which still returned a long list, but I started reading the descriptions of the first few entries. I wrote down the numbers of five boxes on a slip of paper and went to the back room.

Karen came over and asked, "What are you doing?"

"I'm doing research. We're at the state archives, that's what you do here, research stuff," I replied, feigning an annoyed attitude.

Karen followed me to the back. Three workers sat silently in front of computer terminals at a long desk. I stood in front of the woman in the middle and awkwardly asked, "If I want to see a few boxes of archives, how would I do that?" Karen still had a quizzical look on her face.

I was fully prepared for her to say, "I'm sorry, sir, you must be confused or a complete idiot. We don't let people walk in off the street and look at whatever they want. Certainly not someone who hasn't shaved in a week and is wearing a *Smokey, Established 1944* t-shirt." I glanced at the other two workers to see if they were reaching for the silent alarm button as I stood there holding out my slip of paper.

The woman gave me a confused look and replied, "Um, I'm not sure, maybe you should talk with Becky."

I knew it, I thought. I was sure Becky was going to introduce me to the security staff. I almost turned to Karen and shouted, "Go! Save yourself!" but I played it cool.

I walked over to Becky and repeated my question. Becky hesitated as she finished whatever she was doing on her computer, and then looked up at me. She took the slip of paper and said, "I can get those for you. If you want to have a seat at one of those tables over there, I'll bring them out. I just need you to fill out this form."

The form asked for some basic information: name, address, phone number, etc. I filled it out and handed it back to her. She glanced at the form and set it aside. Becky then disappeared into the archive storage area while Karen and I found a table, took off our jackets, and sat down.

"What are we doing?" Karen asked.

"We're looking at Klondike archives. I've no idea what's in the boxes, but I thought it would be fun to find out."

"Yeah, can't hurt to try. It beats walking around town in the rain."

A few minutes later, Becky emerged from the back pushing a rolling cart with five boxes on top. I reached for the boxes and she said, "Wait. You can only take one box at a time. I'll keep the others by my desk while you look at the first one."

I grabbed the nearest box, and while Becky carefully wrote down the number, I shot Karen a look of surprise. *Can you believe they're letting us look at their stuff?*

We opened the first box and inside were four over-sized file folders, each with a reference number written on its tab. I pulled the first folder out and set it on the desk. When I opened it, a thick stack of legal-size paper was on top. It looked like a transcript of a diary. Carefully, I paged through the document and read a couple of the entries.

"This is a transcript of someone's diary while they were on their way to Dawson in 1898!" Karen said. "How cool is that?"

She gently picked up the document to take a closer look. Beneath the transcript was another folder, a plastic one. "What do you think that is?" I asked. Inside the see-through folder was an item was wrapped in white tissue paper.

I opened the folder, pulled out the item and unwrapped it. "It's the diary." We both looked at each other incredulously. I opened the leather-bound book and flipped through the first couple of pages. The handwritten entries matched the typed transcript. Then I set it down and went back to where Becky was sitting.

"Is it OK if we touch the archives?" I asked.

"Yeah, just be careful," she said.

"Do you want us to wear gloves?"

"No, you're fine."

I walked back to the table where Karen was carefully looking at page after page of the diary. "I can't believe this," she said. "This is the actual diary. Look at some of these entries. And look at how perfect the handwriting is. This diary went to the Klondike."

We looked through all five boxes. Each had an original archive or two inside, most of them diaries, but there were other items as well. In one box we found several original sales receipts for supplies that were purchased for the journey from Seattle to the Klondike. In another was a complete deck of playing cards from the White Pass Railroad. The words "The White Pass and Yukon Route – Gateway to the Yukon" were printed on the backs.

"Can I take photos of these items?" I asked Becky as she walked by.

"Sure," she said. "And if you need anything copied we can do that for you."

"They must think you're someone important," Karen said.

"Yeah, I'm a guy off the street wearing a Smokey Bear t-shirt, that's who. The bear commands respect."

As we looked through the boxes, I photographed several items with my phone. Now, I wished we'd stayed longer and taken more photos. We also photocopied a couple of the diary transcripts. We had a blast geeking out on the Klondike archives, but after three hours we needed a break. It was 2:00 pm when we walked out.

"That was pretty amazing," Karen said. "We may have to come back here again next year."

It was well past lunchtime, and we were both starving. Karen had her heart set on eating at a Russian dumpling restaurant on the waterfront named Pel'meni. It's not a surprise to find Russian influence in Juneau; 150 years ago, this *was* Russia.

Pel'meni was small. About half the customers took their food to go. We ordered at the counter; our only choices were meat or veggie, spicy or not spicy, and with sour cream or without. The food was good, I think. I was so hungry I inhaled it.

After lunch we walked through the streets in the heart of downtown and saw few people. About half the retail stores looked like they were closed for the season. Karen and I ducked into a bookstore and looked through their selection of books about Alaska. I bought another book about the Klondike and a long, narrow, fold-out map of the Inside Passage.

"Hey, there's a gift store down the street I'd like to go into," Karen said to me as I paid. We'd walked past it earlier; it looked touristy, not the kind of store I spend a lot of time in. Karen knew this, so she tried to entice me by adding, "They might have pelts in there."

Pelts, the magic word. On the first floor of the gift store were several cases of jewelry. Karen quickly looked through everything they had. Much of it was silver and there were dozens, if not hundreds, of bracelets in the cases. The manager was very attentive to Karen. We may have been the only customer in his store all day. "The artists make these right here," he said to her.

"That's cool," she replied. "You sure have a huge inventory."

"We need to have a lot on hand for the busy season. When the cruise ships come in, it's crazy around here," he replied.

I was looking for animal pelts, of course. I found a few fox and coyotes. They were in good shape, but the prices were much higher than what I'd seen in Montana. He also had a couple of bear rugs. Again, good quality, but way too expensive.

Both Karen and I were ready to leave when the manager said, "We have more stuff upstairs. You have to go out the front door there and then enter the next door to get to our shop on the second floor."

Even before we reached the top of the stairs, I knew that this is where they kept the good stuff. Hanging over the bannister above the stairs were at least fifty caribou pelts, maybe more—several stacks of them. Karen ran her hand across one. "Feel how soft and thick the fur is."

The woman minding the upstairs store saw us and said, "You can sort through those if you want. Take them off the pile and lay them on the floor to get a good look. People do that all the time. Each hide is different, especially the coloring. The darker fur means the animal was hunted before the weather turned cold. And some of them are almost entirely white. Those would have been hunted in the fall or winter."

Karen flipped through the hides, smoothing each one. "These look like reindeer hides. Are caribou and reindeer the same animal?" Karen asked me.

"No," I said. "They're completely different."

"Are you sure? I think they're the same. What's the difference?"

"They're just different. They're not the same species."

Karen shrugged and said, "I think they're the same," as she continued to look through the hides. The store clerk came over and joined her.

"These are really nice hides. We get them from subsistence hunters up north."

"They're beautiful," Karen replied. "I've always wondered, are caribou and reindeer the same animal?"

Before I could interrupt with something stupid like, "Go ahead and tell her that they're completely different animals," the woman said, "Yes, they're the same species. A reindeer is a domesticated caribou, that's all."

"They're the same?" Karen asked loudly so the woman would repeat the answer. "Did you hear that, Matt? Caribou and reindeer are the same animal. Imagine that."

For the rest of the day, if there was a lull in the conversation, Karen would say, "You know what I learned today? Caribou and reindeer are the same animal. Yep, same species."

I had to ignore her ribbing; I was concentrating on which hide to purchase. Once I had it narrowed down to two, I asked Karen, "Which of these do you like better?"

"I like this one; it looks more like a reindeer than a caribou. Wait, never mind, they're the same animal, I almost forgot."

"OK, you're no longer allowed to help choose the hide."

I handed my final selection to the woman and asked her to set it aside for me while I continued to look at their other pelts. They had weasels, ermine, wolves and a large selection of pine martens. Karen noticed that I was spending a lot of time looking through the pine marten pelts and came over to move me along. "What are these?"

"They're pine martens."

"What's a pine marten?"

"It's a type of a weasel."

"Are you sure?"

I sensed that after my caribou/reindeer gaffe, I was dangerously close to losing all the pelt cred I'd built this summer. After a long pause, I replied, "No. I'm not sure it's a type of weasel. But it looks like it could be in the weasel family doesn't it?"

Karen could tell that I was on the verge of buying one of every type of pelt in the store. "I think the caribou satisfies our dead animal quota for the trip, don't you?"

She was right; it's better to go slow with accumulating the animal hides. I'm still not sure how much room we'll have for the interpretive pelt collection in our visitor center.

Toward the top of the hill in downtown, we found a new distillery. Two young guys had started it and they were using local ingredients in their product. By the look of the crowd at 4:00 pm on a Wednesday, we figured they were starting to attract a following to their new venture.

Being less than a year old, all they had ready for sale was gin. Their gin had a distinctive flavor and a floral aroma. We spoke with one of the owners and he told us they use Devil's Club as their flavoring. He brought out a sealed plastic bag, took a stalk out, and showed it to us. We'd never heard the name before, but we've hiked past it countless times. It's a plant that grows in the forests in Alaska and the Pacific Northwest. The canes of the plant are covered with small spikes, hence the name. If you ever walk through an area in the forest thick with Devil's Club, you'll most likely smell it. The plant puts off a floral scent, the same that we tasted in the gin. It's hard to imagine how anyone looking at this ugly plant in the forest would ever think to use it for making gin.

As we stood at the bar chatting with the owner, we noticed a sign that said, "No sitting at the bar, no dancing, no singing, no playing games, two-drink limit."

"We can't dance?" I asked him.

He shook his head. "It's an Alaska state law. I guess they had a hard time passing the law allowing distilleries in the state, so part of the compromise was to make sure no one has fun while they're here. Crazy, isn't it?"

"Are you planning on branching out into whiskey?" I asked.

"Oh, yeah. We've already made a batch."

I was looking for bottles of whiskey on the shelves behind him, but all I could see was gin. "Where's the whiskey?"

"It's right there," he said pointing to a single barrel sitting on the floor. "Come back in a couple of years and you can try it."

"Making whiskey is a slow business, isn't it?"

"Yep, that's why we're making gin."

Once we had two drinks, I asked Karen if she was ready to go. "We can't order any more drinks, and we can't sing or dance, so yeah, I'm ready to go," she said,

"Oh, I thought the two-drink limit was a minimum. I was ready for another," I said.

"No, we're out of here. Let's go to the Red Door Saloon for an early dinner."

"Did you mean Red Dog Saloon?"

"Yeah, Red Dog. That's what I meant," she replied. "And by the way, today I learned that caribou and reindeer are the same animal. How about that?"

This was a sure sign that it's time to go home. It's been a great trip, but we're ready to sleep in our own bed. We're not traveling again for about six weeks. Right after Thanksgiving we leave for Zion National Park to celebrate our 35th wedding anniversary. It seems like the park would be a romantic place during the holidays. I'll write you from there unless we're too "busy."

Your friend,
Matt

From: **Matt Smith**
Subject: **Celebrating 35 Years**
Date: **November 27 (Monday)**

Dear Bob and Sue,

When we planned our anniversary trip to Zion months ago, Karen had images in her head of snowshoeing through a snow-covered valley and drinking wine by the fireplace in our cabin at Zion Lodge. It was sixty-nine degrees when we got here yesterday; more like flip-flops and beer weather.

We didn't set an itinerary for this trip; we're going to do whatever sounds right at the moment. Last night we decided this might be a good time of year to try to get a walk-in permit for The Wave. Right after Thanksgiving, most people are more focused on holiday shopping or trying to get their family members off their living room couch than hiking—so we thought. This morning, at 7:00 a.m., we were in our rental car driving toward the Grand Staircase-Escalante National Monument Visitor Center in Kanab. It was about an hour drive, so we gave ourselves plenty of time to get there before the 9:00 am lottery drawing.

From the lodge, we drove east out of the park. On our way through the valley, before we reached the tunnels, the rising sun lit the mountains to the west. It was an incredible sight. The scene quickly earned a Karen Smith "Magical Place" designation. She made me stop the car about every ten feet so she could take photos of the glowing cliffs. It was a good thing we'd left early.

The BLM issues twenty permits to hike to The Wave each day. Ten of those permits are awarded through their advance, online system, and the other ten are issued the day before the hike date through a walk-in lottery held at the visitor center in Kanab. From mid-November through mid-March, they award ten walk-in permits on Monday through Thursday for hikes on Tuesday through Friday. On Fridays, they conduct the walk-in lottery for hikes on Saturday, Sunday and Monday.

The Wave has become so popular that large crowds show up for the lottery drawings. There's no advantage to putting your name in early to the lottery pool; as long as you register by the time the drawing begins, you've an equal chance to win. Despite our hopes that the crowd would be small today, there were over thirty groups wanting permits this morning. Each permit allows one person to hike the trail, and today the total requests for permits equaled about 110. I asked one of the BLM staffers if this number of people was typical for this time of year. She said, "We never know how many people will show up. There's really no 'normal' anymore. I looked at our records this morning and saw that last year on this date we had about ten groups requesting a total of thirty permits."

We wandered around the visitor center, waiting for the lottery to begin. One of the rangers behind the desk cleared his throat and said, "Listen up everybody. In a few minutes we'll all go into that room over there where you'll fill out a form and we'll get started. Just to be clear, today's drawing is for hiking permits for tomorrow. There is no trail to The Wave, so you must have a GPS and route-finding skills. If you win the lottery, we'll give you the coordinates. Everyone got that?"

I was hoping a few people might leave after the ranger's comments but no one did. One person from each group filled out the required form and the lottery administrator sorted through them, assigning each group a number. We were number six. When the time came to choose the winning groups, he pulled numbered balls out of a hopper, like you would for bingo. By the time he called the first three numbers, only two permits were left. The fourth winning group was a party of three, so the administrator issued an eleventh permit. He assured the crowd that they don't usually issue more than ten walk-in permits each day.

The final group didn't seem too excited to have won. It was a young couple who'd carried their two-year-old, still asleep and in her pajamas, into the visitor center. They were more concerned about not waking their child than collecting their permits. There were a lot of quizzical looks from the hundred losing permit seekers when the couple's number was called. We thought to ourselves, *how are they going to take that child on a strenuous eight-mile hike in the desert?* Regardless, given the size of the crowd, we weren't surprised we didn't get a permit. We'll keep applying for the online lottery and trying for walk-in permits whenever we're in the area again.

At 9:15 am, we had a full day ahead of us and nothing planned. We asked one of the rangers about hikes in the area and he suggested we take a drive through the monument on Cottonwood Canyon Road and do one of the hikes along that stretch. He gave us a map showing where all the trailheads were, as well as some other points of interest. The turnoff for Cottonwood Canyon Road was on the north side of Highway 89 about thirty miles east of the visitor center. It's a forty-six-mile dirt road that can be impassable when it rains, but the ranger assured us we wouldn't have any trouble today. We decided to take it all the way to Highway 12 and then circle back toward Zion.

The drive took us through a desolate landscape, but we enjoy getting off the paved road now and then to see the "path less traveled." Less traveled by humans that is; we ran into a lot of cows—not literally of course. At one point we came to a dead stop at a cattle guard. On the other side, about twenty cows blocked the road, staring at us with their big brown eyes. A cowhand was trying to coax them around the guard and onto the road where we were. I rolled down the passenger window and yelled out to the man, "What should we do?"

He said, "Just keep going, they'll move out of your way."

I looked at the cows a few feet in front of me and then back at the cow hand. "I can't go any farther without hitting them."

"Just go slow, they'll move. You might have to nudge them a bit," he said.

By "nudge" he meant for me to physically nudge them with my car. I wasn't comfortable doing that, but I kept creeping up on them slowly. Eventually, they all moved out of the way, although I spooked a couple of them so much that they climbed precariously above the road onto the side of a dirt hill. They looked like they'd tumble down the loose dirt at any time and land on us. I was glad to get past them without getting a cow-shaped dent in the side of our car. That would be hard to explain to the rental car company.

Shortly after, we pulled into a parking area just off the road by Cottonwood Canyon, and hiked a few miles through the narrows. The hike wasn't challenging, but it was a nice break from driving. We only saw one other couple on the trail.

Farther up the road, we turned off at the sign for Grosvenor Arch, where we stopped and made sandwiches at a picnic table. After we ate, we hiked to the arch to take a few pictures. It's actually two arches side-by-side, towering over 150 feet above the ground. Karen went off the paved path in hopes of getting an interesting angle for her photo. I followed her, assigning myself snake-patrol officer while we picked our way through the desert scrub. After our snake encounters this year, I imagine there's a rattler beneath every bush.

From there we drove past Kodachrome Basin State Park and continued north through the town of Cannonville. Had we not already visited Kodachrome on a previous trip, we would've stopped there to look around. But the days are short this time of year and we wanted to have enough time to hike in Bryce Canyon National Park, so we kept driving.

Past Cannonville, we turned west on Highway 12 and followed it to Bryce. Pulling into the parking lot next to the lodge, which was closed for the season, we were surprised to find it deserted. We hiked down into the amphitheater at Wall Street and took a several-mile loop through the hoodoos that brought us back up to the rim of the canyon at Sunrise Point. The entire time we were there we saw fewer than twenty people, which is amazing because, as you know, the park is usually overrun with hordes of people.

Matt hiking in the Bryce Canyon Amphitheater,
Bryce Canyon National Park

Back at Zion, we had a romantic dinner and evening at the lodge. It was nice to get out and see parts of Escalante we hadn't seen before and to do a few hikes. But it was a lot of driving as well. Tomorrow we're staying in the valley and doing a hike that we can walk to from the lodge.

Your friend,
Matt

From: **Matt Smith**
Subject: **Angels Landing, Not**
Date: **November 28 (Tuesday)**

Dear Bob and Sue,

I've lost count of the number of times Karen and I've been to Zion. Being hikers, you'd think we'd have hiked to Angels Landing by now, but we haven't. After hearing descriptions of the trail—steep drop-offs, chains to hold onto, crowds of tourists—we had zero interest. Maybe we've reached a point where we don't feel pressure to do something because it's popular. Either that or we're chickens.

Even though she doesn't want to go all the way up to Angels Landing, Karen said she'd like to at least hike up to the point along the trail where the chains start, so she could get a better look at it. From our cabin this morning, we walked north along the road for about half a mile and then crossed it and joined the West Rim Trail, which starts at the Grotto Trailhead.

At that point there's a trail sign with a picture of Angels Landing and a drawing of a man falling. The sign warns that since 2004, six people have died falling from the cliffs on this route. I'm not sure how often they update this sign, but I'd guess that number is even higher by now. The sign only reinforced our decision to pass on this hike.

The first part of the trail is relatively flat and runs next to the Virgin River before it turns into a series of uphill switchbacks. They weren't very steep or difficult, but it was still a relief when the trail flattened again and we reached the shade of Refrigerator Canyon. When we got to the end of the canyon, we ascended twenty-one short, steep switchbacks, called Walter's Wiggles.

A view of Angels Landing (center) from the West Rim Trail,
Zion National Park

A mile and a half after starting the hike, we'd climbed
1,000 feet and were ready for a break. We stopped at Scout
Lookout where we could see the Virgin River and the park
road directly below us to the east. It was a straight down
vertical drop.

It's at this overlook that the trail splits. If you turn to the
right (south), the trail up to Angels Landing is a half a mile
hike onto a narrow, exposed fin. On either side of the
landing, the drop-offs are as much as 1,400 feet. To the left
of Scout Lookout, the West Rim Trail continues to the north
end of the park.

As we were marveling at the view, a man approached us and asked if we were looking for the condors. He said he was a volunteer who gives interpretive talks at the overlook. "If you stick around for another ten minutes you can hear my talk about condors."

"I didn't know condors live in Zion," Karen said.

"Yeah, around seventy live in Utah and Arizona," he replied. "This is a great place to spot them."

"California Condors, right?"

He nodded his head. "They were almost extinct in 1982; only twenty-two were left in the world. The remaining condors were captured and a captive breeding program was set up to save them. Now there are over four hundred."

"We'll keep our eyes out for them," I said. "We're hiking farther up the West Rim Trail."

"Good plan," he said. "Everyone wants to go up to Angels Landing, but there are better views if you keep hiking along the West Rim Trail. Nobody hikes in that direction, you'll feel like you're in the wilderness by yourself."

We thanked him and continued on. About a mile farther up, we stopped for lunch at a rock outcropping that was in full sun. Sitting there looking in the direction of Angels Landing we understood what the condor guy had told us; from our perch, we had unobstructed views of the park to the southeast. We could see the top of Angels Landing and the valley beyond. It was spectacular in the mid-morning sun, and we were the only ones there.

The West Rim trail runs for seventeen miles, but we weren't prepared for a long hike, and certainly not for a backpacking overnight. If it were summer, I would have loved to continue along the trail to the end, Lava Point, at the northern boundary of the park. It sits at almost 8,000 feet elevation, so it's probably covered in snow this time of year. Maybe we'll come back and do that someday.

As we started back toward the trailhead, I spotted a woman who was off the trail and standing at the very edge of a tall cliff. She had her back to the drop-off and was taking a selfie. I was so shocked by how precarious her stance was that I wanted to shout at her to move away from the edge, but I figured if I'd startled her in the least she might have fallen off the cliff.

"Are you seeing this?" I asked Karen.

"Uh huh. That's insane. I can't even look. I don't want to see her fall," she replied.

"We need to leave her alone. I don't want to walk toward her, or make eye contact, or talk to her while she's standing there. The smallest distraction might cause her to go over."

"What some people will do for a selfie," Karen said, shaking her head.

The rest of the hike back to the lodge was a pleasant, downhill trip. When we were about half way through Walter's Wiggles, we passed a man and woman who were resting at the side of the trail. The man looked like he was ready to continue hiking, but the woman was sitting on a rock, red-faced and breathing heavily. From a short distance away, we heard the woman angrily say, "Boy, are you gonna owe me big time for this." He didn't respond.

Once we were out of earshot, I said to Karen, "Sounds like she's pissed at him for making her go on this hike."

"See how lucky you are?" she replied.

"Lucky?"

"Yeah, because I don't complain like that."

I must not have responded quickly enough because Karen followed up with an insistent, "Well?"

"Yes," I said.

"Yes, what?"

"Yes—I don't remember the original question. Wait. Yes, I'm lucky," I said.

"Why are you lucky?"

"Because I've been married to the love of my life—a non-complainer—for thirty-five years," I replied.

"Good answer."

I don't know why it took us so long to discover the West Rim Trail. By avoiding Angels Landing, we were missing one of the epic hikes in Zion, one where we have a low risk of becoming a statistic on a park sign.

Your friend,
Matt

~.~.~.~.~.~.~

From: **Karen Smith**
Subject: **Becoming Rock Hounds**
Date: **November 29 (Wednesday)**

Dear Bob and Sue,

Two items were on our to-do list this morning before we left Zion and headed for Vegas. The first was to take our picture in front of the park sign at the entrance for old times' sake. The second was to visit a rock shop in town.

When we arrived at the park sign, we found the parking area torn up. Construction crews have been rebuilding the main street through Springdale, State Route 9, and it's down to one usable lane. A few days ago, when we drove through Springdale on our way to the park, a flagger stopped us for about ten minutes to let oncoming traffic pass. This road construction (a new road and wider sidewalks) is supposed to wrap up in spring of 2018, but it's causing a pretty big headache for visitors trying to get in and out of the park.

Matt had to make a quick U-turn before the oncoming, single-file line of cars trapped us on the wrong side of the road. He was forced to park in the dirt, pretty far back from the park sign, which made it difficult for him to put the camera on the hood of the car, set the timer, and run to the sign before the camera took the photo. We did a couple of takes where Matt was a blur with his back to the camera. We finally got a halfway decent picture so we could move on to rock shopping.

Springdale has a couple of shops along the main road that have brightly colored rocks and gems stacked on tables outside. We pulled into one we'd visited on our first trip to Springdale years ago and were immediately drawn to their piles of petrified wood. It was everywhere. They had chunks the size of tree trunks, and wire cages filled with pieces the size of a deck of cards.

"If petrified wood is so plentiful, why are visitors stealing it from Petrified Forest National Park?" I asked Matt as we rummaged through the bins.

"Because they want to be cursed and have bad luck for the rest of their lives," Matt replied while trying to budge one of the tree trunk-sized behemoths.

"You know we can't take that on the plane, right?"

"I know, I'm seeing how heavy it is. Next time we drive my truck down here, we'll come back and buy one."

Matt wandered into the store. Five minutes later when I joined him, he was deep in conversation with the woman behind the counter.

"We only buy petrified wood that's been collected legally," she was telling him.

"And what does that mean, exactly?" he asked.

"We make sure that the person we buy from is a commercial collector with the proper licenses and permits."

"OK, so you have to be a commercial enterprise to collect petrified wood?" Matt asked.

"No. Individuals can also collect petrified wood in this area, but you need a permit. You have to go to the BLM office in St. George, buy the permit, and then you're allowed to collect up to twenty-five pounds a year on BLM land."

"*Anyone* can collect petrified wood?" he asked slowly.

"Sure, as long as you're collecting for personal use; there's a different process for commercial collectors," she said.

"Once you have the permit, where's a good place to look for petrified wood?" he asked.

"The folks at the BLM office can tell you the best places to go, and they sell maps of the area."

Uh oh, I thought. We might not make our flight home tomorrow.

I put the rocks I wanted to buy on the counter next to Matt's. He paid for them all and thanked the woman. "We really appreciate the tip. We'll stop at the BLM office and check them out."

As we walked to the car I said to him, "You're not serious, are you? We have to drive to Vegas."

"We're going right through St. George on the way. It won't take long to make a stop and get some information."

When we got there, we found the main BLM office closed for renovations. Fortunately, in their parking lot was a temporary office open to the public. Once inside, I made a beeline for the book section. Matt was on his own. He waited in line at the counter while the ranger finished talking with the person in front of him.

I was thumbing through a pioneer cookbook from Pipe Springs National Monument when I came across a recipe for something called "Lumpy Dick." I took it to over to Matt and showed him the name of the recipe. "What, are you like fourteen years old?" he said, feigning disinterest.

"You just wish you found it first," I replied.

"Karen, I have important business here. We need to learn how to become rock hounds. I can't be distracted with pioneer cookbooks and bumpy dicks," he said.

"It's called 'Lumpy Dick,' but suit yourself, I guess I won't be making any of these pioneer dessert recipes then. They have a mean-looking pineapple upside-down cake recipe that you cook in a Dutch oven, but you wouldn't be interested in that."

Before I put the book back on the rack, I read through the list of ingredients and the instructions for Lumpy Dick. It looked like some kind of homemade pudding. The "Lumpy" part of the name comes from the lumps of flour left after cooking, and I bet the "dick" part of the name probably refers to the husband who criticized the lumps of flour. I may write my own cookbook; all of the recipes will have "Matt" in the names. As a matter of fact, I may call it *Lumpy Matt*.

I rejoined him at the counter when it was his turn with the ranger.

"We heard that we can get a permit here to collect petrified wood in the area," he told the ranger.

"Yes, you can. It costs ten dollars and is good for a year. You can collect up to twenty-five pounds during the year."

"That's great," said Matt. "Can you tell me where we'd find petrified wood?"

The ranger brought out a map from behind his desk and opened it. "Let's see here…"

He smoothed out the map and put his finger on an area. "There's a good spot on Little Creek Knolls, off Highway 59. And there's petrified wood up on Dalton Wash, east of Virgin. Just make sure if you're collecting there that you don't cross into Zion National Park. The boundary is real close."

"How will we know if we're in the national park? We don't want to accidentally take something out of the park and be cursed for life," Matt asked.

"There's a fence up there marking the boundary. If you find rocks on the park side of the fence you should leave them be."

Matt took some photos of his finger pointing to the spots on the map where the ranger suggested we look for petrified wood.

The ranger said, "Now if you'll step into the next room, they'll write you up a permit. And remember, you can only collect rocks within the jurisdiction of this office. If you're in other parts of Utah, you'll have to check with the BLM office that manages that area."

Five minutes later, permit in hand, we walked out to the car. "Can you believe it?" Matt asked. "We're rock hounds!"

"You're not thinking that we'll go looking for rocks right now, are you? Because our rental car might not do so well on dirt roads and we don't have a lot of time."

"No, we'll do it in March, when we come back."

On the two-hour drive back to Vegas, Matt looked at me every ten miles or so and said with a big smile on his face, "Can you believe it? We're rock hounds."

I didn't want to throw a wet blanket over his excitement by pointing out that we're not rock hounds yet; all we had was a permit—no rocks. I also didn't mention that we know nothing about rocks and probably wouldn't recognize a piece of petrified wood in the wild if it bit us on the toe. I think I'll get him some rock identification books for Christmas and maybe one of those little hammers that you see rock people using. This should be a hoot. We're going to be rock hounds.

Your friend,
Karen

~.~.~.~.~.~.~

From: **Karen Smith**
Subject: **Mt. Rainier Snowshoeing**
Date: **December 17 (Sunday)**

Dear Bob and Sue,

They say that Mt. Rainier makes its own weather. We've found that to be true on a few occasions when it's been a pleasant summer day in Seattle, and we've driven two hours to do a hike at Rainier only to be enveloped in fog and rain when we got there. So when our friends Craig and Aya asked us to go on a snowshoe weekend with them to Mt. Rainier, we were hoping the mountain would be making snow for us.

Even though the park is open year-round, all of the roads are closed to car traffic in the winter, except the road from the Nisqually Entrance, which is open year-round unless the park gets extreme weather. I was excited we were able to book rooms at the historic National Park Inn in Longmire because we'd never been there before. We've stayed at Paradise Inn a few times, but it's now closed for the winter.

Craig and Aya picked us up early Friday morning, and after stopping for coffee, we drove south on I-5. Matt noticed something attached to Craig's visor and asked him what it was. "It's a tool you can use to break your car window if you're ever in an accident and the door is stuck," he explained.

"What's the little razor for?" Matt asked.

"You can use that to cut your seatbelt," he said.

"I'm ordering one of those as soon as we get home," Matt said.

I didn't know that such a tool even existed. Matt calls Craig "The Gadget Guy;" it's a term of respect—Matt wants to be The Gadget Guy, but he's no match for Craig who has everything you'd need for any emergency. Every time we hang out with him, we always see something new that he's purchased and wonder how we could have possibly survived so long without owning that particular gadget.

When we got within thirty minutes of the park, we stopped for brunch at a diner. It looked like a down-home authentic kind of place that truckers and lumberjacks might frequent. When the waitress came to our table, Matt ordered pigs in a blanket without even looking at the menu.

The waitress responded, "I'm sorry, we don't have those."

Matt dropped his shoulders and said to me, "Are we on another planet?"

"Ignore him," I said to the waitress. "He doesn't get out much."

"OK, OK, no big deal. Do you have pancakes and sausage?" Matt asked.

"We sure do," the waitress replied.

"Then I'll roll my own," he said.

The waitress looked at me as if she needed an interpreter. "That means he'll have the pancakes and sausage," I said.

"Wait, are they link sausages?" Matt asked.

"We have both, which would you prefer?"

"Links. They have to be links. Sausage *patties* and pancakes? I don't know what you'd call that," he chuckled.

The waitress looked confused. I said to her, "Have you seen the movie *Rain Man*?"

"What's that supposed to mean?" Matt asked.

"It means the 'D' is about to catch up to your OC," Craig said.

"I think the 'D' has already caught up," said Aya.

When our food came and he started rolling the sausages inside the pancakes, I knew I shouldn't ask but I couldn't help myself. "Wouldn't it taste the same if you cut a piece of pancake and put a slice of sausage on top and ate it?"

Matt sighed deeply. "Karen, the sausage needs to be surrounded by the pancake. It's the blanket. Actually, it's more like a sleeping bag. Then the butter and syrup go on top of the whole thing. Otherwise, it would just be a pig and a pancake. Doesn't have the same ring to it as 'pigs in a blanket,' now does it?"

"Yep, the D has officially joined your OC, Matt," Craig said.

When we got to the park entrance, an inch or two of snow was on the ground, but the road was clear. Six miles past the entrance station we arrived at Longmire, a national historic district. All of the buildings were designed to harmonize with nature, and the style became known as "National Park Service Rustic." I'm not making that up. It's a thing. When Mt. Rainier was made a national park in 1899, Longmire became the park headquarters. The headquarters eventually moved out of Longmire, but the original building is still there, operating now as a museum. The area has other historic administrative buildings, a ranger station, a general store, and the inn.

Before we checked in, we stopped at the ranger station to get information about snowshoeing that afternoon. We were the only people there, and we had plenty of time to chat with the ranger.

"In the Longmire area, there's not really enough snow right now to snowshoe," the ranger explained. "But you could hike. The Rampart Ridge Trail is a great four-and-a-half-mile hike if you want to get some elevation gain, but it's going to be drizzly today. You'll need to have some rain protection."

"We're thinking about going up to Paradise," Craig said. "How's the snow up there today?"

"It's a lot better than it is down here," the ranger laughed. "We're at twenty-seven hundred feet elevation here at Longmire, and Paradise is about fifty-four hundred. That makes a huge difference in the snowfall all winter long. You'll have lots of trail options up there."

The ranger took out a map and started marking areas with a highlighter. "The Skyline Route, Reflection Lake, Narada Falls, I'll mark those for you. Just a couple of warnings though: First off, there's moderate avalanche danger today. Snowshoers can trigger avalanches up there, so stay away from these areas." The ranger marked X's on those areas of the map.

"Secondly, make sure you can always see where you're going. People have become lost in whiteouts and have fallen to their deaths." Aya and I looked at each other with wide eyes.

"And lastly, the gate up at Paradise closes at four. You'll want to be back in your car by then. We give people time to drive down and then we close this lower gate at five." He gestured out the window behind him. "It re-opens at nine each morning."

"Got it," said Matt. "Thanks for the info."

As we walked back to Craig's truck, I said, "Avalanches and white-outs? I'm not sure Aya and I signed up for that. What are you guys getting us into?"

We drove the fifty yards to the inn's parking lot and went inside to see if we could check in early. This historic hotel is much smaller than the other national park lodges we've been to—it only has twenty-five rooms—but it had a cozy, warm feel and was decorated for Christmas. While Matt and Craig were at the front desk, Aya and I wandered around and looked at the historic photographs on the walls. We saw a picture of the original National Park Inn, which was much bigger. It was destroyed by fire in 1926, leaving only the annex, which became the current National Park Inn. It was remodeled in 1936 and in 1990.

Chairs out on a porch faced the park road. You could sit there and enjoy a perfect view of Mt. Rainier, when it's not hidden by clouds or fog like it was that morning. The lobby didn't have a great room like many of the other national park lodges; it only had a few chairs to sit on, but around the corner we found the Guest Library, which had a huge stone fireplace with comfortable seating in front of it. The half dozen round tables in the room were perfect for playing cards or board games or for doing puzzles. "I see wine, whiskey, and cards right here tonight," I said to Aya.

"That sounds a lot better to me than avalanches and white-outs," she replied.

The guys appeared with room keys, so we grabbed our luggage out of the truck and found our rooms, agreeing to meet in thirty minutes.

"Do you want to come with me to the general store?" Matt asked. "I forgot my belt and I'm hoping they sell them."

The general store was right next to the inn and was filled with all kinds of gifts and souvenirs and snacks. Matt asked the woman behind the counter if they had any belts.

"No, I'm afraid we don't," she said.

"That's too bad," he told her. "I forgot mine this weekend and there's a good chance my pants might fall down. I guess I should have eaten more pancakes this morning."

She laughed. "We sell bandanas. Maybe you could buy a couple of those and tie them together to use as a belt."

"I'll see what else you have," he said, picking up a can of Pringles as he moved toward the back of the store.

"Hey, this might work," he said to me. I wandered over to see him holding a package of shoelaces. "I could tie these together. What do you think?"

I couldn't contain my laughter. "You're going to hold your pants up with shoelaces?"

"Not just any shoelaces! These are hiking shoelaces; they're thick and strong."

He took the shoelaces, Pringles, and a small box of Cheez-Its, and walked toward the check-out counter. "Wait a minute. I found it!" he exclaimed.

"What did you find?"

"A forty-four-inch utility strap with a buckle. A package of two for $2.39. It's perfect."

"Yeah, you could connect them and make a belt."

"My belt size is thirty-six inches, not eighty-eight. But thank you for the compliment."

After he paid for his things, he opened the package and threaded one of the thin nylon straps through his belt loops and buckled it. "I'm so proud of you, honey," I said. "You'll never need to buy another leather belt for the rest of your life. Think how much money you'll save us by wearing your utility strap. I bet Craig doesn't have one."

We reconvened with Craig and Aya and drove the ten miles up to Paradise. The park requires that all cars carry chains in the winter. Fortunately, we never needed to chain-up. The road was covered in a thin layer of hard-packed snow, and plows were out doing their maintenance loops, trying to keep the roads as clear as possible. When we got to the parking lot at the top, there was plenty of snow, but I was disappointed that the incredible view of Mt. Rainier was completely obscured by fog.

Between the fog and the lightly falling snow, visibility was low. Regardless, we decided to put on our snowshoes and try to go as far as we could without falling off a cliff. We snowshoed counter-clockwise on the Skyline Trail Loop, the trail climbers take to Camp Muir on their way to summiting Mount Rainier.

As soon as we got on the trail, we passed Paradise Inn on our right. The snow was piled up to the roofline of the inn in places; a couple of chimneys and a line of dormers poked through massive drifts. It was an eerie scene that made me think of the movie *The Shining*.

We snowshoed along the trail for about twenty minutes, heading in the direction of the summit, even though we couldn't see it. As we climbed steadily in elevation, it didn't take long for the visibility to drop to about twenty feet. Most of the trees disappeared and the horizon vanished; we couldn't tell where the snow ended and the sky began. There was nothing but white in every direction.

"This must have been what the ranger meant when he said to make sure you can always see where you're going," I called out to Matt, who was in the lead.

"I can't see anything. I've no idea which direction we should go. Maybe there's a reason there are no other snowshoe tracks to follow. We better turn around," he said.

Luckily, we could still see *our* snowshoe prints, which we followed back down to the point where the visibility improved. We found another trail close to the parking lot and followed it for a while until it too, started to climb up into whiteout conditions. When we decided to turn back, Craig looked at his GPS and said, "Let's take a left here and we can take a different trail back to the parking lot."

We all followed Craig, and when I looked back, I could barely make out the trail we'd come up on through the fog. Fifteen minutes later, we came to the top of a steep hill and the trail we were following disappeared. Other than going back the way we came, we had no choice but to follow Craig down the steep slope, stepping sideways in the deep snow to descend. When we got to the bottom, we were standing in an untracked snowfield with no sign of civilization—or a trail. Craig pulled out his GPS again and studied it.

"Are we lost?" Aya asked.

"No," Craig replied. "I can see where we are on my GPS, and I can see where the parking lot is. I'm just not sure how we get there from here without jumping off a cliff."

"Or falling off a cliff," Aya said.

"Maybe, to be on the safe side, we should retrace our steps and go back the way we came," I suggested.

Everyone's heads turned to look at the steep hill we'd just struggled down.

"No, we'll be fine," Matt said. "Craig can get us back. Right, Craig?"

"We need to go that way," Craig said as he pointed, and we were moving again.

I have to admit I was scared. You read stories all the time about people who get lost, and their bodies are eventually found within a mile of civilization. I was almost in full-panic mode when we crested a hill and ran across the original trail we'd been on a half an hour earlier.

When we got back to the inn, the wine, whiskey, and cards scenario played out as we'd hoped, in front of a roaring fire, followed by a nice dinner in the dining room. Before calling it a night, we agreed that the next day we would snowshoe from Paradise to Reflection Lake. Instead of going toward the summit, the trail to the lake follows an unplowed park road and descends to a lower elevation, so the chance of being in a whiteout again would be less.

Saturday morning, the Paradise parking lot was much more crowded. Families sledded on the hills and people wandered in and out of the visitor center, which was open for the weekend. There was still no view of Mt. Rainier.

Our snowshoe trek to Reflection Lake along the snow-covered road was longer than we'd expected, but at least it was downhill. At a sharp turn in the road, we tried to get lost by taking a shortcut straight through the forest rather than following the road. Hitting a dead-end and then having to snowshoe back to the road added an unnecessary half of a mile to the trip.

At the lake, we took a break for lunch. It's hard to eat meals when snowshoeing. Usually, it's cold and we're sweating, and we don't want to stop moving for very long. We couldn't find a decent place to sit, so we ate standing up while looking at the lake. Within five seconds of taking food out of our backpacks, birds starting landing in the trees and on the ground next to us. They had white heads and black wings. I think they may have been what people refer to as camp robbers, but I can't be sure. We have nothing against birds, we just don't know their names: Our life list of birds is still blank.

I bent over at one point to look for something in my pack, and Matt and Craig started laughing. "Aya," I said. "What are they laughing at?"

"You have a bird on your back," she said.

Matt poured a few pieces of trail mix in his hand, and before he could toss them into his mouth, a bird landed on his hand, grabbed an M&M and flew away. They became so bold and obnoxious that we put our food away and turned back toward Paradise. We snowshoed on a different trail, one that took us through the forest instead of along the road. The new path was narrow in places, with trees close to the trail. Evergreen branches, heavy with fresh snow, looked like they would break. Bumps in the snowfields marked where smaller trees had already been buried for the winter. It felt like we were hiking through a Christmas card.

Matt snowshoeing on our way back from Reflection Lake,
Mount Rainier National Park

The trek back to Paradise was almost all uphill. The climb
had wiped us out by the time we could see the parking lot in
the distance. A group of people with big packs and shovels
were standing in a circle by the side of the trail. Aya called out
to them as we walked past, "Hey, are you guys going camping
in a snow cave? I want to come with you!" One of the men
looked at her and said in a quiet voice, "Yeah, we're going
camping, and this is our avalanche training session."

"Oh sorry!" Aya said and then turned toward me. "Karen,
don't you want to go with them and camp in a snow cave?
You and me! Let's do it!"

"Aya, I don't even want to snowshoe the remaining quarter mile to the car," I told her. "I'll never want to dig a cave in the snow and then sleep in it. You're on your own on that one."

After a quick stop in the visitor center, we loaded our gear into the back of Craig's truck. A lot of people were leaving at the same time, and we followed a slow line of cars down to Longmire. The final big excitement of the day was seeing a fox trotting right by the side of the road. All the cars stopped, and people were hanging out of their windows taking pictures of it, including me.

When we got back to the lobby of the inn, Matt asked the woman behind the desk, "Is there any place around here to eat that you'd recommend? We had dinner here in the dining room last night, and it was really good, but we'd like to try someplace different."

Without hesitation, the woman replied, "Copper Creek Inn. Best homemade pie in the state of Washington. It's nine miles from here in the little town of Ashford. When driving away from the park, it'll be on your right-hand side."

That was all he needed to hear. For Matt, few things rank higher than homemade pie. Copper Creek was rustic and charming, and the food was great; just what we needed after a strenuous day of snowshoeing. We rolled out of there fat and happy. It was a good thing Craig was driving; I think Matt fell asleep in the car on the short drive back to the inn.

Early this morning when Matt came back to our room from wherever he goes to get coffee, he said, "I have a surprise for you."

"An egg sandwich?" I asked hopefully.

"No, you'll have to come downstairs to see it."

"But I'm still in my pajamas."

He stood there holding two cups of coffee. "You look fine. No one else is up yet."

I struggled out from underneath the blankets and pulled on a pair of jeans and a sweatshirt and brushed my hair. You never know who you might run into.

"Oh, and you'll need your coat and hat," he said.

This just keeps getting better, I thought.

We went down the stairs and Matt turned toward the back porch. He held the door open for me and said, "Out here."

I stepped onto the back porch and it was like stepping into a winter wonderland. An inch or two of snow had fallen overnight and it was pristine, sparkling like crystals in the sunlight.

Matt took my hand and said, "Look up."

"Oh, wow." There was the sight I'd been hoping to see all weekend: Mt. Rainier in all its majesty, brilliant white under the blue sky, with wisps of clouds racing past it.

We stood there for a while, sipping our coffee. I could hear the faint sound of Christmas music coming from inside the inn. It was one of those perfect moments in life—an early Christmas gift.

"Thank you," I said. "This is magical."

He squeezed my hand. "Merry Christmas, sweetie."

We stood and looked at the mountain until it disappeared behind the clouds. After a leisurely breakfast with Craig and Aya, we packed and headed for home.

This trip was our last one of the year. Now it's time to focus on Christmas. When we got home from Rainier, we went right back out to get our Christmas tree. We put it in the same place we always do in our living room, even though it's under construction. The visitor center remodel has started, and the raised floor is covered with plywood. The old fireplace is a gaping hole until the stonemason does his work, but we're pretty sure Santa will make it down the chimney anyway.

Wising you and the kids a merry and magical Christmas.

Your friend,
Karen

From: **Matt Smith**
Subject: **Happy New Year!**
Date: **December 31 (Sunday)**

Dear Bob and Sue,

It's about time for New Year's resolutions. While we were drinking our coffee together this morning, Karen said, "If you tell me your New Year's resolution, I'll tell you mine."

"Alright, I was going to discuss this with you sooner or later, but now is as good a time as any. I've reached that age when I shouldn't have to live with certain disappointments, especially ones that I can do something about. I'm going to make a change."

"I agree, honey. You deserve to be happy. What change are we talking about?"

"I'm no longer going to eat fake pancake syrup."

"What do you mean by 'fake?'"

"That colored corn syrup stuff that they serve at hotels," I said.

"I see."

"Remember when we were on the ferry to Alaska? The syrup episode?" I asked.

"I remember. Do we have to talk about that again?"

"When I turned the syrup container upside down and the syrup never came out? Ever?"

"Yes, never, I remember now. Your food got cold while you waited for the syrup and you had to eat cold, dry pancakes."

"Dry pancakes! At my age? I don't have that many pancakes or waffles left in my future."

"You're in your mid-fifties. You probably have more than you think."

"Dry pancakes!" I said.

"OK, what are you going to do about this… disappointment?" she asked.

"Thank you for asking. I plan on taking maple syrup with me wherever I go."

"And how would that work?"

"Since we already have the big jug from Costco, I'll fill up small bottles with real syrup and carry a few with me at all times. I'll take them with us when we travel," I said.

"That's not a bad idea, although you can't use your own syrup in restaurants. They wouldn't like it if you brought in your own."

"If they don't have real maple syrup then I'm pulling out my little bottles. They don't have to like it," I said.

"Alright, it seems that you've given this a lot of thought. Maybe you could get some of those small Nalgene bottles at REI to put your syrup in."

"Don't need 'em. I already have little bottles, a bunch."

"Really? Where did you get them?"

I disappeared into my office and brought the bottles out to show Karen. "Here you go. They're a perfect size."

"Those are airline-sized whiskey bottles. Won't it look odd if you're standing next to the waffle grill at Hampton Inn waiting for the timer to go off and you're holding a small bottle of Jack Daniels in your hand? With the syrup inside it'll look like whiskey."

"And?" I asked.

"You don't see this as a problem?"

"Have you ever tasted fake syrup?"

"OK, here's the thing; bringing maple syrup with you when you travel is not really a New Year's resolution. You're supposed to change a bad behavior or accomplish a goal. Something that improves your life."

"Trust me, maple syrup will improve my life."

"I was kind of embarrassed to tell you my resolution, but after hearing yours I feel much better."

"Great, can't wait to hear it."

"I've decided I'm not going to take my hair straightener anymore when we travel," she said.

"Ha! What are we betting?" I asked.

"It's not a bet, it's a New Year's resolution."

"No hair straightening when we travel, huh? That's pretty bold."

"And no hair curling either."

"You're not taking your hair curler either?" I asked.

"No, I also use the hair straightener to curl my hair."

"You straighten your hair, then curl it? Couldn't you do nothing and end up in the same place?" I asked.

"No, the straightener makes the waves. You know the waves I have in my hair?"

I knew better than to answer this question truthfully. "Oh yeah, the waves, the waves. You make those with your hair straightener, do you?"

"Well, not anymore when we're on the road. I'm leaving it at home from now on. Instead of worrying about how my hair looks, I'm going to try to be more outdoorsy."

"I like the outdoorsy look on you. I can't wait for our next trip. In February we're going to Las Vegas. *Outdoorsy in Vegas*, maybe that'll be the title of our next book."

"Hmm, I forgot that was coming up. I might have to start my resolution after that trip."

"What did we bet again?" I asked.

"It's not a bet," she replied.

So, Bob and Sue, based on our resolutions, next year should be filled with introspection and personal growth. You might not even recognize us when we meet in Rocky Mountain National Park in May. Karen will be the one with the not straight/not curly hair, and I'll be the one with a fistful of little whiskey bottles.

Have a Happy New Year!
Your friend,
Matt

The End

ABOUT THE AUTHORS

Matt and Karen have been married for over thirty-five years and live in the Seattle, Washington area. They have three adult children: Rachel, Emily and Matthew. Rachel and her husband Justin have two children of their own: Hadley and Clara. Having both grown up in the Midwest, Matt and Karen met at the University of Kansas and have been together ever since. *Dear Bob and Sue: Season 2* is their third book project together.

HOW TO CONTACT US

Email us at mattandkarensmith@gmail.com
Or visit one of our websites:
www.mattandkaren.com
www.dearbobandsue.com

INDEX

OTHER WORKS BY MATT AND KAREN

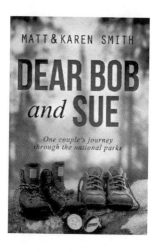

Dear Bob and Sue is the story of our journey to all fifty-nine U.S. National Parks. We wrote the book as a series of emails to our friends, Bob and Sue, in which we share our humorous and quirky observations. It is at times irreverent, unpredictable and sarcastic, all in the spirit of humor. We describe a few of our experiences in each park but do not provide an exhaustive overview of each experience or park. We didn't intend for this book to be a travel guide nor a recommendation for how to visit all fifty-nine of the U.S. National Parks although many readers have said they've found it to be a useful guide. Rather, it is our story about how we did it.

If you enjoy quirky humor set in the magnificent U.S. National Parks, this book may be for you. If you are looking for eloquent descriptions of the natural beauty we encountered or detailed descriptions of every activity you can do in each park, there are many other books available where you can find that information. All that said, many readers have commented that it's "laugh out loud" funny and a light-hearted glimpse of our journey through the parks.

OTHER WORKS BY MATT AND KAREN

Travel with Matt and Karen as they float down the Colorado River through the Grand Canyon. In September 2016, they experienced the trip of a lifetime with fourteen friends and a crew of ten while traveling in wooden dories through the canyon. *Dories, Ho!* is a story of their adventure and discovery. Similar to their first travel memoir *Dear Bob and Sue*, this book is as much about their relationship as it is their fantastic trip. Matt and Karen's quirky writing style is both humorous and irreverent. It's fun, laugh out loud, and an easy read.

While not intended to be a traditional guidebook, anyone contemplating a river trip through the Grand Canyon will benefit from this firsthand account. The reader will feel as if they've traveled with the authors on their journey to and through Grand Canyon National Park. If you are looking for a story that will make you laugh and inspire you to get out and see our incredible national parks, *Dories, Ho!* is for you.

34359375R00224

Made in the USA
Columbia, SC
14 November 2018